Differentiating
with
Graphic
Organizers

Tools to Foster
Critical
and
Creative
Thinking

Patti Drapeau

CORWIN PRESS
A SAGE Company

For information:

Corwin Press
A SAGE Company
2455 Teller Road
Thousand Oaks, California 91320
www.corwinpress.com

SAGE Ltd.
1 Oliver's Yard
55 City Road
London EC1Y 1SP
United Kingdom

SAGE India Pvt. Ltd.
B 1/I 1 Mohan Cooperative Industrial Area
Mathura Road, New Delhi 110 044
India

SAGE Asia-Pacific Pte. Ltd.
33 Pekin Street #02-01
Far East Square
Singapore 048763

Printed in the United States of America

Library of Congress Cataloging-in-Publication Data

Drapeau, Patti.
Differentiating with graphic organizers : tools to foster critical and creative thinking / Patti Drapeau.
    p. cm.
Includes bibliographical references and index.
ISBN 978-1-4129-5975-9 (cloth)
ISBN 978-1-4129-5976-6 (pbk.)
   1. Graphic organizers. 2. Critical thinking—Study and teaching. 3. Creative thinking—Study and teaching. I. Title.

LB1044.88.D73 2009
371.33—dc22
                                         2008025415

This book is printed on acid-free paper.

12   10 9 8 7 6 5 4 3

Acquisitions Editor:	Carol Chambers Collins
Editorial Assistant:	Brett Ory
Production Editor:	Veronica Stapleton
Copy Editor:	Taryn Bigelow
Typesetter:	C&M Digitals (P) Ltd.
Proofreader:	Dennis W. Webb
Indexer:	Sheila Bodell
Cover Designer:	Rose Storey

Contents

Acknowledgments

I would like to thank the many educators, colleagues, friends, and family members who supported me as I made my way through the idea generating, field testing, and writing stages of this book. I would like to recognize the work of educators who have influenced this material and in particular Richard Paul, Lorin Anderson, David Krathwohl, Robert Marzano, Matthew Lipman, Carol Ann Tomlinson, Sandra Kaplan, Eric Jensen, and Mel Levine.

I would like to thank the following teachers who field tested the graphic organizers at the elementary, middle, and high school levels: Terrance Gould, Melissa Antrim, Jen Blair, June Lajeunesse, Leah Matvay, Danae Secunde, Marianne Stephenson, Cindy Thorne, Heather Chambers, Doreen Carson, Ed Disy, Melanie Ekstedt, Janice Fickett, Celeste Frisbee, Joshua Gagnon, Kristen Gentile, Katie Knox, Michael Levine, and Lynn Mercier.

I would like to thank my colleagues who provided support when this book was still in manuscript form. They are Dr. James Curry, Dr. Diane Heacox, Karen Shible, Pam Lester, Ira Waltz, and Dr. Cecilia Boswell.

I would like to thank the staff at Corwin Press who enabled this book to come to fruition. I am grateful to Alison Sharp for her commitment to the book. Thank you to Carol Collins for her editing efforts and her help in structuring the book. I would like to thank Brett Ory for her assistance and feedback. I would also like to thank copy editor Taryn Bigelow for her ability to edit with an eagle eye. Her comments were invaluable in moving the book into its final stage. I would also like to thank the production editor, Veronica Stapleton, for her guidance and support.

Thank you to my family and friends who were incredibly supportive of me while I was writing this book. Their love and support helped me on my journey and continue to enrich my world.

PUBLISHER'S ACKNOWLEDGMENTS

Corwin Press thanks the following reviewers for their contribution to this work:

Sarah Miller
Resource Teacher
Baldwin County Schools: Orange Beach
    Elementary
Orange Beach, AL

Jennifer Sinsel
Science Teacher
John Marshall Middle School
Wichita, KS

Joseph Staub
Resource Specialist Teacher
Thomas Starr King Middle School
Los Angeles, CA

Brigitte Tennis
Head Mistress and Seventh
    Grade Teacher
Stella Schola Middle School
Redmond, WA

Robert E. Yager
Professor of Science Education
University of Iowa
Iowa City, IA

About the Author

Patti Drapeau is teacher, trainer, author, an internationally known presenter, and educational consultant. She has more than twenty-five years of classroom experience teaching students and coordinating programs in Freeport, Maine. Patti currently serves as adjunct faculty at the University of Southern Maine where she teaches graduate courses in Differentiation, Critical and Creative Thinking, Curriculum Integration, Education of the Gifted and Talented, and Curriculum and Methods for Teaching Gifted and Talented Students. Patti is also a certified trainer for the IIM (Independent Investigation Method) Research Model.

Patti developed a curriculum model for the regular classroom called "Affective Perspectives: Combining Critical Thinking, Creative Thinking, and Affect." She has authored a variety of articles for the *Maine Exchange* and is the author of two books published by Scholastic, *Great Teaching With Graphic Organizers* and *Differentiated Instruction: Making It Work.*

Patti is an international presenter in the United States and Canada, where she has appeared at many national, state, and regional conferences. As an educational consultant, she conducts district and school workshops focusing on different ways to meet the needs of all students. She may be contacted through her Web site, www.pattidrapeau.com.

This book is dedicated to those teachers who seek and are willing to risk change. May your courage and spirit endure.

Introduction

From Potential to Performance

Educators are and I hope always will be concerned with their students' level of achievement. We believe an overarching goal in education is to help all students move from potential to performance. To this end, we have spent millions of dollars and hours conducting scientifically based research studies to find the magic answer to the age-old question: What can we do to help our students achieve? What can we do to bring students up to grade level or challenge them beyond grade-level expectations? How can we help students achieve all they can achieve?

I have come to realize that one basic problem exists. Our definition of achievement is relative: What one person says is an acceptable level of achievement another thinks is unacceptable. Sometimes a student has an exceptional personality or a singular talent, but can't achieve academically. In school, such a student is viewed as unsuccessful. The student feels like a failure. In fact, from a purely academic viewpoint, their grades and their inability or unwillingness to meet state standards verify this. In school, it is what you do academically that counts. But we cannot separate who the learner is and what the learner does, because achievement affects self-esteem and self-confidence, and self-esteem and self-confidence affect achievement. Achievement cannot be easily or narrowly defined or measured.

TRENDS IN ACHIEVEMENT

In the search for answers, many educational fads have come and gone. In the 1970s, "thinking skills" was the latest fad. Educators claimed that teachers weren't asking their students to think deeply about content. The fear was that students were learning information at a rote level, quickly forgetting what they learned or never really learning it at all. The thinking skills movement took hold and "high-level verbs" became the rage. Bloom's Taxonomy became the guiding light and teachers classified their questions accordingly.

But soon, some teachers protested: If we spend too much time focusing on thinking skills, content will be compromised. There won't be enough time to teach content. Articles began to appear in educational journals with titles such as "Content Versus Thinking Skills." The debate continued for years.

The thinking skills movement took a back seat, staff development no longer focused on thinking skill models, and teachers sometimes used Bloom's Taxonomy to address high-level thinking objectives, while others no longer thought much about it. State tests continued to focus on low-level thinking and teachers went back to targeting this level of thinking because that is what the tests were designed to evaluate. Textbook companies targeted low-level thinking in the name of reaching all students. Only their enrichment activities focused on high-level thinking. Many teachers stopped questioning whether this level of achievement was acceptable.

When the thinking skills movement passed, the learning styles movement took its place. Researchers such as McCarthy, Dunn and Dunn, Meyers Briggs, and others were now telling us that if we just looked at the student's style of learning, we could vary our instructional strategy to accommodate it. Thus, learning styles became the key to achievement. About this time, Howard Gardner (1993) came out with his multiple intelligences. Teachers were now excited about this new way to classify learners. Teachers began to allow students to show what they knew in a variety of ways according to their intelligences. Brain research supported the notion that students learn through a variety of pathways. Neuroscience confirmed that the brain is affected by stress, emotion, and physical activity and that this also affects our ability to learn; therefore, teachers were encouraged to promote active learning rather than passive learning. The stage was set for the differentiation movement.

Among the variety of instructional strategies that became popular at this time, one that held great promise was the graphic organizer. They were easy to use and everyone liked them. They seemed to be a great aid for the many visual learners in the classroom, as well as a useful way to help all students organize and review information. A plethora of graphic organizers emerged, with formats ranging from simple to complex. Teachers liked using them because they provided students with structure. In fact, some teachers became graphic organizer junkies: They used them a lot and were always searching for a new graphic organizer to complement a lesson.

Graphic organizers were, and still are, engaging and useful tools. They enable students to be successful with information they would otherwise have struggled to learn. They've also raised awareness among teachers that students have a variety of needs that can be met through a variety of graphic tools. It became apparent that one graphic organizer will not work in all situations, just as one type of instruction will not suit all students.

DIFFERENTIATION: ANOTHER FAD?

Fast forward to the last ten years or so, when differentiation has become popular. The term originally described the types of curriculum modifications teachers made for gifted and talented students. Teachers were trained to modify the content, process, and/or product of a lesson to meet the needs of the gifted learner. Soon, however, differentiation made its way into the regular classroom, as an instructional approach that targets the needs of all students.

Excitement mounted. Could *this* be the answer to the achievement question? As many schools jumped on the differentiation bandwagon, staff development focused on changing teaching habits—and the results were mixed. Effective change in classroom practice requires careful support and ongoing staff development. After providing one- or two-day workshops or even one-week trainings, many school districts were discouraged when their teachers slipped back into old habits of whole class instruction. But in districts that had the finances and commitment to set up long-term goals and extended training programs, more teachers effected significant changes in their teaching styles and many schools experienced an overall increase in student achievement.

I believe differentiation is here to stay because the wide variety of needs of the children in our classrooms is here to stay. No longer do we have classrooms where everyone speaks English as a first language, and no longer are these students necessarily low-performing students. Research conducted by the National Foundation for American Policy shows that 60 percent of the nation's top science students and 65 percent of the top mathematics students are children of recent immigrants (Friedman, 2005, p. 270). In an age of inclusion, no longer are students with disabilities separated from their peers. Advanced Placement classes are promoting equal access at the high school level. Different languages, different ability levels, different thinking styles, and different special needs all contribute to the general call for differentiated instruction.

THE FRAMEWORK: INTEGRATING WHAT WE KNOW

Differentiated instruction is not a passing fad, but it is difficult to do well. Differentiation requires that we modify our instructional approach, as well as the content, process, and products of the curriculum. It requires that we learn new types of questioning and interactive strategies. It requires a new approach to grouping, grading, and evaluating students. Because we continually gain knowledge about student achievement, differentiation practices need to be continually refined.

In the past, I improved my differentiation practice by developing and using tiered questions in the classroom. I integrated what I knew about learning styles into these questions. I provided options and choices for interactive activities. I tried out different systems of assessing differentiated activities and assignments. Still, I continued to search for better ways to improve my effectiveness with students. That search has culminated in this book, in which the goal is to provide teachers with tools to promote student achievement.

Why a Book About Graphic Organizers?

My first reason for writing this book is to help you raise the level of your students' academic achievement—and graphic organizers are powerful tools in promoting student performance. Research indicates that students who use them show improvement in overall achievement and in specific content areas (Institute of Advancement of Research in Education, 2003). They are effective instructional tools to use in science, social studies, reading, writing, math, and foreign language, with students who have learning disabilities, and with English Language Learners. Graphic organizers are often more effective than traditional forms of instruction, such as lecture, note taking, and question and answer.

Why Target Verbs in a Graphic Organizer Book?

My second reason for writing this book is to help you increase students' abilities to engage in critical and creative thinking, habits of mind long known to be essential to academic achievement. The three highest, roughly equivalent cognitive domains out of the six outlined in Bloom's Taxonomy (Bloom, Englehart, Furst, Hill, & Krathwohl, 1956) are synthesis (creative thinking), analysis, and evaluation (or critical thinking). Each was associated in that groundbreaking work with certain verbs, as a way to understand the thinking processes involved at these high levels of thinking. For this book, I have chosen to target nine verbs that correlate with critical and creative thinking skills: assume, infer, analyze, prioritize, judge, brainstorm, connect, create, and elaborate.

The graphic organizers in this book can be used with students to discuss what a verb means and to describe the thinking processes or steps we go through when we use a particular verb. For example: How do we analyze something or evaluate something? How do we make an inference? The shared language between teachers and students, noted in the steps on the graphic organizers, makes it clear what these words mean and how to do this type of thinking well. It is the process involved—you as the teacher modeling, what the verb means, student-teacher discussion, and practicing feedback—that appears to consistently correlate with learning improvement (Alvermann & Boothby, 1986; Anderson-Inman, Knox-Quinn, & Horney, 1996; Boyle & Weishaar, 1997; Bulgren, Schumaker, & Deshler, 1988; Carnes, Lindbeck, & Griffin, 1987; Clements-Davis & Ley, 1991; Darch, Carnine, & Kame'enui, 1986; Gardill & Jitendra, 1999; Idol & Croll, 1987; Scanlon, Deshler, & Schumaker, 1996; Willerman & Mac Harg, 1991, all cited in Strangman, Hall, & Meyer, 2003).

WHAT THIS BOOK IS ABOUT

The graphic in Figure I.1 presents the topics covered in the book. By focusing on the nine high-level verbs noted on the bottom of the figure, teachers challenge students to think critically and creatively. Using the tools in this book, teachers can meet different learners' needs by changing the organizer, prompts, or resource materials noted at the top of the figure. Above all, teachers must create a classroom environment that is safe, caring, and conducive to critical and creative thought. The elements in the figure sit on top of the classroom environment because without such an environment, a higher level of teaching and thinking cannot occur.

The book is divided into four parts. In Part I, Chapter 1, I discuss the power of graphic organizers to promote student achievement and describe how the nine verbs that are the focus of the graphic organizers were chosen. In Chapter 2, the topic is differentiation and how students' needs determine how graphic organizers are used in the classroom. Six ways to differentiate using graphic organizers are presented, including steps to create your own graphic organizers.

Figure I.1   The Content of This Book

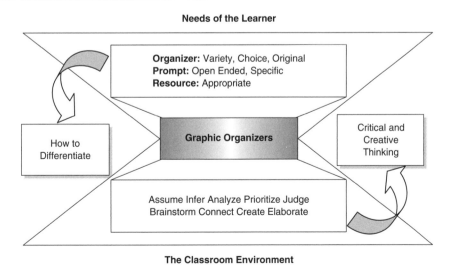

In Parts II and III, I describe the nine cognitive graphic organizers and how to use them. The graphic organizers in Chapters 3–7 are designed to promote the critical thinking skills associated with the five verbs assume, infer, analyze, prioritize, and judge. Those in Chapters 8–11 are designed to encourage the creative thinking skills represented by the four verbs brainstorm, connect, create, and elaborate. Sample lessons demonstrate the application of the graphic organizers in a variety of content areas and grade levels. Rating scales and rubrics are specially designed for each graphic organizer and can be used to provide feedback.

Finally, in Part IV, Chapter 12, I'll show you how to put graphic organizers to good use in your classroom, whether you are following a particular curriculum model, a textbook series, or designing your own lessons. I will show you how to develop and use activity grids to plan graphic organizer activities. Chapter 13 lists some frequently asked questions and answers to help you on your path to using graphic organizers as tools to foster critical and creative thinking.

TEACHERS AS CRITICAL AND CREATIVE THINKERS

The graphic organizer designs created for this book are simple and easy to use. They are designed so that all students can be successful with any format. Although the language that goes along with each graphic organizer has been researched, of course, not all of the graphic organizers will fit all situations all of the time. If this were true, I might have found "the answer" to achievement.

Do not be afraid to look at the ideas presented in this book and think "so what," "what if," "what else?" This is a book that encourages critical and creative thinking! Question what you do in your lessons and what you say to your students so that you can help all of them achieve to the best of their abilities—not only in your classroom but also in the classroom we call life, where strong thinking skills will help them on their journeys.

PART I

Graphic Organizers, Critical Thinking, and Differentiation

1

Graphic Organizers

Tools to Promote Critical and Creative Thinking

Graphic organizers provide teachers with tools to help students on the road to higher achievement. Graphic organizers that target critical and creative thinking verbs are vehicles to help develop students' cognitive abilities and provide formats for students to process their thinking about content. Graphic organizer formats also allow teachers to diagnose where students' thinking has gone awry. Teachers can pinpoint areas in which students' thinking is weak, illogical, or unclear. The structure and language of the organizer allows teachers to be able to coach students and move them beyond where thinking has fallen apart. Graphic organizers provide new language that facilitates classroom communication, as well as deepen understanding of the content that teachers work to transmit.

For certain students, the use of graphic organizers is particularly beneficial:

- For students who easily fall victim to faulty reasoning, they are an aid to the thinking process.
- For students who have difficulty expressing their thoughts, they provide a format for expression.
- For students who have difficulty processing information, they provide a structure within which to state content and support for ideas.
- For students who are visual learners, they provide a visual aid.
- For students who ramble, they help focus the response.
- For students who are English Language Learners, they can enable the expression of depth of thought through the use of limited written responses.

EVIDENCE SUPPORTING GRAPHIC ORGANIZERS

Many studies have established the value of graphic organizers as cognitive tools. Stiggins (quoted in Gregory & Kuzmich, 2004, p. 142), for example, states that "When graphic organizers are used, students show increases in retention and comprehension, and they demonstrate higher levels of achievement on content-based assessments."

A number of studies have focused on Hyerle's (2004) Thinking Maps, which target eight thinking skills. Each map includes a visual structure with shared language and procedures. Studies using his eight maps have been conducted in a variety of schools and content areas, and they indicate many positive outcomes, including an increase in student achievement in all content areas.

The effectiveness of graphic organizers is also supported in the meta-analysis conducted by Marzano, Pickering, and Pollock (2001) in which they identify nine ways to increase student achievement. I discuss these nine strategies in the following list, which includes the percentage rates of improved student achievement according to the study. The list also contains the names of graphic organizers presented in this book that can be used as instructional strategies to target each area.

1. Recognizing similarities and differences, using metaphors and analogies: Students trained in these skills showed a 45 percent gain over students who were not. The ability to recognize similarities and differences is crucial to connecting new information with known information. In Chapter 9, the Rose-Colored Glasses graphic organizer enables students to draw analogies by relating similar content characteristics and attributes to an animal, place, object, and/or themselves. In Chapter 4, the Paint Jars (inference) graphic organizer can be used to find differences. In Chapter 5, the graphic organizer called the Framed Puzzle can be used to not only recognize differences but also analyze them.

2. Summarizing and note taking: Trained students showed a 37 percent gain. Most of the graphic organizers in this book can be used as summarization tools. Students use the graphic organizers to organize their notes by making judgments (Chapter 7) or perhaps prioritizing (Chapter 6) them.

3. Reinforcing effort and providing recognition: Trained students showed a gain of 29 percent. Teachers can address this category by using strategies that give specific feedback, which includes recognition for effort. Every graphic organizer in the following chapters has accompanying feedback tools. These tools are not meant to be used only as grading mechanisms. They are designed to give ongoing direction and feedback, so that students have guiding tools for processing information and a system in place for refining their responses. In this way, students are recognized not just for complete, correct answers but also for partial answers.

4. Homework and practice: Trained students showed a 28 percent gain. Any of the graphic organizers in Chapters 3–11 can be used as a homework assignment to review content or in the classroom as a way to rehearse or practice new learning.

5. Nonlinguistic representations: Trained students showed a 27 percent gain. This category addresses the importance of using strategies that use pictures, diagrams, and organizers. All of the graphic organizers in this book target critical and creative thinking, and can be used to differentiate instruction.

6. Cooperative learning: Trained students showed a 27 percent gain. As you read about the graphic organizers in the following chapters, the idea of flexible grouping (students working with different groups of students periodically) is promoted and encouraged. We cannot create cooperative learning groups all of the time, and we know that for some types of learners, such as introverts, this type of learning can feel exhausting. Most students, however, are very social. They like to work with their peers. This type of learning is motivational and engaging. Many students need help moving their thinking beyond a literal level and the teacher is

not always available to help out. Cooperative learning can provide a management system that enables students to help one another by working on the graphic organizers together.

7. Setting objectives and providing feedback: Trained students showed 23 percent gains. The language and structure provided in the graphic organizers in this book provide clarity as to how the teacher wants the students to think about what they know. The use of cognitive graphic organizers makes the objectives clearer and also serves to provide guided feedback. Brain research also indicates that feedback needs to be specific for it to be most effective. Graphic organizers presented in this book use procedural language, structured formats, and rating scales and rubrics that provide teachers with the direction necessary to give quality feedback.

8. Generating and testing hypotheses: Trained students showed a gain of 23 percent. By asking students to come up with a hypothesis and then support it, students are encouraged to use both critical and creative thinking skills. Many of the graphic organizers in this book serve as ways to test hypotheses. In Chapter 7, students are asked to make a belief statement and then justify it in the "judge" graphic organizer. In Chapter 3, students are asked to state an "assumption" and then support their statement. In Chapter 4, students are asked to make an "inference" statement. They then reflect on facts and prior knowledge supporting this inference and draw a conclusion.

9. Using questions, cues, and advance organizers: Trained students showed a 22 percent gain. Throughout this book, the importance of word cues and shared language is discussed. High-level questions promote deep thinking and long-lasting learning, but word cues help students know what we are looking for. By paying attention to both the content and the verb in prompts, students learn just how important word cues are.

THE USE OF VERBS

There is wide consensus that graphic organizers are useful tools to promote critical thinking and boost student achievement. But why provide graphic organizers that focus on verbs?

The use of specific verbs is considered a cognitive organizer because it directs students to think about content critically and creatively, as well as in an organized way. Obviously, students could use an organizer like an outline to help with their thinking. The organizers in Chapters 3–11, however, have the added advantage of focusing students on the action suggested by the verb. For example, some students have difficulty prioritizing. If they are asked to decide which event had the greatest impact in the presidential election, students can apply the four-step process they learned by using the Prioritizer graphic organizer. The knowledge of *how* to prioritize, along with the content knowledge, helps students to make logical, informed responses with precision.

Graphic organizers that use verbs are also useful to differentiate teaching because they help to pinpoint when and where students get stuck. Is it a lack of content information? Does the student understand the question? Can the student express an answer? I examine each of these possibilities in turn.

1. *Does the student lack content information?* If the student cannot fill out the graphic organizer or has only partial responses, try changing the verb in the prompt. Simplify the verb to the knowledge or comprehension level and see if the student can give you at least a partial answer. In this way, you can glean whether the student has a minimal understanding of the information. She may need more practice and review of the content information before she is able to be successful with a high-level thinking graphic organizer.

2. *Does the student understand what the question is asking her to do?* If, after simplifying the verb, the student gives you quite a lot of information but still has trouble with the graphic organizer, it may indicate that the student is having difficulty responding to the verb in the question or prompt. This means the student needs help understanding how to process the verb. Once this happens, the students will know what the question is asking. For instance, if the teacher asks students to make an inference based on an article they read on pollution, then this assignment assumes students can read and understand the article as well as know how to make an inference. If the student knows information but is unable to make inferences, then the teacher can use the Paint Jars graphic organizer to demonstrate how to make inferences. Students can continue to use the graphic organizer until they no longer need to write out the process.

3. *Can the student express her answer so that it is understood?* Some students do not have the writing skills or expressive language to write essays and reports. A major advantage of using these graphic organizers is that they require limited written responses. This is an effective tool for students who have difficulty writing or are English Language Learners. They may have a good grasp of the content information, but are not successful at conveying their knowledge when asked to make written responses. According to Reiss (2005 p. 75), "The graphic organizer allows ELL students to give a maximum amount of information with only a minimum amount of language." In short, the graphic organizer allows the teacher to assess to what degree the student actually knows the content information without having language problems interfere with communication.

WHY THESE NINE VERBS?

You might wonder how I decided to focus on the specific verbs described in this book. It's clear that the teaching of thinking and reasoning is critical to student achievement (Futrell, 1987; National Education Goals Panel, 1991; National Science Board Commission, 1983). It's not always clear, however, how thinking and reasoning should be taught. To answer this question, Marzano and Pollack (2001) analyzed an exhaustive study by Kendall and Marzano (2000), who looked at national standards across content areas to identify what skills were used in multiple standards. Marzano and Pollack identified the following six thinking and reasoning skills that come up again and again:

1. Identification of similarities and differences

2. Problem solving and troubleshooting

3. Argumentation

4. Decision making

5. Hypothesis testing and scientific inquiry

6. Use of logic and reasoning

The verbs used in Chapters 3–11 of this book are linked to the six thinking and reasoning skills identified by Kendall and Marzano (2000). These include five critical thinking skills—assuming, inferring, analyzing, prioritizing, and judging, and four creative thinking skills—brainstorming, connecting, creating, and elaborating.

For Skill 1, identification of similarities and differences, teachers can use the "connect" graphic organizer to help students identify similarities. Or, the "inference" graphic organizer encourages students to look for similarities and differences that aren't immediately apparent.

When teachers focus on problem solving and troubleshooting (Skill 2), they can use the "brainstorming" graphic organizer to help students generate ideas, the "elaboration" graphic organizer to help students develop their ideas, and the "analyze" graphic organizer to help students differentiate between the parts of problems.

For argumentation and decision making (Skills 3 and 4), the "assumption" graphic organizer can help students sort out points of view and perspectives, as well as identify important decisions that need to be made.

For hypothesis testing and scientific inquiry (Skill 5), brainstorming helps get the processes going and the "create" graphic organizer helps bring the idea to fruition.

Finally, for tasks involving logic and reasoning (Skill 6), the "analyze" and "judge" graphic organizers are useful.

The target verbs in each graphic organizer were also chosen because they are commonly used in the classroom but are not readily available in a graphic organizer format on the Internet or in other books. Over many years, I've asked my university students, who are teachers, to identify the verbs they focus on in their classrooms. Some teachers said they expected their students to make inferences, but they didn't really have a good way to explain how to make an inference. Some teachers said their students made assumptions, which contributed to their reaching erroneous conclusions. These teachers wanted a way to help students distinguish between new information and prior assumptions that interfered with new learning. High school teachers could not believe their students still could not write a good analysis. Elementary teachers wanted to help students make meaningful judgments. Teachers at all grade levels said their students needed help prioritizing information. The nine verbs emerged as a response to the needs of these practitioners. Once the verbs were identified, pilot graphic organizers were field-tested across grade levels and content areas.

PURPOSES OF GRAPHIC ORGANIZERS

Graphic organizers can and should be used in a purposeful way. If teachers consider the objectives of the lesson and the strategies to reach those objectives, then they can decide which graphic organizer to use with all, some, or individual students. In Figure 1.1, six main purposes of graphic organizers are listed. These are discussed below.

1. Many practitioners have experienced the usefulness of graphic organizers, both in and outside of the classroom. As we've seen, the overriding reason for teachers to use graphic organizers is to **improve student achievement**, but there are at least five other reasons to incorporate them into classroom practice.

2. We use graphic organizers to help students **make sense of information**. Merkley and Jefferies (2001) state the benefits of using graphic organizers as (1) enabling students to verbalize relationships, (2) allowing students to connect information from past learning to new learning, (3) allowing students to anticipate new learning by previewing information, and (4) allowing students the ability to decode and apply structural analysis in reading. Making sense of information encompasses all of these things and more.

3. This leads us to another significant reason why teachers should use graphic organizers; they help students **chunk information**. In the Information Age, information overload is a problem. It's critical for students to be able to sort through expanses of material accrued through research. Graphic organizers help students sort through information, prioritize it, sequence it, evaluate it, and build on it. Without the ability to structure information, the management and retrieval of information can be overwhelming.

4. A fourth reason for using graphic organizers is to **promote depth of learning**. In 1997, Caine and Caine wrote, "Deep meaning refers to whatever drives us and governs our sense of purpose" (quoted in Howard & Fogarty, 2003, p. 190). If students don't know what the learning means, or why it is relevant, then they will have little drive to think about it. Deep understanding has to do with understanding information and being able to apply it in context. This context may be a novel situation where the learning goes beyond the application of regurgitated information.

5. Graphic organizers also help us to **construct mental models** from which we can organize and make sense of information. These models provide a framework for metacognitive learning. Hyerle (2004, p. 23) says, "When students repeatedly associate a concrete visual pattern with an abstract thought process, they learn patterns for what thinking looks like." Cognitive graphic organizers lay out specific procedures that delineate thought processes, so that students know what the teacher is expecting for a response. Students practice these processes in a variety of contexts and, after time, are able to use them independently of the graphic organizers. They can actually visualize the processes and formats. For example, students can visualize the "prioritize" graphic organizer and know there are four steps to prioritize. First, list the ideas; second, narrow the ideas to four; third, order the ideas in terms of greatest importance; and fourth, give reasons for their top priority. Visual learners will

Figure 1.1   Purposes of Graphic Organizers

Purposes of Graphic Organizers
1. Improve student achievement.
2. Make sense of information.
3. Chunk information.
4. Promote depth of learning.
5. Construct mental models.
6. Foster motivation.

associate the process with the graphic organizer design. For example, they will visualize the "prioritize" machine on the graphic organizer and then remember the steps to prioritizing. Metacognition takes place as a result of students making mental models, practicing in different contexts, receiving specific feedback, and transferring the formats to other situations on their own. Perkins, in 1995, said, "Transfer occurs when a person applies knowledge or skills acquired from some earlier context in a new context" (quoted in Howard & Fogarty, 2003, p. 164). By promoting cognitive graphic organizers across content, students are able to see the generalized applications of these tools and their personal relevance to their own world.

6. For most students, graphic organizers are fun to use and provide variety; thus, they **foster motivation**. This book looks at nine different graphic organizers in detail. I hope you will not use the same one over and over again. Tweak your verbs and provide students with choices. Most often, you can reach the same objective by asking a critical thinking question as with a creative thinking question. So, mix up the verbs and let students choose which graphic organizer they want to use to create a response.

Graphic organizers also lend themselves to small group learning. Students work together to share ideas, discuss viewpoints, and come up with a group response for an organizer. Graphic organizers can also be tailored to fit with students' individual learning styles. Remember, these are enabling tools. Whereas most students will find the graphic organizers useful and motivational, there will be some students who do not like them. If the student is able to process the information without the guide, then by all means let her answer questions in the style that best suits her.

The graphic organizers described in the following chapters target high-level thinking, but it isn't high-level thinking alone that will help students attain depth in learning. It's the level of content, along with the thinking process, that achieves this depth. Therefore, teachers need to supply the appropriate content prompt that promotes high-level thinking.

CONTENT APPLICATIONS OF GRAPHIC ORGANIZERS

Graphic Organizers and Reading

Graphic organizers are effective strategies to promote reading comprehension. The National Reading Panel (2000) cited graphic and semantic organizers as one type of instructional strategy that is effective in the improvement of reading instruction. Findings from seven research reports concurred with this conclusion (Berkowitz, 1986; Bowman et al., 1998; Darch et al., 1986; Davis, 1994; Gordon & Rennie, 1987; Reutzel, 1985; Troyer, 1994, all cited by the Institute of Advancement of Research in Education, 2003). Of twelve studies reviewed by Strangman et al. (2003) at the National Center on Accessing the General Curriculum, nine studies found that graphic organizers increased reading comprehension.

The graphic organizers presented in this book will work well before, during, and after reading. Pre-reading activities can be used as a hook to engage the reader. Teachers might ask students what assumptions can be made about the book by reading the title or the chapter titles. Or, students might be challenged to infer the author's purpose in writing a book after they have read the author's biography.

The graphic organizers can also be used during reading to check ongoing comprehension. For example, part way through the story, students might be asked to make inferences and judgments regarding the character's actions in the story so far. They could be asked to elaborate on the character's relationships with the other characters in the story.

Finally, graphic organizers can be used as a summative activity to assess comprehension after students finish reading. Students might be asked to create a gift for the main character or analyze the actions of the antagonist in the story from the protagonist's point of view.

Graphic organizers can also be used to review vocabulary in various content areas. Students gain facility with new words when they use the Wheel of Words (elaboration) or Rose-Colored Glasses (connect) graphic organizers. Both of these organizers focus on creativity and therefore promote a more playful approach to learning vocabulary, which is far more effective than rote memorization.

Graphic Organizers and Writing

Graphic organizers are great tools to help students improve their writing. In 1999, 84 percent of fourth graders at Brookshire Elementary School passed the FCAT (Florida Comprehensive Assessment Test) in writing. After receiving training in Hyerle's Thinking Maps, the number of students who passed the FCAT writing section soared to 97 percent within one year (Hyerle, 2004). For many years now, teachers have been using graphic tools as pre-writing activities and seeing great results. For example, webbing has been used as a pre-writing activity with expository, persuasive, and narrative writing. A more conventional graphic organizer is an outline, which also helps students organize their thinking. A great computer program called Inspiration uses both webbing and outlining. This computer program takes brainstormed ideas and reformats them in outline form. Whether students have difficulty generating ideas, using elaborative language, or organizing their thoughts on paper, critical and creative thinking graphic organizers can help them develop fluency and provide organizational structures that will enable them to become more effective writers.

Graphic Organizers and Math, Science, and Social Studies

Critical thinking organizers can help students improve math skills by analyzing and judging their answers and reflecting on assumptions. Graphic organizers can be used to review information and review for a test or quiz. According to one study by Dickson, Simmons, and Kame'enui (1995), students who were taught how to use graphic organizers for test preparation retained significantly more information than did other students (cited in Kenney, Hancewicz, Heuer, Metsisto, & Tuttle, 2005). Because graphic organizers can also be a motivational tool, creative thinking graphic organizers, such as the Rose-Colored Glasses (connect) graphic organizer, can give students a fun way to learn or practice math vocabulary. For example, a teacher could prompt students to think of ways that a drawing of a trapezoid is like a drawing of a book. Student responses might be that they both have four sides, they both have four corners, they both come in many sizes, they both can be drawn three dimensionally, and so on.

In both science and social studies, students can use graphic organizers to take an issue and make assumptions and inferences. They can analyze information, prioritize it, and judge it. They can brainstorm ideas related to the issue, look at the flexibility of those ideas, and make connections to things they know. Finally, they can create a solution to resolve the issue and they can elaborate on it.

SOME CAVEATS AND CLARIFICATIONS

Graphic organizers are most often not the end product of a lesson. They may be used as tools to process thoughts before individuals join a group or to guide a group discussion. This process can improve a writing piece or written response, for instance, or be used to analyze and evaluate ideas before students use them in a product. In these situations, the organizers would rarely be assessed. The rating scale and rubrics that are included in Chapters 3–11, however, can still be used to provide valuable feedback. When a graphic organizer is the end product of a lesson or the follow-up for a homework assignment, teachers may grade the graphic organizer itself.

Once the verb processes are internalized, some students stop using the graphic organizers and just write the steps out on paper. Other students begin to visualize the process in their heads and do not feel the need to fill in a graphic organizer or even process their thoughts in writing. This is particularly important: We actually want students to wean themselves off graphic organizers and internalize the thinking processes that they foster. The goal is to have students become independent of the graphic organizer yet able to engage in the high-level critical and creative thinking skills that the organizers are intended to facilitate.

Not all lessons warrant using a graphic organizer. A graphic organizer is useful when there is a lot of information to sort through or when the information is at a complex level for the student. There is no need, for example, to have students fill out an "assume" graphic organizer (Chapter 3) when we are asking them to make a simple assumption. Similarly, graphic organizers are often helpful as aids to memory; but if the student does not really have to remember the information on a particular topic and can just Google it, then a graphic organizer is unnecessary. The graphic organizer is there to help students make meaning. It should never be used as busywork.

The graphic organizers described in Chapter 3–11 are not visually complex, and this is intentional. They delineate simple structures and processes so that all students can use them easily. But they also allow for advanced levels of content to be processed through their visual frameworks. They allow students to construct mental models that organize information. The formats facilitate both deductive and inductive reasoning and a variety of creative thinking processes. They are designed to be flexible tools or working templates. They are not meant to be prepackaged worksheets for which teachers verbalize scripted language and students fill in the blanks. Rather, they are meant to be dynamic models that can be adjusted according to your students' needs.

 ## KEY POINTS TO REMEMBER ABOUT GRAPHIC ORGANIZERS

1. Graphic organizers that target critical and creative thinking verbs are vehicles to help develop students' cognitive abilities and provide formats for students to process their thinking about content.

2. A graphic organizer that focuses on a specific verb is considered a cognitive organizer, because the organizer directs students to think about content critically, creatively, and in an organized way.

3. Cognitive graphic organizers provide new language that facilitates classroom communication, as well as deepen understanding of the content.

4. The overriding reasons for teachers to use graphic organizers are to increase student achievement, make sense of information, chunk information, promote depth of learning, construct mental models, and foster motivation.

5. Graphic organizer formats allow teachers to diagnose where students' thinking has gone awry.

6. Graphic organizers are most often not the end product of a lesson.

7. Graphic organizers should never be used as busywork.

? PAUSE FOR REFLECTION AND DISCUSSION

1. Compare and contrast graphic organizers that target critical and creative thinking processes with other types of graphic organizers.

2. Analyze the evidence that suggests the use of graphic organizers increases student achievement.

3. How can high-level thinking graphic organizers be used in the classroom? Prioritize your ideas in terms of their applicability to your classroom.

4. What is the relationship between graphic organizers and high-level thinking?

5. Judge whether you believe this statement to be true: Graphic organizers that delineate critical and creative thinking skills provide flexible formats for student responses.

2

Graphic Organizers

Tools to Promote Differentiation

Cognitive graphic organizers are one of the more powerful tools we have to support differentiated instruction. Many teachers, however, use these graphic organizers as whole class activities. Although this may be effective teaching practice, whole class lessons can sometimes be limiting because they only address some of the learner's needs some of the time. The versatility of the graphic organizers makes them perfect tools for differentiation. If teachers think about why they differentiate, then they can figure out how to use the graphic organizers to address students' interests, styles, and abilities.

Below, I have listed ten principles of differentiated instruction (adapted from Tomlinson, 1999; Tomlinson & McTighe, 2006), and paired these principles with the ways in which graphic organizers can be used to support them (see Figure 2.1 and the discussion that follows). These principles are not listed in a prioritized fashion. They are all important and they often interrelate.

1. *Addressing readiness, interests, and styles.* A high-level thinking graphic organizer can be used as soon as students are ready to think about content at a sophisticated level (Drapeau, 2004; Howard & Fogarty, 2003; Jensen, 2006; Tomlinson & Edison, 2003). Students who are not ready to apply information at this level may receive the graphic organizer a few days later than other students. In this way, they will have extra time to review basic content with other instructional strategies before they are expected to apply the information at a high level of complexity. We know that some students are more interested in certain topics within a subject area (Gregory & Chapman, 2002; Tomlinson & Edison, 2003). Students use different graphic organizers to tailor their work to their areas of interest. We also know that most of our students prefer a visual style of learning. "Research conducted by 3M Corporation in 2001 found the brain processes visuals 60,000 times faster than text, and visual aids in the classroom have been found to improve learning up to 400 percent" (Gangwer, 2005, p. 24). Gangwer recommends the use of color, graphs, tables, and pictures for visual learners. When memorizing information, visual learners are often the ones who write information over and over before it is encoded and stored in their long-term memory. Visual learners who are not usually successful with high-level thinking have more of a chance for success with the visual format of graphic organizers.

Figure 2.1   How Graphic Organizers Support Differentiated Instruction

Principles of Differentiation	Graphic Organizer Application
1. Modify the content, thinking process, and/or product when addressing student readiness, interests, and styles.	1. Use high-level thinking graphic organizers with different students at different times.
2. Adjust pace of instruction to accommodate rate of learning.	2. Students who use graphic organizers may work faster because of their increased learning rate or slower because of delays in processing information.
3. Provide different levels of assistance.	3. The graphic organizer itself provides a level of assistance because it directs the learning process.
4. Offer controlled choice as much as possible.	4. Open choice is great, but no choice is OK, too. Control the choice by offering just two or three graphic organizers when necessary.
5. Foster active learning through varied grouping practices and different types of instructional strategies.	5. Formats provide a guide for small group and paired discussions.
6. Provide feedback and different types of assessment.	6. The graphic organizer lets the teacher see how the student is thinking. Rating scales and rubrics provide feedback guides.
7. Allow for resource variety and text modifications.	7. Based on expanded resources or limited resources, organizers are useful tools.
8. Modify assignments by length, time, and complexity.	8. Simplify the organizer, allow more time to fill it out, integrate different levels of content complexity.
9. Provide a supportive classroom environment that fosters individual differences and promotes individual successes.	9. Honor both critical and creative thinking, offer choice, and allow for modifications.
10. Devise management strategies for both teachers and students.	10. Use file folders to store graphic organizers and use spreadsheets to keep track of student choices.

2. *Adjusting the pace of instruction.* We know that some students take longer to learn things than others. It takes a gifted and talented learner a shorter amount of practice time than other learners to know, understand, apply, and remember information. It takes an average student seven to fourteen meaningful exposures to a word before it becomes part of his or her working vocabulary (Beers, 2003). Graphic organizers can be used to help students through areas of the curriculum where they are stuck or slower.

3. *Providing different levels of assistance.* The graphic formats and the accompanying language presented in the organizers in this book can serve as a support for students. Not only do students do their work more efficiently, they also require less help from the teacher. The cognitive graphic organizers walk students through thinking processes, so that students are provided with cues to move from

step to step. Students who have difficulty writing responses or young students with minimal writing skills, however, will still need teacher or peer support to make their thoughts known.

4. *Offering controlled choice.* Choice enhances engagement (Howard & Fogarty, 2003; Jensen, 2006) and motivation (Glasser, 1999; Sprenger, 2005). It's important, whenever possible, to foster critical and creative thinking by offering students a choice of graphic organizers that will promote deep learning. Because students feel empowered when they have choice, we can expect it to increase student motivation. Choice, however, doesn't mean giving over total control of the learning process. Teachers can offer students a limited choice between two or three graphic organizers.

5. *Fostering active learning through grouping practices and instructional strategies.* Each group may address the same content, and they may use a different graphic organizer. The use of the graphic organizer format provides a structure that promotes productive small group discussion. The group doesn't have to figure out how they will structure their responses. They have a tool that does this for them.

   Without a basic structure to get the group going, some groups don't get going! Whether students work in pairs or individually, the graphic organizer helps keep learners on task. In some cases, students modify the organizer to create space for their responses. Each group successfully reports out to the whole class, and their responses are discussed with the other groups.

6. *Providing feedback and different types of assessment.* The cognitive graphic organizers presented in this book allow for specific feedback because the structure of the organizers provides a window into the students' reasoning. The framework lets both you and the student see how the student is thinking (Burke, 1994). The teacher is able to see just where the student needs help in coming up with a more complete or better answer. Wiggins (1998, quoted in Tomlinson and McTighe, 2006, p. 77) suggests "the use of real feedback in allowing the student to make self-adjustments." The rating systems and rubrics that are used with the graphic organizers give teachers tools to demonstrate to students how to check to see if their answers are logical, rational, and/or creative. Because the tool provides shared language, students more readily understand feedback.

7. *Allowing for resource variety and text modifications.* Some students may need resource variety and text modifications (Forsten, Grant, & Hollas, 2003). For high-end learners, this means they utilize information from many and varied resources, and organize and synthesize it. For struggling learners, this might mean they read only key passages. In both instances, graphic organizers help learners think more deeply about content at their ability level.

8. *Modifying assignments by length, time, and complexity.* This might mean shortening or altering the graphic organizer, instructing students to use some but not all of the steps on the organizer. Too many steps are just too much for some students!

   Some students, however, like to break information down into detailed steps. Some students may need more "think time" to complete the graphic organizer. Students who use critical and creative thinking may need more time to answer a prompt than when they're answering factual questions.

9. *Providing a supportive classroom environment that fosters individual differences and successes.* The best graphic organizer is not going to work in an environment

where students are afraid to express their ideas. Teachers connect with students by showing that they care and can express emotions (Intrator, 2004, p. 23). Because graphic organizers lend themselves to more than one correct answer, students need to trust their teacher. They need to understand that the teacher is asking them to think about the content and then state their own ideas, which is different from stating the one right answer.

In a supportive classroom environment, you will need to model critical and creative thinking. "Of all the instructional strategies, modeling is by far the most effective" (Fogarty, 1994, p. xiv). One way to honor individual differences is to accept both critical and creative reasoning. Both types of thinking are important and necessary. Cognitive graphic organizers help teachers demonstrate to students that they value all kinds of thinking.

10. *Devising management strategies.* It's important to make sure that differentiation does not overwhelm teachers or students. Graphic organizers can easily be managed in a file folder system (Drapeau, 2004) and kept in a particular area of the classroom. Students can access the folders when they need a new graphic organizer. If you offer a lot of choice, you have to watch out for students choosing the same type of graphic organizer again and again. Although a particular thinking skill might be the student's preferred thinking style, it's still important to make sure that students experience a variety of thinking skills.

A simple spreadsheet with student names or numbers down one side and verbs across the top can help you keep track of who is choosing what type of graphic organizer. On a master list, older students can check off the type of graphic organizer they choose. With younger students, teachers will need to do the record keeping. In order to promote variety, you might make up rules, for example, students may not use the same graphic organizer more than three times in a row or more than five times a semester. Rules may not apply in your situation but are something to consider.

Another issue is managing the paperwork. In other words, it takes a lot longer to grade a variety of papers than it does if everyone uses the same graphic organizer. Do what works for you. If you feel you can correct only one or two organizers at a time, then offer limited choice. Try to offer one organizer based on critical thinking and a second based on creative thinking. In this way, you are offering different cognitive style choices.

Also remember that not everything has to be graded (Wormelli, 2006). This especially holds true if graphic organizers are used to review for a test, as tools for discussion, as part of a rough draft, or to organize information for a culminating activity.

SIX WAYS TO DIFFERENTIATE USING GRAPHIC ORGANIZERS

I have identified six ways to differentiate using graphic organizers. Five of these focus on modifying the organizer itself, the prompt, and/or the resources based on the needs of your students. A sixth way to differentiate involves creating your own graphic organizer, when existing ones just won't work in a situation. Both teachers and students can use the steps to create their own formats. Let's take a look at the advantages and disadvantages of these six ways to differentiate.

The Open-Ended Prompt

- All students use the same high-level thinking graphic organizer.
- All students hear the same prompt.
- All students use the same resources.

Note: Students are able to respond at their own level of understanding.

The first way to differentiate involves an *open-ended prompt*. A prompt is a directive that students respond to on a graphic organizer. The prompt usually is in statement form but can include a question. For example, the teacher asks students to "use the Framed Puzzle graphic organizer to analyze Stanley's actions in the beginning and middle of the story." Such prompts allow teachers to use the same graphic organizer, the same prompt, and the same resources with the whole class. The graphic organizer provides an open-ended structure that allows for a basic level of differentiation. The teacher expects student responses to reflect their level of understanding of the character's actions. This is differentiated because students are able to respond at their own level of understanding. All students, not just those with stronger abilities, should be encouraged to think deeply.

Using open-ended prompts works well for teachers who are just beginning to differentiate in their classrooms and are comfortable with whole class instruction. When teachers ask an essential question, they often want all students to respond at the same time. They can then use the responses to build a class discussion, so that all students gain a comprehensive understanding of the answers to the question. This is only fair, however, when all students have the knowledge to respond to the prompt and the activity is equally challenging for all. Since it is difficult to create a prompt that is equally challenging for all students, this option should be used with caution.

This basic level of differentiation, however, is an easy way for teachers to get used to using new graphic organizers. Teachers may feel awkward at first addressing the verb, and the students might wonder why the teacher is spending time going over what the verb means. It is good teaching practice to discuss the verbs with your students, show them how to fill out the graphic organizer, show them how to use the rating scale or rubric, and model a sample lesson. They can fill out an organizer as a whole class, and the teacher can record responses on the board, overhead, or flip chart. When the students understand how the format works and the expectations are clear, then, in most cases, the students are ready to use an organizer on their own.

The advantages of using a graphic organizer when students receive the same organizer, hear the same prompt, and use the same resources are many (see Figure 2.2). First of all, students have access to the same activity. Teachers do not have to worry about students' perception of fairness. Students often think if their assignments differ from those of classmates, that other students have it easier or are having more fun. Another advantage is that students may experience success because they can work with others if they need or want to, because everyone is doing the same task based on the same information. Therefore, there is more opportunity for help if they need it. Students also like to work together for the social aspect of learning, which leads to greater success. Finally, it is important for all students to experience high-level thinking.

A major drawback to this way of differentiating is that we don't always get the level of response we're looking for. Have you ever felt a student could have answered a question more completely or with more detail? Perhaps you ask the student to revise her answer. In all fairness to the student, she did answer the question correctly. Some students don't even know how to make the answer more complete. They may feel they disappointed you because their answer wasn't good enough. For these reasons, it may be better to differentiate the prompt.

Figure 2.2   Advantages and Disadvantages of Using the "Open-Ended Prompt"

Pros	Cons
1. All students have access to the same activity.	1. The teacher does not always get the level of response that she wants from the student!
2. All students have the potential for success.	
3. Provides an opportunity for grouping arrangements.	
4. All students are exposed to high-level thinking with content.	

The Directed Prompt

- All students use the same high-level thinking graphic organizer.
- Students receive differentiated prompts.
- All students use the same resources.

Note: Students' responses are focused and specific.

In the next differentiation scenario, the *directed prompt*, only one graphic organizer is used, which means all students are using the same high-level verb, and all students read or interact with the same resources. All students read the same chapter or hear the same lecture or watch the same video. They might be reacting to the same assignment or the same Internet research materials. This time, however, the prompts are different for different students. For example, all students in science class are required to read a chapter on the respiratory system. But some students might be asked to analyze how the lungs function while other students are asked to analyze the respiratory system. The first prompt demands a comprehensive understanding of the chapter information. The second is appropriate for students who are ready to deal with more complex information because they are able to analyze the chapter content information and fit it in with prior knowledge of the respiratory system as a whole. This is not to say that the student who answers the first question will never answer the second question. It will just happen at a different time, perhaps one or two days later, or in a different way, such as through a lesson in which students listen to other students present information and then they talk about it.

The prompt provides the set-up for the student response. When providing two different prompts, check each one to make sure it asks what you want it to ask. The first thing to check is the content-specific language used in the prompts. Although specialized language helps make the prompt clear, you may be assuming the student has an understanding of a vocabulary word that she does not have. If she does not, the student is unable to respond to the prompt. Therefore, it's important to make sure all students understand the vocabulary before using it in prompts.

Even some of our most common words mean different things when used in different content areas. In looking at the math content area, a study conducted by Kathryn Sullivan (1982, cited in Kenney et al., 2005) showed that even a brief, three-week program centered on helping students distinguish the mathematical usage of small words can significantly improve student mathematics computation scores. Students need to understand that even small words can take on different meanings in different content areas. For example, "add" in math does not always result in an increase. Therefore, make sure all students understand what the words in the prompt mean.

Be aware also that students may not even be able to read the vocabulary word. The NASSP Bulletin (Barton, 1997, cited in Jacobs, 2006) reported 35 percent of all achievement test errors were fundamentally reading errors, in that many of the words were not part of the student's day-to-day language. Even if they can read the words, students may not use verbs such as "infer" or "analyze" often enough to actually remember what they mean. They do not say to their mother, "I need to analyze what to bring on my field trip tomorrow." Yet we expect students to conduct these processes and respond to question prompts using such verbs. Students need to learn and use "school language."

I recommend using key words and phrases to help you create directed prompts. These words inserted into an existing prompt can make it even more specific. Richard Paul's (1999) concepts can be particularly helpful to teachers who like to have a list of prompts to bump up content. Paul identifies eight elements of reasoning (see the first column of Figure 2.3) that drive understanding and promote depth of learning in a meaningful way. In this figure, you can also compare the difference between the open-ended prompt and the directed prompt.

Let's take a closer look at how Paul's elements are used as key words to direct the prompt. Take the first row in the figure: When we ask students to analyze the different forms of government, as in the third column, we are asking them to compare the different forms and describe their relationships to one another. But if we ask students to analyze the *purpose* of having different forms of government, then we move the content to a more conceptual level of knowing (Anderson & Krathwohl, 2001). By adding the word "purpose" to the prompt, we make it more specific and conceptual. This may be appropriate for students who need more challenge.

Another element of reasoning is to target questions, solve problems, and resolve issues. If you want to move the prompt from a basic level to a more complex level, change the prompt to include one or more of these concepts. For example, a more difficult and more specific prompt would ask students to "analyze the problems the character has in the story and how these problems create issues." If you want to keep the prompt simple and more open ended, the prompt might ask students to "analyze the character in the story." In both cases, students could use the same "analyze" graphic organizer, but one group focuses on the character in general while the other group focuses on the character's problems.

Figure 2.3   Using Key Words

Element of Reasoning (Adapted from Paul, 1999)	Directed Prompt	Open-Ended Prompt
Purpose (goals, objectives)	Analyze the purposes of having different kinds of government.	Analyze the different forms of government.
Issues or problems	Analyze the problems the character has in the story and explain how these problems create issues in the story.	Analyze the character in the story.
Information (facts, observations, experiences)	What might you infer from the animals' experiences regarding the pros and cons of zoos to draw conclusions about zoo effectiveness?	What inferences can you make after reading this article on the pros and cons of zoos?
Interpretation or inference (including conclusions and solutions)	How might we analyze different interpretations of Seurat's paintings?	Analyze Seurat's paintings.
Concepts	Elaborate on the different theories of dinosaur extinction.	Elaborate on why you think the dinosaurs died out.
Assumptions (that which we take for granted)	Judge the assumptions the character makes and how they help drive the action.	Judge the character's actions in the story.
Implications/consequences	Prioritize the implications or consequences of the character's action in the story.	Prioritize the events in the story.
Point of view (frame of reference, perspective, orientation)	Brain-write: How do the lungs function from the point of view of a surgeon, and from the point of view of an asthmatic?	Brain-write: How do the lungs function?

Sandra Kaplan (2005) is another who advocates the use of key words and phrases to promote complexity and depth. Her words and phrases can also be used to differentiate a prompt.

- Define over time.
- Note patterns.
- State trends.
- State ethical considerations.
- Define unanswered questions.
- View different perspectives.
- Identify rules.
- Recognize multiple points of view.
- State generalizations, principles, or big ideas.

Not all of your students will be ready for this level of abstraction. Such language can be eliminated for your struggling learners. They can still be successful thinking at a high level, if the content is addressed at a basic level. For advanced learners, when a prompt does not include such language, it is helpful to have the key words by Paul (1999) and Kaplan (2005) readily available to help you differentiate. It is easier to complexify a prompt when you have a word list to refer to than to create something from nothing.

There are advantages and disadvantages in differentiating with directed prompts (see Figure 2.4). First, every student uses the same graphic organizer. Because students can follow the step-by-step procedure on the graphic organizer, they have more chances to be successful when responding to the question. The biggest advantage I see with using this type of differentiation is that all students are challenged, because they all use critical or creative thinking. Just by tweaking the question with one or two words, the teacher creates harder and easier questions. This is also important because, in some cases, teachers are required to use the same text with all students. Teachers can easily differentiate textbook questions or questions in a teacher's manual by tailoring the prompt. All students will be challenged to think beyond the literal information to one degree or another.

Of course, some students do not want to be challenged. This becomes a disadvantage because it is sometimes difficult for the teacher to convince a student to work to her potential. By using familiar formats and providing support through shared language and commonly used procedures, the reluctant learner may find she has the tools to engage comfortably at the challenge level.

Another negative aspect of the second way to differentiate is that it takes longer to correct responses from graphic organizers with different prompts. As Nunley (2006) acknowledges in her list of general teacher complaints, the paperwork can be overwhelming. In addition, there is no answer key. Teachers have to take the time to determine what an acceptable level of response is and create their own answer keys. Because teachers do like the organizers but find them difficult to correct, they often use them as tools to generate discussion and do not correct them. This is unfortunate because students benefit from specific feedback.

A final drawback is it takes time and hard work to come up with differentiated prompts, particularly more difficult prompts. That is why I like the key words by Paul (1999) and Kaplan (2005) in which one or two words can easily change the level of complexity.

Figure 2.4   Advantages and Disadvantages of Using the "Directed Prompt"

Pros	Cons
1. All students have access to the same activity.	1. Some students do not want the challenge.
2. All students have the potential for success.	2. Teachers complain this type of activity takes too long to correct.
3. All students experience high-level thinking with content.	3. Teachers complain it's too hard to come up with challenging prompts.
4. All students are challenged!	

Different But the Same

- Students use different graphic organizers.
- Students receive differentiated prompts.
- All students use the same resources.

Note: Students may have to read the same material but responses to the material can target more or less depth of understanding at a particular point in time.

A third way to differentiate using high-level thinking graphic organizers is to use different graphic organizers with different prompts, even though students use the same resources (Figure 2.5). I call this type of differentiation *different but the same.* This works well when teachers are using a prescribed reading series or textbook and are required by the district to follow the published materials. Teachers in this situation often feel there is little time for students to do additional readings, and the teachers often do direct teaching in a whole class setting. Once the teacher has presented or reviewed the content, however, the teacher may be willing to differentiate the follow-up activities by providing students with different prompts on different graphic organizers. Teachers can either assign different graphic organizers or let students choose the ones they would like to use.

Given a choice, students most often choose graphic organizers that match their cognitive style. Robert Sternberg (1996), professor of psychology and education at Yale University, calls analytical thinkers "school smart." They are the students that do school well. They are the learners that will choose graphic organizers based on critical thinking. They like to make judgments and evaluate, as well as to compare and contrast things. Sternberg's research indicates that people still need to be taught, even in their areas of strength, to become better within their cognitive thinking disposition. Therefore, whether teachers allow students to choose a graphic organizer and they choose to stay in their comfort zone, or whether the teacher assigns particular graphic organizers, students will benefit from explicit instruction either way.

Figure 2.5   Advantages and Disadvantages of Using "Different But the Same"

Pros	Cons
1. Differentiation is hidden.	1. Teacher has to prepare more than one organizer.
2. May allow for student choice.	2. Teacher has to keep track of who does which one.
3. Allows for variety in the classroom.	3. May take different amounts of time for students to finish.
4. All students are challenged!	

One wonderful advantage in differentiating with different but the same is that students expect to be doing different graphic organizers. It becomes the class norm and it's fair. Rather than have one group of students working on graphic organizers and another group doing something else, all students are doing the same type of activity. Teachers can assign different organizers or allow student choice. Of course if you allow choice, students may choose the organizer with an easier prompt. Preadolescent and adolescent learners may choose only the formats that their friends choose, *but that's OK because they get their work done.* All learners like to work with their friends, and we know that social learning helps change our stress level, our confidence, and even our content knowledge (Jensen, 2006).

Whenever you're unsure about allowing students choice in working together, err on the side of choice. Remember—choice empowers students and gives them control over their learning. For some students, this may be the only sense of control they have over their lives. Do not, however, sacrifice learning in the name of choice. This sounds obvious, but you might be surprised that teachers, in their efforts to differentiate, offer choice when this may not be the best way for students to learn. Remember, you can control choice. That is, give students a choice between two graphic organizers that are geared for their levels of understanding rather than total free choice.

Similar to the directed prompt, the different but the same approach also requires the teacher to make up more than one question to go on more than one graphic organizer. Even though this is more work for the teacher, you will likely see that the payoff is worth it. The students will be more engaged and student achievement will increase. It's also more work if the teacher has to keep track of the graphic organizers that the students choose; but this will eliminate the possibility of the student doing the same type of graphic organizer over and over again. Once a student finds a formula for success, it's tempting to keep repeating the same type of thinking. Teachers should discourage this. Look at the example of the simple spreadsheet (Figure 2.6) with students noted by number down one side of the page and the different thinking skills across the top. This allows the teacher to keep track of the students' choices. When students choose a graphic organizer, put the date in the cell next to their number, and watch for patterns of choice. This will minimize redundancy.

Figure 2.6   Sample Spreadsheet for Tracking Use of Graphic Organizers

	Assume	Infer	Analyze	Prioritize	Judge	Brainstorm	Connect	Create	Elaborate
1	3/12	3/09		3/10	3/07				
2						3/12, 3/07	3/09		3/10
3	3/12			3/09		3/10	3/07		
4		3/12			3/09		3/10		3/07
5	3/12	3/09		3/10	3/07				
6		3/12			3/09	3/10	3/07		
7			3/12	3/09	3/10	3/07			

After looking at the chart, the teacher makes sure that Student 1 does some creative thinking activities next time. Student 2 will be required to do some critical thinking activities, and perhaps Students 1 and 5 will not work together next time. I wouldn't want to pair Student 1 with Student 2 for the next few activities because I know the one who prefers to think in a particular manner might take over the lesson and do all the work. This would undermine the teacher's attempt to make sure all students do different types of thinking at least some of the time.

A final concern for teachers with the different but the same way to differentiate is that students finish filling in the graphic organizer at different times. This is actually a problem with any type of differentiation. Make sure students who finish earlier know what to do while they are waiting for others to finish. Asking them to fill out another graphic organizer is NOT A GOOD IDEA. Students will soon learn that if they finish early, the teacher will just ask them to do more of the same. Watch how quickly your students slow down so that they don't finish before the others. Instead, let them move on to the next activity or give them time to look at extension materials.

Resources Make the Difference

- All students use the same graphic organizer.
- All students receive the same prompt.
- Students use different resources.

Note: Students respond at their level based on their engagement with different material.

In this fourth way to differentiate, *resources make the difference,* all students use the same graphic organizer with the same prompt, but they use different resources This is a great approach if you want everyone to focus on the same content, but you need to modify the print material for students who are struggling readers or extend the print material for advanced learners. This is also most effective when the teacher pretests students and finds out the student's prior knowledge. Differentiation entails finding entry and exit points to learning (Gardner, 1999; Heacox, 2002). If the pre-assessment indicates that no students have prior knowledge, then the teacher can focus on whole group instruction with students doing different follow-up readings.

Some students may need to read the content information at a lower level than the one being used by most of the students in a classroom. In the average third-grade classroom, ten reading levels exist. At the high school level, "A textbook with a 10th grade readability level means that 50% of 10th graders can read and comprehend this textbook with teacher assistance" (Nunley, 2006, p. 117). This does not take into account students who can read the material, but who do not understand or remember what they read.

This is a particular problem for teachers who use a required reading or math series, or a required textbook. They may not be allowed to use alternative print material. In this case, adjustments will need to be made for some students to successfully deal with the content. Teachers might minimize the passages that struggling students read, or they may buddy them up with a more advanced partner so they can work together.

Figure 2.7 Advantages and Disadvantages of Using "Resources Make the Difference"

Pros	Cons
1. Whole class can discuss the process.	1. Teacher has to collect a variety of reading materials.
2. Easy for teacher to correct.	2. Teacher modifies materials.
3. Students use materials commensurate with their abilities.	3. May take different amounts of time for students to finish.
4. Teacher does not have to keep track of who is doing what.	4. Students may see this as unfair.

There are actually many advantages to the resources make the difference way of differentiating. The whole class is doing the same lesson, so students can process information and discuss ideas as a whole group. Those students who read more sophisticated material can add information that others might not have read. In this way, struggling students gain additional information without actually having to read the material. The graphic organizers are easy to correct because everyone is using the same format. Students are also reading materials at their ability level, which enables them to be more successful. Teachers really do not have to keep track of who is doing what because everyone is doing the same graphic organizer with the same prompt.

The biggest drawback to this way of differentiating is the teacher needs to find many different resources or reading materials. As we all know, doing an Internet search on a topic can also mean hours of looking at layers and layers of materials at different Web sites. However, once the teacher takes the time to compile a list of resources that students can use, she won't have to do this again or will only have to modify the search the next time. Collecting resources for a particular unit is usually a one-time investment if the teacher teaches the same content year after year.

Even when teachers find articles on the Internet, they may still need to modify the information because they might not want students spending a great deal of time on one article. There might be only a portion of the article that applies to the content. In this situation, copy the article, cut it into sections, and throw away the parts that don't relate to the assignment. In some cases, teachers might actually have to highlight important information for the students. This helps the struggling reader a great deal. The average- and high-ability reader should be able to tackle the whole article and sort through relevant and irrelevant information without the teacher's assistance.

It is important to consider whether the objective of the lesson is for the student to apply the content information or to discern important information. The objectives in a science or social studies lesson are usually content-specific, whereas discerning important information is a specific skill area. If your lesson objectives do not include the specific skill area, then help out your struggling readers by doing this for them. It is not the intent of the lesson to have them bogged down in the skill area. There may be other lessons to practice discerning important information.

Another drawback, as I mentioned before, is that students may take varying amounts of time to finish. By modifying the resources, however, teachers can anticipate how long it will take students to read the materials. Most often, instead of the struggling learners taking a longer time than others to get through print material, now all students take a similar amount of time to process differentiated print information.

Finally, if the fairness issue surfaces—Why does one student only have to read an article and another an entire chapter?—I recommend being honest with your students. Tell them that students are reading what they can handle at that time. This isn't really news. Students know who can read smoothly and who struggles. If you're matter of fact about it, students will accept this as the norm. Help them to understand that by modifying resources or providing different resources, some learners may not have such a hard time keeping up with other learners. High school teachers, in particular, often feel this backfires in the classroom and affects the struggling learner's self-esteem. The danger of changing resources in the content areas is not only that the struggling learner is jealous and wants to read the harder material, but that the proficient reader doesn't want to work that hard and would prefer to coast. This is minimized if all the print materials "look" age appropriate. Then the different levels of reading are not so obvious.

Variety Plus

- Students use different graphic organizers.
- Students receive different prompts.
- Students use different resources.

Note: Students' needs are met in a variety of ways.

I call the fifth way of differentiating—using critical and creative thinking graphic organizers—*variety plus,* because it offers the most variety. Students use different graphic organizers with different prompts as well as different resources. The teacher can assign a type of graphic organizer or the students can choose, although this may not involve unlimited choice. The teacher provides different prompts for each graphic organizer in use. Finally, students may be reading from different sources, or may have modified reading passages from a text. The key factor here is that every element is targeted to meet individual needs.

In practice, this fifth form of differentiation is not as complicated as it sounds and its benefits can be numerous. Imagine a language arts class that is studying the fairy tale genre—specifically, the many different versions of Cinderella and how it translates in various cultures. Some students read *The Salmon Princess: An Alaskan Cinderella Story* by Mindy Dwyer. Other students read *The Golden Sandal: A Middle Eastern Cinderella Story* by Rebecca Hickox. Another group reads *Ella's Big Chance: A Jazz Age Cinderella* by Shirley Hughes.

The students who read *An Alaskan Cinderella Story* use the Paint Jars graphic organizer to create inferences about the main character's life in Alaska. The students who read *A Middle Eastern Cinderella Story* make "assumptions" about the main character based on their knowledge of the basic story line and Middle Eastern culture. The third group that read *A Jazz Age Cinderella* uses the "create" graphic organizer to design the shop that Ella and Buttons will have when they live happily ever after.

Notice that not every person is using a different resource. The whole class is broken down into three groups that use different resources, have different prompts, and complete different organizers. Eventually, they come back together as a whole class, summarize their stories for the other students, and share their graphic organizers. Ideally, the whole class discussion will entice at least some students to read the other versions of the story that classmates read!

The variety plus way of differentiating can be extremely motivating when teachers allow students to choose their own reading material and graphic organizer. For example, a boy might choose a modern-day fairy tale that targets his interest or at least has a boy as a main character. Another way to use the variety plus method with older students is to place the learning objective on the white board or overhead. Ask the students to choose a graphic organizer and create a question that uses the verb on the organizer and addresses the objective. Students are more invested in their learning when they come up with their own questions. It's quite difficult, however, for students to create their own questions based on the learning objective; so, make sure you are available to help students or else they may just sit there and waste time.

The variety plus approach hides differentiation because many students are doing different things. It allows for student choice and variety. It is important, however, for the teacher to introduce the verb, explain the procedural steps used to process the verb, and show students how to use the graphic organizer. Before students can work independently, the teacher should model lessons and demonstrate just what the expectation is.

The variety plus approach allows for different levels of challenge, because all aspects of the lesson can be geared specifically to the individual student. Teachers can reach all learners, because the graphic organizer activity is matched to what each student needs. If some students need to be motivated, teachers can target different materials and perhaps use one of the creative thinking graphic organizers. If some students need to review information, you can modify required readings and choose a graphic organizer like "adding details." This activity will reinforce the learning and build on the lesson's vocabulary and concepts. Some students who can read sophisticated material may like to analyze the information. All students are working on the same standard or objective but at different levels. The different levels are targeted through the learning activities, which are adjusted by all three elements—the graphic organizer, the prompt, and the resource.

The negative aspects of this type of differentiation include having to prepare more than one graphic organizer and coming up with many different prompts. This can be tedious even for the most dedicated teacher. So that you do not feel overwhelmed, begin by taking the standard or objective and changing the verb to one of the graphic organizer

Figure 2.8   Advantages and Disadvantages of Using "Variety Plus"

Pros	Cons
1. Differentiation is hidden.	1. Teacher has to prepare more than one organizer.
2. May allow for student choice.	2. Teacher has to keep track of who does which one.
3. Allows for variety in the classroom.	3. May take different amounts of time for students to finish.
4. Allows for different levels of challenge.	4. Students can fall through the cracks.
5. Reaches all learners.	5. Difficult to grade.

verbs. Turn this into a question or prompt and make sure it makes sense. Then, check to make sure the question maintains the content elements. If it loses the content thread, the question should not be used. The content connected to the standard must be an integral part of the newly revised question. Continue to substitute the different graphic organizer verbs to see which organizers will work. Then offer these as choices. With practice, you can quickly tweak the questions to use with various graphic organizers.

Of course, when students use different graphic organizers it does, again, create the problem of keeping track of who does what, and some students finishing earlier than others. Handling these issues has been discussed previously. The greatest danger with the variety plus approach, however, is that some students can slip through the cracks. They appear to be busy but do not accomplish much. They're quiet and do not draw attention to themselves. If you grade graphic organizers, then it becomes apparent who is not finishing their work. If you do not grade papers, give feedback, or at the very least check off who is doing what, these students may stay under the radar and do very little.

This brings us to a final problem, which is that it may be difficult to grade the graphic organizers when using a variety plus approach. This is true for many reasons. One graphic organizer appears easier than another; therefore, is an A on the easier graphic organizer worth the same as an A on the harder graphic organizer? If there's a rating scale or rubric that guides the scoring, then that gives you a place to start. If not, then the teacher scores each paper in terms of the responses. If the organizers are not graded, some teachers feel their students will either not do the work or not take them seriously.

Effort is always a factor. Did the student really think about the responses or just fill in the graphic organizer to complete the assignment? One student's answers may be basic, but could be a big improvement when compared to prior work as opposed to being compared to another student's work. Grading is a philosophical issue and most of us, whether we agree with our district's guidelines or not, grade according to the school's philosophy.

Regardless of what grading system you use, students need to know what the rules are. In the book, *Fair Isn't Always Equal: Assessing and Grading in the Differentiated Classroom*, Rick Wormelli (2006) describes effective assessment and grading practices. He suggests giving feedback on practice papers and only grading summative work.

Most of the time, the graphic organizers in this book are not used as truly summative work. I think of summative work as being more encompassing than responses on graphic organizers. Therefore, my intent in providing you with rubrics and rating scales in Chapters 3–11 is to give you tools you can use to provide students feedback so that their work with graphic organizers can lead to higher achievement and enhance their ability to use critical and creative thinking.

Create Your Own Organizer

- Create a graphic organizer when no graphic organizer exists to meet your needs.
- Target the critical and/or creative thinking verb.

Note: Teachers create graphic organizers to focus on a specific thinking skill area. Students create graphic organizers as a metacognitive skill to show how they think about what they know.

Perhaps the ultimate way to differentiate using high-level thinking graphic organizers is to create your own, to better suit your students' needs. You might adjust a graphic organizer with little difficulty, but find the idea of creating your own overwhelming. Creating your own graphic organizer is really not that hard! First of all, unless you are a graphic artist or a computer whiz, let go of the idea that it has to look great. As long as it works and is neat, students can use it. Here are some recommended steps that will help you create your own tool:

1. Identify the verb around which you want to create an organizer. Let's use the verb "predict" as an example.

2. Search through graphic organizer books to see if a "predict" graphic organizer exists. If one does exist, decide whether you need to modify it for the whole class or for some students. If one is not available, then move on to the next step.

3. Do an Internet search or book search to find out if others have identified a process for "predict" that you are comfortable with. These processes may be in language form and not yet in graphic organizer form. For example, Nancy Polette, in her book *The ABCs of Books and Thinking Skills: A Literature-Based Thinking Skills Program K–8* (1987, p. 109), identifies four steps for prediction: "Clarify what is to be predicted; analyze data to find a basis for predicting; make a tentative predication; and consider related data and modify predictions as necessary." Barry Beyer, in *Teaching Thinking Skills: A Handbook for Elementary School Teachers* (1991) and *Teaching Thinking Skills: A Handbook for Secondary School Teachers* (1991), defines the process in seven steps. Other books that delineate thinking skill procedures are *Thinking Skills Resource Book* (1990) by Lorene Reid and *Assessing Student Outcomes: Performance Assessment Using the Dimensions of Learning Model* (1993) by Marzano, Pickering, and McTighe. If you find useful material identified with the verb you are researching, choose which process you like best for your students or come up with your own process. If you have to come up with your own language to help students process the thinking skill, move on to the next step.

4. Think about what you do when you make a prediction. It's best to work with a colleague on this because you'll be able to bounce ideas off each other. Whether you're working alone or with a colleague, write down the process that you expect your students to use. Here is an example of the procedure that I might use:

    Step 1. Write the prediction statement.

    Step 2. Give reasons for your prediction based on the information presented in the text.

    Step 3. Give reasons to support your prediction from information that exists outside of the information presented in the text.

    Step 4. Consider other possible predictions and modify your prediction if necessary.

    Step 5. Determine the likelihood that your prediction will occur.

For instance, let's say I'm a language arts teacher teaching a fairy tale unit to my fourth graders, and the students are reading *Cinderella*. I might ask them to predict her chances for long-term happiness with the prince (Step 1). One prediction statement might be "I predict she will be happy with the prince." This assertion can be supported (Step 2) by giving examples from the story that describe what a nice person Cinderella is and how happy she always is regardless of her situation. Next, I might ask them to consider their prediction based on other sources or information (Step 3). Students might support their prediction by saying that fairy tales always end happily ever after. In Step 4, students have the opportunity to reconsider predictions and modify the original prediction. For example, someone may have raised doubts about Cinderella's chances for long-term happiness because they think of Princess Diana and how she was not perceived as happy in her marriage. It may occur to students to consider what demands royalty would place on a peasant girl such as Cinderella. This might lead some students, who started out believing she would have long-term happiness, to change their prediction. In Step 5, one group of students may be 100 percent certain their prediction is correct. Another group that came to a different conclusion may be equally adamant. Of course, we will never know who is right. I do like this last step, however, because I want my students to think about the likelihood that their prediction is correct. Most of my fourth graders would not know percentages, so I would use a Likert-type scale that goes from "not sure" to "positive" that the prediction is correct. It really doesn't matter to me where the students make a slash mark, because I've added this step for our enjoyment. I do reflect on the lesson, however, to make sure it meets my objective: for students to review the story and their own knowledge to find supporting evidence to support their prediction.

5. The next step is turning the process into a graphic organizer. This is where teachers tend to get very nervous. They think they could never come up with a visual they could really use. But you can and here's how. First of all, think of the number of steps you used in your process. In my example, I used five, which means I need five places for my students to make a response. If I can't draw and have limited computer skills, I can always use boxes, circles, and arrows. High school teachers prefer these types of formats because their students often think pictorial formats are too cutesy and are only for elementary students. This is unfortunate because students often remember images. It's more likely they will remember the predicting process if it is embedded in labeled steps in a picture (Figure 2.9) as opposed to isolated boxes and lines (Figure 2.10).

When I created the Birthday Wishes graphic organizer, it started out as a staircase. After I made the steps, I thought it looked like a birthday cake, so I named it that. This is easy to draw on the computer but I could have drawn it by hand or asked the art teacher for help. When I use this organizer with students, the first thing they say is that it's an awesome birthday cake because it's so big.

I like to create two graphic organizer formats. One is usually pictorial and the other is a linear format. One style format may appeal to you more than another. But make sure you create different styles of organizers because if you always use boxes and arrows, you will be shortchanging learners who prefer to see pictorial formats. If you use a whole lot

Figure 2.9 Birthday Wishes Graphic Organizer (Predict)

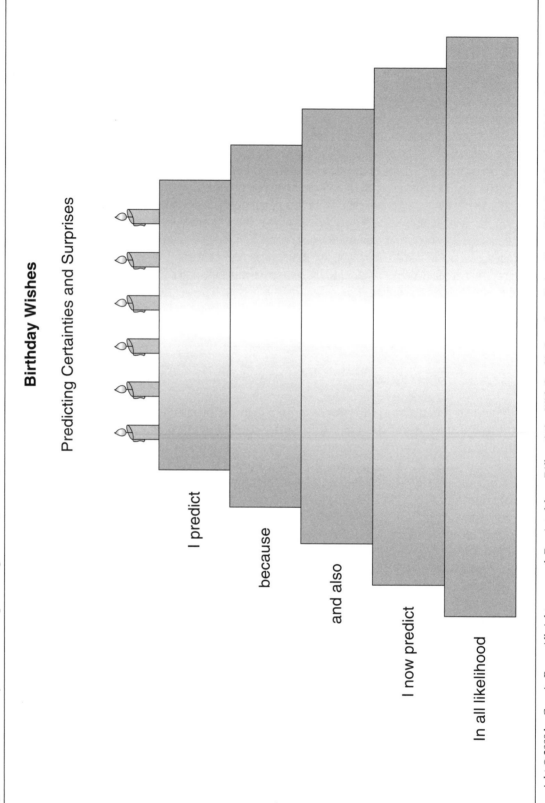

Birthday Wishes

Predicting Certainties and Surprises

I predict

because

and also

I now predict

In all likelihood

Figure 2.10   Linear Graphic Organizer (Predict)

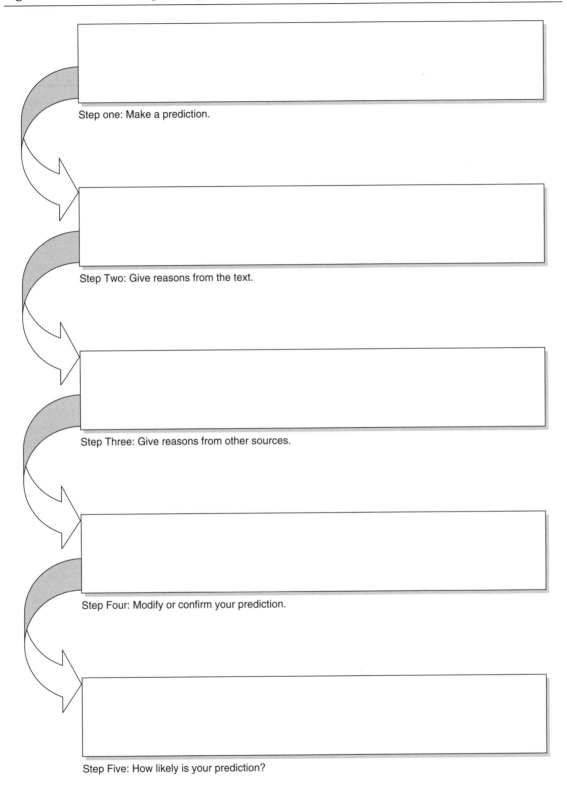

Step one: Make a prediction.

Step Two: Give reasons from the text.

Step Three: Give reasons from other sources.

Step Four: Modify or confirm your prediction.

Step Five: How likely is your prediction?

of pictures, you won't be helping learners who prefer information presented in simple, linear sections. Through variety, you reach all learners.

Once you know the steps for creating graphic organizers, you can help your students create their own. You may be surprised to discover that some students are really good at this. In fact, they may be better at it than you are. In *Great Teaching With Graphic Organizers* (Drapeau, 1998), there are examples of fourth-grade, student-generated creative thinking graphic organizers. Even though students can be successful doing this, they still need teacher support to understand how to analyze the verb, create procedural steps to process the verb, think about the information they are studying to make sure it works in the content area, and come up with a graphic design. Not all students will be up for this challenge. Perhaps students can generate their own thinking tools and share them with one another. Any tool that helps students be successful in the classroom is always welcome.

The pitfalls (see Figure 2.11) of allowing students to create or modify graphic organizers are numerous: Some of their creations will not make sense, and some students will simply be unable to create organizers. They may not be able to come up with logical steps, create a visual from the words, or the visual may be random and confusing to use. You will need to review the organizer (which of course is not part of the curriculum content), understand what the student is trying to say or do, and provide feedback. This takes time and can be a frustrating experience for both you and the student. Unless doing so is part of the curriculum, I do not recommend a whole class activity that asks students to create organizers. There should be opportunity to do this, but no requirement.

The benefits of students creating or modifying their own organizers, however, are numerous and can be well worth the time and effort. Students who can do it show evidence of developing awareness of their own thinking, the ability to articulate their thinking processes, and the ability to articulate this process visually. This is motivational for some students and fosters their self-esteem because they are usually proud of their original work. It is an opportunity for students to not feel restricted by someone else's design and for visual learners to see how the thinking process looks on paper. Students really learn about quality thinking when they come up with their own visual. Often, when they see the process, they understand it and remember it. Once it is embedded, they have access to the process whenever they want to use it again. This transference does not happen quickly—it takes practice across content and over time (Black & Black, 1990, cited in Burke, 1994).

Figure 2.11   Advantages and Disadvantages of Student-Created Graphic Organizers

Pros	Cons
1. Customize to fit responses.	1. Some of the original graphic organizers will not make sense.
2. Great for creative learners.	2. Takes time to correct original formats.
3. Great for visual learners.	3. Not all students will be able to or want to create their own graphic organizers.
4. Students and/or teachers create formats.	
5. Fosters self-esteem and motivation.	

DECIDING WHEN TO USE WHICH DIFFERENTIATION APPROACH

We've examined six different ways to differentiate using cognitive graphic organizers, but it should be noted that not all of the graphic organizers work well in every context in all content and with every student. Therefore it is important to consider some factors before you decide which differentiation approach to use in a lesson with a graphic organizer.

First, you need to consider nonnegotiable factors and situations, for example, the time allotted for a lesson. Consider how to use your time efficiently and effectively and to maximize the payoff. If you turn a graphic organizer lesson into a great activity that takes 45 minutes (because the discussion based on the responses on different organizers takes more time), as opposed to just having students fill out the same graphic organizer in 15 minutes and moving on, the 30 extra minutes was time well spent. When students create their own graphic organizers, it usually takes more time than any of the other options.

Next, consider at what point in the lesson students begin to really show a difference in what they know, remember, and can apply content. At what point in the lesson do some learners understand the information, whereas others need to review it? Use the directed prompt approach to address these different rates of learning.

If you choose to deepen the instruction by providing advanced extension resources, you need to have the resources or find them. When remediating the material, you might seek out supplemental materials. If you do not have the resources readily available or do not have time to search them out, then this is not a viable option. This creates a problem when your target differentiation approach is resources make the difference.

Factors to Consider When Selecting Graphic Organizers

- Time when lesson must end
- Point in lesson when students learn at different rates
- Point in lesson when supplemental or extension information is needed
- Point in unit that is not interesting and needs a lift
- Meeting needs of the students
- Meeting needs of the teachers

Brain research consistently supports the notion that learning must be novel, challenging, and meaningful (Jensen, 2006). In looking at a unit of study, take note of when activities, questions, or lessons fall flat. This might be a great place to give your unit a lift by substituting graphic organizer lessons for the ones that you previously used. If it's an introductory lesson, an open-ended prompt might spark discussion. If it's a lesson that occurs midway through a unit, different but the same might be an effective activity. Have students use different organizers with different prompts based on the same reading material. They can then come back as a group and share their ideas. In a follow-up lesson at the end of a unit, use the variety plus approach so that students can recap the information they have learned in their preferred style.

Meeting the needs of students can feel overwhelming. That is why it is important to collect data and form groups of students who have similar abilities, interests, and styles.

Student inventories are helpful in collecting data (Gregory & Kuzmich, 2004; Heacox, 2002). This information helps teachers to form groups of students and target their cognitive styles. Students who have a creative thinking preference can use the "brainstorm," "connect," "create," or "elaborate" graphic organizers, while the critical thinkers can use the critical thinking graphic organizers. In this situation, teachers can use the different but the same approach.

Teachers should consider their own needs as well. Research shows that if you're happy and enjoy teaching, you will be more effective in the classroom. Enthusiasm is contagious—the role of emotion in the classroom is well documented (Sousa, 2001; Sylwester, 2003; Wolfe, 2001). These graphic organizers can help you make changes in your teaching and differentiation practices.

CREATING A RATING SCALE OR RUBRIC

Once you've selected a graphic organizer, decide if you want to create a rating scale or rubric to go with it. The rating scale or rubric is based on a specific verb and provides guidance and direction for the student (see specific examples in Chapters 3–11). Let's take a look at how a rating scale might be created for our prediction example. Think about each step of making a prediction and ask questions about it based on the various criteria. For example, in Step 1, when the student is asked to make a prediction, the first question you might think about is: How *relevant* is the prediction? In Steps 2 and 3, you might want students to consider how *important* are the reasons found in- or outside of the text supporting this prediction? This might be a particularly important criterion for students who give reasons based on minutia or inconsequential facts. Another criterion you might want students to consider is how logical their final prediction is based on their reasons and sources. You can then ask students to score their responses on a 1 to 5 scale, with 5 being highest. The rating scale might look something like Figure 2.12.

There is no set number of criteria and probing questions that teachers need to use. Figure 2.13 presents a list of possible criteria and probing questions. This list is meant to help you get started in considering criteria that you can use with graphic organizers. You and/or your students can develop criteria and questions that are age-appropriate and specific to your content.

Have students use the rating scale to check their thinking, or, after they hand in their work, you can also use the rating scale to assess the graphic organizer and provide the student with feedback. When students rate themselves, the questions are personalized. They sound like this: How clear are my statements or how relevant are my predictions? A third way to use the rating scale is to have both the teacher and the student fill it out. If the two scores are discrepant, the teacher should meet with the student to discuss why.

Figure 2.12   Sample: Critical Thinking Rating Scale (Predict)

Criteria	Probing Questions	Rating
Relevancy	How relevant is the prediction?	5
Importance	How important are the reasons?	4
Logic	How logical is the prediction?	5

Figure 2.13   Generic Rating Scale Criteria and Prompts

Criteria	Probing Questions
Clarity	How clear are the statements?
Relevancy	How relevant are the statements?
Importance	How important are the reasons?
Logic	How logical is the reasoning?
Consistency	How consistent are the statements?
Reasonableness	Do the statements seem reasonable?
Connections	To what degree are connections made?
Accuracy	How accurate are the examples?
Creativity	To what degree are the ideas unusual?
Detail	To what degree are details included?

Figure 2.14   Sample: Critical Thinking Rubric (Predict)

1	2	3
The prediction is irrelevant.	The prediction is somewhat relevant.	The prediction is relevant.
Reasons reflect lack of evidence.	A few of the reasons are not that relevant.	All reasons are relevant.
The conclusions are not logical.	The conclusions are logical.	The logical conclusions reflect inferential reasoning and informed judgment.

Some teachers prefer to use a rubric rather than a rating scale. In Chapters 3–11, I include samples of both. The rubric provides more description and guidance than the rating scale. In Figure 2.14, the prediction rating scale is converted into a rubric that addresses each of the probing questions from the rating scale and describes a range of performances.

I design my assessment tools to be used as feedback. I rarely use them to grade the graphic organizers, although some teachers do. I generally use other summative performance tools for grading purposes. Most of the time, I use graphic organizers as a stepping-stone for the next activity. By that, I mean I use them as a pre-writing tool, a tool for a discussion format, a review for a test, a homework assignment, and so on. I often decide whether to grade or not based on the use of the graphic organizer. When I use the graphic organizer as a pre-writing tool, I grade the writing piece, not the graphic organizer. When I use the graphic organizer as a format for a shared discussion, I use the graphic organizer as a way for students to organize their thinking so that they can effectively participate in the discussion. I do not grade the discussion. When I ask students to use the graphic organizer as a tool to review for a test, it is the test I grade. When I ask them to use the graphic organizer as a homework assignment, I might grade the graphic organizer or I might just check off the homework as complete. I also do not use rating scales or rubrics every time I use a graphic organizer. That would be overkill! Just decide when the lesson or activity warrants using feedback tools such as these. In quick lessons, it is often not necessary to use the assessment tools, as opposed to in-depth lessons, where students are sorting through a lot of complex content.

KEY POINTS TO REMEMBER ABOUT DIFFERENTIATING WITH GRAPHIC ORGANIZERS

1. The six ways to use graphic organizers presented in this chapter are effective instructional techniques that help us apply the principles of differentiation.

2. Through the many applications of graphic organizers, teachers are able to modify the content, process, and product of a lesson; adjust pacing of instruction; and provide different levels of assistance.

3. Teachers can offer controlled choice by focusing graphic organizer options according to student needs, and foster active learning through group work.

4. Rating scales and rubrics provide specific tools that can be used for feedback.

5. The different ways to use the organizers allow for resource variety and assignment modifications.

6. The teacher provides the supportive classroom and creates a management system for this to work.

? PAUSE FOR REFLECTION AND DISCUSSION

1. Summarize what you know about the six ways to use graphic organizers as differentiation tools.

2. How do you decide which graphic organizer to use and when?

3. In what situation or unit might you decide to create your own graphic organizer and who might you need to help you accomplish this task?

4. Do you think the use of rating scales will help your students to create better, clearer, more logical responses? Why or why not?

PART II

Five Critical Thinking Verbs and the Graphic Organizers to Use With Them

Assume

Infer

Analyze

Prioritize

Judge

3

"Assume"

Exploring What We Take for Granted

Name:_____ Date:_____

Assume

1. State an assumption. _____
_____
_____

2. Justify your assumption with information. _____
_____
_____
_____
_____

3. Evaluate your assumption: Is it reasonable? Why? _____
_____
_____
_____

Assume!

⇨ Graphic Organizer: Thought Bubble

⇨ Verb: Assume

⇨ Synonyms: Believe, suppose, take for granted

⇨ Define the Steps:

1. State your assumption: List an assumption or what you believe to be true.

2. Justify your assumption: Verify your assumption with information or data.

3. Evaluate your assumption: Make conclusions regarding the assumption.

DEFINITION

An assumption is a belief or fact that we accept as true. It is something we take for granted, something we once learned that we no longer question. We make unconscious assumptions every day. Paul and Elder in their book, *Tools for Taking Charge of Your Learning and Your Life* (2001), describe assumptions as part of our belief system. Because we assume our beliefs are true, we view the world through this lens. For example, students might look at a text that has few pictures and small print and assume it will be hard to read. This assumption is made based on prior knowledge. The students don't ask other students who have read the text what they think of it. They don't ask if the text has difficult words or if it is hard to understand. They just take it for granted that it will be hard for them.

As students identify assumptions in their thinking, they become aware that both unconscious and conscious assumptions affect point of view and decision making. When students study to get good grades, they may make a conscious assumption, perhaps based on past experience, that studying will help them perform well on their assessments. Practical experience along with logical thinking often leads to well-founded assumptions. Conversely, a student might make an unconscious assumption about studying by assuming, "I'll never get good grades no matter how hard or long I study, because I'm just not as smart as other kids in my class." The unconscious assumption here is that good grades are an indication of intelligence alone, rather than the result of persistent effort.

People make reasonable and unreasonable assumptions, and this applies to teachers as well as students. A reasonable assumption is based on evidence and can be justified or reasoned according to that evidence. For example, if a student has completed all her homework assignments from September through April, it is reasonable for the teacher to assume she will continue to complete all of her homework assignments to the end of the year. Of course, the student may become sick or experience a personal tragedy. The assumption, however, appears reasonable based on past evidence. An assumption may be unreasonable when the evidence is weak or illogical. If a student is taking notes with a pen, the teacher might assume that this student likes to take notes with a pen rather than use a computer, when in fact there could be many other explanations.

PURPOSE

The purpose of pointing out assumptions and teaching the steps of reasonable, conscious assumption making is to help students know that assumptions are used to build comprehension, make good decisions, and construct arguments. In the twenty-first century, students are exposed to information at a rate never experienced before. This is why it is so important for students to be able to read information, sort through it for meaning, and determine assumptions that are being made to judge the accuracy of information.

Once students are aware of assumptions they make and how to analyze them, it can help them realize how assumptions influence their ideas. Students also become aware of where their thinking goes astray. When identifying and analyzing assumptions becomes a habit of mind, students' reading comprehension, oral communication, and writing skills may improve. According to Norris's (1985) review, "Most students do not score well on tests that measure ability to recognize assumptions, evaluate arguments, and appraise inferences" (p. 44). If your state tests do not ask questions that require your students to recognize or analyze assumptions, you might wonder why you should ask students to even think about their assumptions. The answer is that this type of thinking helps students make sense of their learning. Talking about assumptions makes learning more interesting and challenging for all students. Students often find listing facts and comparing them boring, but they are interested in thinking about assumptions they make about these facts. Even though it is harder to think about assumptions, it is deeper learning that will move from short- to long-term memory. Imagine how easy students will think the questions are on state tests if you have them practicing this deeper level of knowing in the classroom.

Because recognizing assumptions is an advanced reasoning skill for students in the primary grades, it is important to keep the practice examples simple. For young children, it helps to give them concrete examples with real objects rather than language-based texts. For example, in science class, teachers might ask students what they assume will happen when they plant seeds in a paper cup. Students will probably respond that they assume the seeds will sprout. The teacher asks them why they believe this to be true.

For older students, the unpacking of assumptions can help them to clarify issues in their content areas. In an energy unit, a student might argue, "The government should encourage homeowners to use alternative energy to heat their homes because when we use oil for home heating, we place ourselves in a dependent position." The hidden assumptions in this argument are that (1) there are no incentives for homeowners to use alternative energy sources, (2) homeowners use only oil to heat their homes, and (3) we are dependent on foreign nations for our total oil supply. The argument stated thus, without support, is weak because not all the assumptions have been shown to be entirely valid. When assumptions are erroneous or unsupported by evidence, an argument lacks credibility. Therefore, it is important for students to know and understand the power of assumptions to apply logical reasoning in an argument or, as in this case, to offer valid supporting evidence.

BENEFITS

Students use many sophisticated thinking skills when they analyze an assumption. Messina and Messina (1999) recommend validating or testing assumptions to see if they are grounded in reality. In the process, students identify inconsistencies, evaluate whether conclusions logically follow from certain premises, and determine whether statements are

- Relevant or irrelevant
- Important or unimportant
- Valid or invalid
- Clear or unclear
- Justified or unjustified
- Consistent or inconsistent

By using an assumption graphic organizer, teachers are able to assess if students are making false assumptions that are influencing their understanding of content, or if their assumptions are true but they are not able to integrate them with new knowledge. If the former is the case, the teacher can analyze the students' ability to articulate sound assumptions and help them use the process articulated on the graphic organizer to improve their thinking and develop correct answers. In the latter case, the teacher can help the student build strong conclusions by showing how to connect the assumption with new learning.

APPLICATIONS

Exploring assumptions is a life skill that can be applied to any content area. The more students practice it, the more it will become a habit of mind. Students are already making assumptions; if they weren't, they would be immobilized in their thinking. By bringing the skill of examining assumptions to the level of consciousness, so that students use it in their everyday engagement of curriculum, our hope is that we can raise students' levels of achievement.

Let's look how the verb "assume" can be used in the classroom. For a start, teachers can take many state standards and ask what assumptions can be made about the standards. The Texas standard, Texas Essential Knowledge and Skills (TEKS), for seventh-grade social studies states, "The student understands the rights and responsibilities of Texas citizens." After classroom readings and discussions on the topic, the teacher might ask her students, "What can we assume about the rights and responsibilities of Texas citizens?" This not only helps to "cover" the standard, it also has students thinking about the standard in a new and different way. The teacher can state an assumption in a question for discussion (in the example above), allow the students to choose from a list of given assumptions, or allow her students to make their own assumption statements and then examine them with the graphic organizer.

Addressing assumptions in the classroom is often particularly motivating for young students, because they like to think about what is "hidden." Primary teachers can capitalize on this by telling their students they can be investigators to try to find hidden assumptions or make predictions. For middle and high school students, an assumption can be used as a hook to pull students into a text. For example, the teacher might say, "The word 'shiver' is used in this story. What might you assume?" Students become curious and want to know who shivers and why.

Here are a few examples to get you started thinking about applying this skill in your classroom (adapted from Connecticut Standards, Georgia's Quality Core Curriculum, Maine Learning Results, National Council of Teachers of Mathematics Standards, National English Language Arts Standards, National Science Standards, National Social Studies Standards, New Hampshire Curriculum and Proficiency Standards, and Texas Essential Knowledge and Skills). In many of the examples, students are asked to come up with their own assumption(s). They verify this assumption and make conclusions about it on the graphic organizer. All of these examples can be used with the "assume" graphic organizer and follow the steps outlined on the organizer.

In the Elementary Grades

Language Arts

o The teacher asks the class what we can assume about the character at the beginning, middle, and end of the story. The teacher lists the assumptions and asks students to justify them.
o What can we assume from the behavior of the character in the story? Students might assume that Charlotte in the story *Charlotte's Web* by E. B. White is a nice spider. They can justify and make conclusions about this assumption and compare it to assumptions they make about real spiders.

Writing

o At the rough draft stage, students use the graphic organizer to identify and verify assumptions in their writing before using them in a formal piece.
o During the revision process, teachers check for valid assumptions. Students can use the rating scale or rubric to ascertain whether assumptions they make in their paper are accurate.

Math

o What can be assumed when making a one-two pattern with blocks? Students might assume that the pattern can be continued so long as alternating colored blocks remain. Students can check their assumption after the teacher adds additional blocks.

o What can we assume when we use estimation? Have students work in small groups to create their own assumptions such as: Estimation is useful. They can then try to support their assumption by citing examples, and they may conclude that their assumption is true.

Science

o What assumptions can we make about the weather. Students may, for example, assume that weather changes. In a whole group activity, the teacher uses the assumption steps and records student responses on chart paper.

o What assumptions can we make about day and night? Students might assume that day and night occur simultaneously, depending on your location. Have groups test this assumption and report their results.

Social Studies

o What assumptions can we make about the different functions of government? The teacher lists functions of government on the board. Students work in pairs to identify, verify, and make conclusions about the assumptions and share them with the class.

o What assumptions can we make about the writing of the United States Constitution? The teacher uses this prompt as a summarizing activity at the end of a unit.

In the Middle Grades

Language Arts

o What can we assume about the controversies surrounding the issues in the story? Have the class identify an issue in the story such as prejudice. Students then work in groups of four to create an assumption statement based on the portrayal of prejudice in the story. Then, have them support their assumption and make conclusions about it on their graphic organizers.

o Halfway through a story, have students identify a problem or issue. Then give them an open-ended prompt to come up with an assumption about the solution.

Writing

o Examine assumptions you made during an expository writing assignment and see if they can be verified through research. Students generate questions to research and identify assumptions that are implied in their questions. After conducting their research, they verify their assumptions.

o What do you assume about an audience you are writing for? Students are asked to write an editorial for the school newspaper. Before they write, the teacher asks them to work in groups to identify assumptions they make about their audience and use the graphic organizer to verify and draw conclusions about these assumptions. The teacher then asks students to think about how their assumptions influence their message.

Math

o What can we assume when using measures of central tendency and range to describe data? Have students use the graphic organizer to reinforce math vocabulary.

o What can we assume when we use generalizations in algebra? This prompt encourages students to synthesize what they know about the principles of algebra. One assumption might be that whatever we do to one side of the equation we need to do to the other side of the equation to hold the value constant. To demonstrate this principle, students could cite many examples using positive and negative numbers, decimals, fractions, and exponents.

Science

o What assumptions can we make regarding the classification of human body systems? The teacher uses this prompt to address assumptions about the meaning of classification systems. After the class generates assumptions, groups of students choose one assumption and process it on the graphic organizer.

o What assumptions can we make about the function of a cell in a multicellular organism? The teacher uses this prompt a few days into a unit on cells. The students create assumptions, analyze them, and reconfirm their assumptions throughout the unit of study.

Social Studies

o What assumptions can we make about political issues during the American Revolution? The students can use the graphic organizer to examine their assumptions.

o What assumptions can we make about interpreting maps and other geographical data to derive information about people, places, and region? The teacher uses this prompt to reinforce lessons on using geographical tools.

In the High School Grades

English

o Examine assumptions you make when you describe relationships between characters. This is a more specific and focused prompt than simply having students compare and contrast characters.

o Confirm assumptions you make regarding the author's purpose. Students work in groups to discuss the author's purpose, and then work individually to create and evaluate their assumptions using a graphic organizer.

Writing

o Review assumptions we make about peer editing. The teacher uses this prompt to illustrate to students how useful peer editing can be if taken seriously.

o Evaluate assumptions we make regarding the use of mood, tone, and voice in a writing piece.

Math

    o Examine assumptions we can make regarding simulations related to probability. This prompt is useful when a student refuses to believe a probability does not just boil down to a fifty-fifty chance.

    o Come up with possible assumptions that can be made regarding translations, rotations, reflections, and scale changes using coordinate systems. Break the class into groups with each one focusing on a different condition of change (i.e., translation, rotation, reflection, etc.). Each group makes, verifies, and evaluates assumptions.

Science

    o What might we assume about the causes of acid rain and the chemical reactions involved? The teacher uses this prompt after students read an Internet article on acid rain.

    o What do we assume in using various methods to measure the speed of light? This prompt serves as a review of the ways light speed is measured and changes in methods of measuring it over time.

Social Studies

    o Identify the facts and assumptions that are used in creating a position paper on an issue of public or foreign policy. This prompt is used to encourage students to reflect on arguments used in defending a position. After using the graphic organizer, students are given opportunity to revise their position papers.

    o What assumptions can be made regarding current international trade issues? Students can fill out graphic organizers individually, and then come together as a class to discuss the results.

GETTING STARTED IN THE CLASSROOM

Addressing thinking skills in the classroom can feel awkward at first. You may not know how to bring up the word "assume" without making it seem like the verb is being taught in isolation. As you introduce or review the meaning of assumption, let your students know you expect them to think about and examine assumptions that are made in a lesson. Make it clear that they will be using critical thinking when they do this and their reasoning will help them understand the material more completely and accurately.

Model the steps on the graphic organizer by doing a practice example with the class or by showing them an example of a completed graphic organizer. Review the steps outlined on the graphic organizers in Figure 3.1 (the "Thought Bubble") and Figure 3.2 (the linear "assume" model). As students identify assumptions or teachers assign assumptions in Step 1, students are expected to consider why the assumption is being made. They should examine what information or evidence supports the assumption in Step 2 and then validate, revise, or invalidate it in Step 3. With clear examples, teachers need to model how to move from Step 1 (identifying the assumption), to Step 2 (providing evidence), to Step 3 (drawing a conclusion about the evidence).

Figure 3.1 Thought Bubble Graphic Organizer (Assume)

Name:_____ Date:_____

Assume

1. State an assumption. _____
_____
_____

2. Justify your assumption with information. _____
_____
_____
_____
_____
_____
_____

3. Evaluate your assumption: Is it reasonable? Why? ____
_____
_____
_____

Assume!

Illustration by Bob Greisen.

Figure 3.2   Linear Graphic Organizer (Assume)

Name _____   Date _____

Assume

1. State an assumption.

2. Justify the assumption with evidence. _____

_____

_____

_____

_____

_____

_____

3. Conclude whether or not the assumption is reasonable and explain why.

_____

_____

_____

_____

_____

SAMPLE LESSONS

In an eighth-grade classroom, students are reading *Julie of the Wolves* by Jean Craighead George. Before they finish the book, the teacher asks the students, "What assumption can you make about if and how Miyax will survive?" Students work independently to create their own assumptions and justify them. One student says she assumes Miyax will survive because the wolves bring her food and warmth. The student supports this assumption by stating, "The wolves already like her and the wolves already bring her food." Although this is true, the evidence is weak because the wolves' behavior could change. The teacher points this out, but the student decides not to change her assumption. She is anxious to finish the book to find out if her assumption is true.

The next lesson includes student responses, which will help you to fully understand the nuances of this graphic organizer. This example involves the book *Because of Winn-Dixie* by Kate DiCamillo. When students are halfway through the book, they are instructed to fill out an "assume" graphic organizer. At this point, students have some information about the premise and the problems posed in the story, but they don't yet know the ending.

One student's "assume" graphic organizer from this lesson is reproduced in Figure 3.3. Her assumption is that Opal, the main character in the story, will find friends. To support her assumption, she says that Opal's father is a preacher who mostly thinks about preaching, Opal's mother left when she was three, and Opal moves all the time. These could be reasons why Opal has no friends, but they do not support the assumption that she will later find friends. The student goes on to say that Opal takes home a dog and is allowed to bring it into the library. Also, the pet owner gives Opal a job. These observations imply that having a dog, being in a library with a dog, and working in a pet store might provide situations for Opal to make friends. This is possible, but her responses only somewhat apply proper reasoning to support her assumption.

ASSESSMENT

Rating scales or rubrics represent a culminating activity with graphic organizers. The teacher uses them to inform students how to process their assumptions more efficiently and effectively. They can certainly be used as a guide when describing what to look for in a quality response. Students can check their responses on a graphic organizer against the descriptors on the rating scale. If any part of their response is weak, they have an opportunity to adjust their thinking and revise their answer. The criteria and probing questions on the rating scale help students understand the power of assumptions. Take, for example, the student whose graphic organizer on the book *Because of Winn-Dixie* was reproduced in Figure 3.3. The prompt for this lesson was to make an assumption about Opal and use the graphic organizer to determine if the assumption was reasonable. After the student filled out the graphic organizer, she was asked to assess her work on a rating scale, which is presented in Figure 3.4. The first step on the graphic organizer, stating or listing an assumption, is evaluated on the rating scale in terms of relevancy. The second step on the graphic organizer, listing information that supports the assumption, is evaluated on the rating scale in terms of importance and validity. The last step, which is to determine if the assumption is reasonable, is evaluated on the rating scale in terms of the student making a logical connection between the evidence and the assumption. The student gave herself the top rating (5 on a scale of 1 to 5) in all four categories—relevancy, importance, validity, and logical conclusions.

Figure 3.3   Sample: *Because of Winn-Dixie* Thought Bubble Graphic Organizer (Assume)

Name: _____ **Date:** _____

Assume

1. <u>State an assumption.</u> *I assume India Opal Buloni will find friends.*

2. <u>Justify your assumption with information.</u> *Opal's father is a preacher who mostly thinks about preaching. Opal's mother left when she was three. Opal has no friends because they move all the time. Opal takes home a dog. Miss Franny, the librarian, allows the dog in the library. Otis, the pet store owner gives Opal a job.*

3. <u>Evaluate your assumption: Is it reasonable? Why?</u> *Yes, Opal will make many friends.*

Because of Winn-Dixie
by Kate DiCamillo

Assume!

When the teacher reviews the student's rating scale, she feels the assumption does relate to the prompt. So, she agrees that the student is justified in giving herself a 5 for relevancy. The teacher, however, disagrees with the student's score in the second category. She thinks that some of the information is weak in supporting the idea that Opal will make "many" friends. Thus, the teacher thinks the student should receive a 4 in the importance category. The teacher agrees with the student that some of the information is valid but not all of it, so the teacher feels a 4 is an appropriate score for validity. The teacher also thinks the student does not really take into account the information. Therefore, the teacher gives the student a 4 rating for logical conclusions.

One weak area for this student is the assumption that all the information she listed is important and valid. This is a common problem. Many students will list their information and then not think about it. Because they have made a list, they think this means that there is important, relevant evidence. They do not think about the relationship between what the list says and the degree of influence the ideas have on their conclusion. The graphic organizer enables the teacher to pinpoint where thinking breaks down. She might, for example, mention the importance of quantifying words like many, all, or some. She might ask the student, "From the information you listed, can you assume she will have many friends? What characteristics enable people to make many friends? Does Opal have these characteristics?"

In Figure 3.5, the language from the rating scale is turned into a three-point rubric. In the lesson on *Because of Winn-Dixie,* the teacher scores the student responses with asterisks in a rubric version of the rating scale because she prefers to use rubrics. The teacher gives the student a 3 because she does make a relevant assumption. The teacher gives the student a 2 because some of her information is not very important. In the next criteria, the teacher gives the student a 2 because some of her information is not really valid in terms of the assumption. The teacher also gives the student a 2 when it comes to making a logical conclusion and explaining why.

Teachers can provide feedback on student responses in a variety of ways. Because you cannot possibly meet with every student every time to give specific feedback, try working with a few students individually on a rotating basis to go over responses on the graphic organizer and the rating scale or rubric. You can also write questions on the student's rating scales or rubrics when you do not have time to meet with them. These questions help prompt students to think more carefully. Some teachers collect the papers, examine the scores the students have given themselves, and score the paper in a different color. Students then have the opportunity to see if the teacher agrees or disagrees with their rating and can ask to meet later if there is confusion.

Once students have used the "assume" graphic organizer and rating scale or rubric a few times with supervision, they should feel comfortable using them on their own. When this happens, the students are ready for the teacher to move away from using the same graphic organizer, the same prompt, with the same resource materials for the whole class at the same time and begin to use the graphic organizers in the variety of ways described in Chapter 2.

Figure 3.4   Sample: *Because of Winn-Dixie* Critical Thinking Rating Scale (Assume)

Criteria	Probing Question	Rating
Relevancy	Does the assumption make sense and is it related to the prompt?	5
Importance	How important is the information in relation to the assumption?	5
Validity	How grounded in evidence is the assumption?	5
Logic	Does the conclusion take into account the information?	5

Figure 3.5   Sample: *Because of Winn-Dixie* Critical Thinking Rubric (Assume)

1	2	3
No relevant assumption made.	Assumption doesn't make sense or is unrelated to the prompt.	Assumption is clear and relates to the prompt. *
No important supporting information.	Two or more supporting pieces of information but one or more may be unimportant. *	Three or more important pieces of supporting information, which are all important.
Does not connect valid information to assumption.	Makes obvious connections between valid information to assumption. *	Makes subtle connections between valid information to assumption.
No conclusion.	Conclusion is reasonable but cannot tell why. *	Conclusion is reasonable and reasons are accurate.

Note: The asterisk indicates where the teacher scored the student on the rubric.

 KEY POINTS TO REMEMBER ABOUT ASSUMING

1. It is something we take for granted.

2. It may be something we learned, do not question, and now believe.

3. We make conscious and unconscious assumptions.

4. Assumptions affect decision making.

5. There are reasonable and unreasonable assumptions.

6. Good critical reasoning involves checking assumptions and verifying their relevancy.

7. Using assumptions in arguments builds point of view.

? PAUSE FOR REFLECTION AND DISCUSSION

1. What do you know and understand about assumptions?

2. How can students improve their achievement by understanding assumptions?

3. How might you differentiate a lesson by using the "assumption" graphic organizer in your classroom?

4. What is the value of using the "assume" rating scale or rubric?

4

"Infer"

Drawing Conclusions

⇨ Graphic Organizer: Paint Jars

⇨ Verb: Infer

⇨ Synonyms: Conclude, gather, deduce, predict, guess

⇨ Define the Steps:

1. Identify the facts: List what you know from the pictures or the text.

2. Provide prior knowledge: Add what you know from other contexts.

3. Create an inference: Draw a possible conclusion, consequence, or implication.

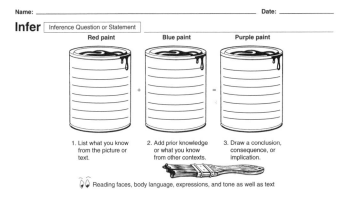

DEFINITION

An inference is a type of conclusion based on facts or assumptions that helps us to construct meaning. An inference is made when one takes information, data, or facts and adds prior knowledge to it to come up with a possible conclusion, or consequence. An inference can be a guess, but one based on reasoning or prior knowledge; that is, we decide something is true based on knowing or assuming something else is true. Teaching about inferences allows students to see the mental steps they are taking and enables them to reach sound, reasonable conclusions. "Reasoning proceeds by steps in which we reason as follows: Because this is so, that also is so or probably so, or since this, therefore that. Any defect in such inferences is a possible problem in our reasoning" (Paul, pp. 3–9, 1999).

According to the revised Bloom's Taxonomy (Anderson & Krathwohl, 2001), "Inferring means to draw a logical conclusion from presented information" (p. 67). Inferring may involve finding a pattern from data, a list of examples, or a group of statements. Take an example from math: Given $2 + 3 = 5$, $3 + 4 = 7$, and $4 + 5 = 9$, what comes next? Here, prior knowledge consists of knowing basic computation and knowing to look for a pattern. Applying that knowledge to the presented information results in a logical answer: $5 + 6 = 11$.

Inferring may also involve making comparisons. This can be demonstrated through an analogy task. A "cat" is to "fur" as a "bird" is to ___. In this example, from a primary grade bird unit, the student must know that fur covers cats' bodies, and also that this relationship between the first and second words provides the clue that must be applied to the third word to come up with the fourth word to complete the analogy: "feathers." If students have this prior knowledge, they can infer a logical answer.

It is important to understand the distinction between assumptions and inferences. Assumptions are beliefs (see Chapter 3) and inferences are interpretations that are based on facts, assumptions, and point of view. For example, in a second-grade lesson, the teacher was reading *The Knight at Dawn* by Mary Pope Osborne aloud to her students. She asked them to use an organizer to infer what the word "precipice" meant in the story. They inferred through the context of the sentence that a precipice is a cave that leads somewhere. This inference is incorrect for many reasons—one of which is the assumption that a cave always leads somewhere. Students who have used the "assume" graphic organizer will already have at least a basic understanding of how to recognize assumptions. Therefore, it may be beneficial to teach about assumptions before moving on to inferences.

In *I Read It, But I Don't Get It,* Tovani (2000) recommends teaching students how to differentiate between opinion and inference. The following definitions can help students understand the difference between opinions and inferences as well as other ways we draw conclusions: "*Predictions* are logical guesses based on facts confirmed or disproved by the text; *inference* is a logical conclusion based on text clues and background knowledge; *assumption* is a fact or a statement that is taken for granted that may or may not be correct; and *opinion* is a belief or conclusion not based on facts that can be knowledgeable or ridiculous because it is based on what one thinks and isn't verified" (Sprenger, 2005, p. 73).

PURPOSE

Students who are good at making inferences build strong conclusions. Although some students naturally use inferential thinking as they get older, many students do not do this on their own. Therefore, it is important for teachers to actually teach students how to become good inferential thinkers. This is important as a school skill but it is also a life skill because we make inferences every day. We need to use these skills to make sense of our world. For example: It's Saturday. What might we infer? Well, among other things, we don't have to go to school. To make this inference, we know schools are closed on Saturdays and our prior knowledge tells us there has never been an exception in our town. Thus, we can logically infer that we will not go to school on Saturday.

Students who are good at inferences understand point of view. They understand people make different inferences because their prior knowledge is based on their own particular experiences. For example,

- Situation: The family is taking a trip to the beach.
  - o Prior knowledge: We have fun at the beach.
  - o Inference: It will be a "good" day.

Or

- Situation: The family is taking a trip to the beach.
  - o Prior knowledge: I hate the feel of sand on my skin.
  - o Inference: It will be a "bad" day.

Let's look at another example.

- Situation: The house is on fire.
  - o Prior knowledge: Firemen put out fires.
  - o Inference: The firemen will save our house.

Or

- Situation: The house is on fire.
  - o Prior knowledge: Our house burned down two years ago.
  - o Inference: Our house will burn down and we will have to move again.

Some of our inferences will be justified based on data or assumptions. Some will not. The skill of processing inferences, in this case through a graphic organizer, allows us to follow a procedure that breaks down the component parts of inferences. The process helps students to recognize how their experiences are shaped by their thinking and their thinking is shaped by their experiences.

BENEFITS

Being able to process inferences, like being able to process assumptions, builds reasoning skills. It helps students to understand point of view and make logical connections. It utilizes the skills of pattern finding, making comparisons, and "reading between the lines." It can also be used to help formulate principles and make predictions and build strong comprehension skills.

Sometimes, special needs students are still working on decoding strategies and the literal interpretation of texts. The stories they read have minimal plot lines. Often the goal is for the student to be able to just understand the main idea. Even though inference seems a long way off for these students, we should not assume they could not learn what inferring means and how to make a good inference. Such limiting beliefs hold special needs students back and maintain gaps in learning. The graphic organizer format provides a clear and easy way for teachers to discuss the process of making inferences with students. It also gives the students a way to process their thinking and a guide to direct their responses.

You can use the "inferring" graphic organizer to see if an inference is mature or premature, reasonable or not reasonable, biased or unbiased, or exhibits gross generalizations.

A premature inference can occur when there is little, if any, evidence or prior knowledge. Students may think they have enough facts, but the facts may be erroneous or worse yet, they may not be facts at all. Using the organizer, students have the opportunity to catch premature inferences.

APPLICATIONS

Inferring is categorized under the "understand" category in the cognitive process dimension in the revised Bloom's Taxonomy (Anderson & Krathwohl, 2001). As such, its focus is on comprehension, and it is frequently applied during literacy instruction and comprehension skill instruction and in content area instruction. Students use this skill when they make conclusions, make predictions, summarize information, and create generalizations.

Some students may have difficulty understanding this skill and moving beyond the literal information. "When beginning to teach the inferring skill, it may be necessary to build from pictures, to words, to sentences, to paragraphs, to complete stories" (VanInwagen, 1997). Begin by having students look at a picture and ask them what they see, what prior knowledge they have, and what logical inference they can make. Cartoons are especially effective because it is through the process of inferring that we actually get the joke. When students do not have any background knowledge or do not connect their background knowledge to the image on the cartoon, they usually do not get the joke. This is a concrete (and entertaining) way to show your students the process of inferring.

You can also ask students to make inferences from sentences. Choose a key sentence from a story, a chapter in a history text, a math word problem, or a student's writing. Take, for example, the sentence "The United States has historically demonstrated economic stability since the Depression." Have students list information from the sentence and from their prior knowledge of economics and U.S. history. Then, students create an inference. If a sentence is too multifaceted for struggling learners, you can differentiate the task. An alternate statement might be "One basis of U.S. economic stability is foreign trade." This is an easier prompt because it focuses on only one aspect of economics.

Students need a lot of practice drawing inferences from sentences before they are able to move on to paragraphs and longer texts. Harvey and Goudvis, in their book *Strategies That Work* (2000), suggest a variety of strategies that can be used for practice. One strategy is playing charades so students will understand that inferring is also about reading faces, watching body language, and hearing expression and tone. They also suggest using a two-column note in which a teacher or student selects a quote or picture from a text in one column and the students write an inference next to it in the other column.

Like assumptions, inferences can be applied to virtually any content. By writing a sentence and making an inference, students can begin to get ideas for a writing piece; they might discover a new idea for a paragraph or a main idea for a story line. Inferences might be used as a jumping off point for a discussion when reviewing content or reviewing for a test. Below are some prompts teachers have used with their students across grade levels and content areas. In most cases, the graphic organizers are used to process information and not as the end product of the lesson. These questions can all be used with the "infer" graphic organizer. They are drawn from Connecticut Standards, Georgia's Quality Core Curriculum, Maine Learning Results, National Council of Teachers of Mathematics Standards, National English Language Arts Standards, National Science Standards, National Social Studies Standards, New Hampshire Curriculum and Proficiency Standards, and Texas Essential Knowledge and Skills.

In the Elementary Grades

Language Arts

- o What might you infer about the main character in the story? The teacher makes the inference statement, and the students use the graphic organizer to support the inference.
- o What might you infer about the relationship between two characters? Above-average readers can develop their own inferences and compare them with other students. Struggling students will complete their graphic organizer under teacher direction.

Writing

- o In the rough draft stage of writing a story, what can you infer about your character to develop him more completely? Have students create an inference and use it as a thread that runs throughout their writing piece.
- o After students complete their writing assignment, the teacher asks them to trade papers and make an inference based on the other student's writing.

Math

- o What might you infer about the blocks? In this example, the students have a pile of multicolor blocks in front of them. The teacher asks them to sort them by color. Then she completes the steps on the organizer in a whole group activity. She asks them what they know, what they have learned in the past, and then to draw a conclusion.
- o The students are given this word problem: There are twelve pencils on the table. Suzie rounds out the number of pencils to fifteen. What might you infer about Suzie? The teacher uses this activity to reinforce the idea of estimation.

Science

- o Describe your invention and infer its uses. In this example, the teacher is encouraging the students to go beyond the obvious use of the invention and think about related uses as well.
- o If alternate energy sources become less expensive, what might we infer? If this were simply given as a question prompt, the teacher would receive a quick answer. Through the use of the graphic organizer, students must use deeper thinking skills to reach conclusions.

Social Studies

- o After students read about the weather of a particular region, ask them to infer what its main crops might be. For example, have the whole class brainstorm crops that are grown in the United States and record their answers on the board. Then assign groups to various regions and have them infer which of those crops might be grown in their region. The next day, the students read their textbooks to learn if their inferences are correct.
- o What might you infer about the implementation of the Constitution? Students work on this individually as a follow-up activity that occurs toward the end of the unit.

In the Middle Grades

Language Arts

- o Read the story and infer what the mother's childhood was like. Students work in their literature circle groups to make their inferences.
- o In the story, the main character had motive and opportunity to commit the crime. After reading part way through the mystery story, students create inferences.

Writing

- o In the rough draft stage of a nonfiction piece, make some inferences about your facts and research their validity. Or, the teacher can have students identify an inference in their writing and verify it.
- o In your revision stage, analyze inferences you made and determine whether these inferences add credibility to your writing piece.

Math

- o The students are given this word problem: Hank creates a model of the physical world using geometry skills. What might you infer about Hank? The teacher uses this activity as an introductory lesson to a geometry unit.
- o What might you infer when you look at the data on this chart? This is an extension activity to a graph lesson presented in math.

Science

- o Make an inference regarding the hunting laws in your state and draw a conclusion based on the inference. After students read about the hunting laws and the reasons why we have them, the teacher asks students to work in groups to make at least one inference. These are shared with the whole class.
- o What can be inferred when a substance goes through a chemical change, the atoms are rearranged, and a different substance with new properties is produced? This is used to reinforce the idea of "What is an atom?" Some students may just be starting to understand what an atom is, and some students may be ready to tackle this challenging question in a group of students of similar ability.

Social Studies

- o What might you infer about the impact of totalitarianism in the twentieth century? This question reinforces the students' understanding of types of government.
- o What might you infer about the impact of landmark Supreme Court cases? Students work in groups to discuss landmark cases and form inferences and conclusions.

In the High School Grades

English

- o What might you infer about the author's use of literary devices in the story? Students make inferences and support them, which helps them to see the purposes of literary devices.

o What inferences can you make regarding the influence of mood and tone of the novel on your perception of the main characters? The teacher breaks the class into groups of those with similar perceptions, and then has them complete the inference process.

Writing

o What can you infer about your use of detail in your writing? The teacher has each student complete an "inference" graphic organizer, and then the students pair up and read each other's pieces. The reader makes inferences about the writer's use of detail and compares her ideas to those written on the graphic organizer. If the responses are significantly different, the writer may need to revise her piece.

o What can you infer about the use of inferential reasoning in your writing? The teacher uses this prompt as a way for students to check on their use of inferences in their writing.

Math

o Make an inference regarding the use of technological tools for graphical and statistical analysis of data. This is a follow-up activity after students have learned about the tools that are used in data analysis.

o What might we infer about the relationship between probability and statistics? The students are asked to make an inference, defend it, and come up with a logical conclusion. The teacher uses this activity to reinforce the definitions of the terms for some students while allowing others the opportunity to think about the relationship between the two math concepts in a meaningful way.

Science

o What might you infer about the interrelationships among organisms? The teacher uses this activity as a way to generate discussion.

o What can you infer about the author's opinion on changes in the ecosystem from the article you've just read? The students are given this as a homework assignment.

Social Studies

o What might you infer about labor practices in 1925? After students look at images of child labor and the situations that existed in factories, they are asked to work in groups to discuss what inferences they can make from the pictures.

o What inferences might you make after reviewing information on cultural characteristics that make specific regions of the world distinctive? In a world history class, students make inferences based on the influences of population increases, geographical conditions, and political climate, and how they affect a region.

GETTING STARTED IN THE CLASSROOM

First, introduce the content of the lesson, emphasize the thinking process, and review the meaning of infer. Then, describe how to make inferences by going over the steps either on the Paint Jar graphic organizer (Figure 4.1) or the "infer" graphic organizer (Figure 4.2). These graphic organizers are designed to describe a basic three-step process. Their simple structure makes them easy for students to use and enables all students to be successful. If you are working with high school students and prefer to articulate a more complex structure, feel free to modify the organizer to fit your students' needs. If advanced students want to include additional steps, they should be allowed to alter the graphic organizer. Remember, the format is meant to be enabling, not constraining. If at any time the process does not make sense to students, you can ask them to show you how they perceive the process. As long as the modified process makes sense, students should be allowed to use their own personalized version.

The paint jars in Figure 4.1 indicate the process that is used to infer. Students know or will learn that if you take red paint from a jar and add it to some blue paint you will end up with purple paint. The visual reminds students to mix two things together to come up with an end result. With the Paint Jar graphic organizer, they mix prior knowledge and acquired knowledge to make a conclusion. This association may help some students remember how to make an inference. Remind students that they can make inferences based on prior knowledge from reading information, by reading facial expressions or body language, and by listening to voice tone; nonverbal messages do influence us.

SAMPLE LESSON

In this sample lesson, a fourth-grade teacher has been reading aloud from *A Series of Unfortunate Events* by Lemony Snickett for about twenty minutes each day. The class is about halfway through the story when she uses an inference activity. The objective of the lesson is character study. So, the teacher asks the students, "What can you infer about Count Olaf in the story?" (see Figure 4.3). The teacher conducts this lesson orally with the whole class to show students how to fill out the graphic organizer. She feels the class needs practice using the graphic organizer before they use it in a differentiated lesson.

Students have their own copies of the graphic organizer and fill it in as the lesson progresses. First, the students write what they know in the red paint jar. They know that Count Olaf is a distant relative who takes care of the children in the story when their parents die. In the blue paint jar, they add prior knowledge. The teacher instructs the students to think about the description of Olaf's face, his body language, expressions he uses when speaking to the children, and any tone that is expressed in the text and to relate this to prior knowledge they have about what this means. Two of the prior knowledge responses from students are, Olaf "has a dirty house," and "There are eyes all around the house." The teacher tells the class that this is not really prior knowledge. It is information they have because they read it in the book. The teacher tells the students they should have placed this information in the first paint can. The students have another response in the prior knowledge paint can. They say, "He is scary looking." This is based on prior knowledge that tells them that in children's stories, bad guys look like bad guys.

The inference the students make is "Because of the way Count Olaf behaves and the way he looks (shifty), it seems that the children may have some problems living with him." Although the students do make an inference, their conclusion focuses on the children, not Count Olaf. This is a wonderful teachable moment that we all appreciate. The teacher addresses the students' answer and relates it to test taking. The teacher knows some of her students have this same problem when they answer prompts on state tests. Students do not always answer what the question asks! The teacher points this out to the students and asks the students to correct the inference by focusing the inference on

Figure 4.1   Paint Jar Graphic Organizer (Infer)

Name: _____   Date: _____

Infer   Inference Question or Statement

| Red paint | Blue paint | Purple paint |

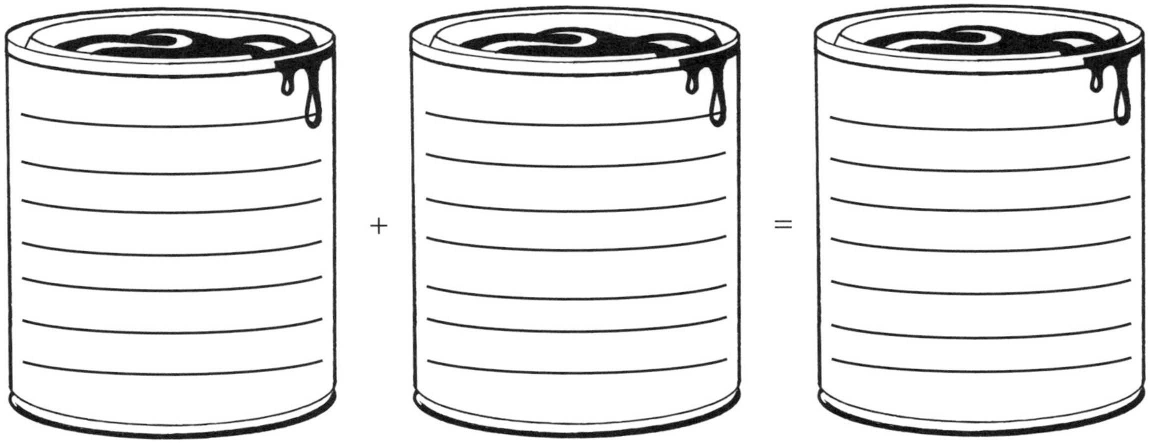

1. List what you know from the picture or text.

$+$

2. Add prior knowledge or what you know from other contexts.

$=$

3. Draw a conclusion, consequence, or implication.

Reading faces, body language, expressions, and tone as well as text

Illustration by Bob Greisen.

Figure 4.2   Linear Graphic Organizer (Infer)

Name: _____ **Date:** _____

Infer

Inference question or statement:
_____
_____

List what you know from the pictures or text.
_____
_____
_____
_____
_____

Add prior knowledge or what you know from other contexts.
_____
_____
_____
_____
_____

Draw a conclusion, consequence, or implication.
_____
_____
_____
_____

Figure 4.3 Sample: *A Series of Unfortunate Events* Paint Jar Graphic Organizer (Infer)

Name:_____ **Date:**_____

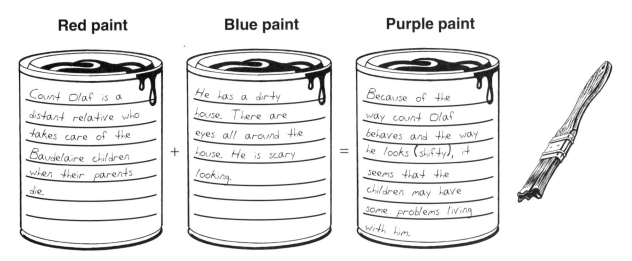

Infer | Inference Question or Statement | What can you infer about Count Olaf in A Series of Unfortunate Events?

Red paint

Count Olaf is a distant relative who takes care of the Baudelaire children when their parents die.

+

Blue paint

He has a dirty house. There are eyes all around the house. He is scary looking.

=

Purple paint

Because of the way count Olaf behaves and the way he looks (shifty), it seems that the children may have some problems living with him.

1. List what you know from the picture or text.

2. Add prior knowledge or what you know from other contexts.

3. Draw a conclusion, consequence, or implication.

 Reading faces, body language, expressions, and tone as well as text

Count Olaf rather than the children. They decide they like their answer so they adjust the wording. They change it to say, "Because of the way Count Olaf behaves and the way he looks (shifty), it seems he might have a problem getting along with the children." At this point in the lesson, the shining star in the room recognizes that the response is just a shift in point of view. The teacher smiles and thinks, "There is hope!"

ASSESSMENT

Of course informal assessment goes on all the time with graphic organizers. When students self-assess and the teacher assesses on the spot, the students have the opportunity to revise and clarify their responses. Although this is wonderful when it takes place, there are times when the students are working without the teacher's guidance. The rating scale is a helpful tool for teachers to give students feedback but it is also useful as a guide for students to use to review their own work. Students may not have the teacher's spoken words to guide them, but they do have the written words on the rating scale. After the teacher thoroughly discusses with students what the words mean on the rating scale and how to use it, students can use it independently.

In the activity using the book *A Series of Unfortunate Events,* students fill out the five-point rating scale together as a class (Figure 4.4). Students give themselves a 5 in the first criterion because they think their inference is clear. The next question asks if the inference is consistent. Students think their inference is mostly consistent with the information, even if they miscategorized some of it. So, the students rate themselves with a 4. The students think about the next criterion. How deep is the inference? They agree it is not really deep. In fact, it is quite obvious. They end up giving themselves a 2 for a score. The last criterion asks if the inference is reasonable. While it is reasonable, the probing question asks if it makes sense. They know it makes sense in light of the information, but not really in terms of the prompt. Therefore, they give themselves a 2. This rating scale provides them with tools to improve their responses.

For a primary rating scale, the teacher simplifies the descriptors and focuses on the basics. Note that the criterion "depth" is not addressed at the primary level (Figure 4.5). Making a superficial inference that makes sense is often the goal at this level.

The rating scale can easily be transformed into a rubric. Teachers transfer the thinking skill criteria from the rating scale to the rubric. The "infer" rubric based on the rating scale from *A Series of Unfortunate Events* lesson with scores marked with asterisks might look like the one in Figure 4.6. This rubric can also easily be modified to fit with the primary rating scale.

As with differentiation, a one size fits all rating scale or rubric will not work with all contents in all grades. Teachers should feel comfortable adapting them in any way. Using simpler language, or adding or modifying criteria is common practice. If students are making particular kinds of mistakes that are not on the assessment tool, then add this criterion to make sure students review their work in this area. If a teacher feels her class is too teacher dependent, then she can add independence to her rating scale or rubric. Eliminate criteria that seem too easy or obvious for students.

Figure 4.4 Sample: *A Series of Unfortunate Events* Critical Thinking Rating Scale (Infer)

Criteria	Probing Question	Rating
Clarity	Is my inference clear?	5
Consistency	Is my inference consistent with the information?	4
Depth	Is my inference deep or superficial?	2
Reasonableness	Does my inference make sense?	2

Figure 4.5 Primary Critical Thinking Rating Scale (Infer)

Criteria	Probing Question	Rating
Facts	Have I listed the facts and my prior knowledge?	1–5
Connectedness	Does my inference connect to the information and the prompt?	1–5
Reasonableness	Does my inference make sense?	1–5

Figure 4.6 Sample: *A Series of Unfortunate Events* Critical Thinking Rubric (Infer)

1	2	3
Inference is unclear.	Inference is somewhat clear.	Inference is clear. *
Inference is mostly inconsistent with information.	Inference is mostly consistent with information. *	Inference is consistent with information.
Inference is superficial.	Inference is obvious. *	Inference is deep or sophisticated.
Inference makes no sense.	Inference makes some sense. *	Inference makes sense.

By knowing and understanding the inference skill, students can increase their ability to become better at critical reasoning. As defined by Chance (1986, p. 6), critical thinking is the ability "to analyze facts, generate and organize ideas, defend opinions, make comparisons, draw inferences, evaluate arguments, and solve problems." Inference is an important skill in helping students better understand content and make sense of their world. The graphic organizer provides visual cues so that students can know, understand, and remember how to make a good inference.

KEY POINTS TO REMEMBER ABOUT INFERRING

1. An inference is a type of conclusion based on facts or assumptions.

2. An inference can be a guess, but one based on reasoning.

3. Inferring means drawing a logical conclusion from presented information.

4. Inferring may involve finding a pattern of data, or making comparisons.

5. Inferences help us construct meaning.

6. Inferences are influenced by point of view.

7. Making inferences allows students to reach strong conclusions.

PAUSE FOR REFLECTION AND DISCUSSION

1. What is the difference between an inference and an assumption?

2. Why do you think the ability to infer is an important skill in your content area?

3. How can learning about making inferences lead to increased student achievement?

4. How might you use the "inference" graphic organizer with your content?

5. In what ways might you differentiate this skill so that all students can be successful with it?

5

"Analyze"

Unpacking the Big Idea

Name: _____ Date: _____

Analyze

1. State the problem: What is to be analyzed? _____

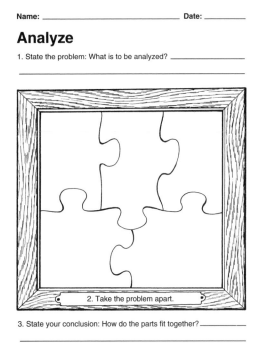

2. Take the problem apart.

3. State your conclusion: How do the parts fit together? _____

➪ Graphic Organizer: Framed Puzzle

➪ Verb: Analyze

➪ Synonyms: Separating into parts, differentiating, organizing

➪ Define the Steps:

    1. Identify the issue, problem, concern, topic.

    2. Break information into parts.

    3. Collect data (if necessary).

    4. Seek relationships.

    5. Draw conclusions as to how the parts serve the overall issue, problem, concern, topic.

DEFINITION

To analyze a topic, students must first understand the topic. Then they can analyze and evaluate it. An analysis involves taking something apart, identifying the elements and their relationships to one another, determining how the elements relate to the overall structure or purpose, and drawing conclusions or making generalizations. In the revised

64

Bloom's Taxonomy (Anderson & Krathwohl, 2001), differentiating, organizing, and attributing fall under this category.

When *differentiating* parts, students determine the importance of the parts of something in relationship to the whole. For example, in science class, the students watch a movie on the water cycle. After the movie is over, the teacher could ask students to identify the parts of the water cycle. By using the word "identify," the teacher is only asking students to use straight recall and name the parts. This is not critical thinking. To move the process into the realm of critical thinking, students are asked instead to analyze the stages of the water cycle. Students have to think about the parts of the water cycle, and consider how these parts relate to each other and to the whole cycle. They differentiate between the parts and seek relationships. The students make a conclusion such as "Each part of the water cycle affects the other parts and each part of the water cycle is critical to the functioning of the cycle." Another example comes from a second-grade language arts class. After reading *Cloudy With a Chance of Meatballs* by Judi Barrett, students are asked to analyze the effects of food falling from the sky like rain. They identify the problem, food falling from the sky. Students identify the parts of this problem as the different times it rains food. They identify the relationship of the parts as each "rainfall" contributes to the overall effect: a very messy town! They conclude that what at first seems like a welcome phenomenon—free food—very soon becomes a logistical problem, because of its size, unpredictability, and destructive effects.

Organizing is also part of analysis. Students must differentiate parts of the topic or event, and then organize them to fit within a structure. This step is critical to constructing meaning. Without this skill, students will break the information apart but will be unable to determine relationships to make sense of the whole. They end up identifying the parts but not analyzing them. This inability to connect the pieces often leaves some students asking, "So what?" They see the parts of something but do not connect and organize them to create an entire picture.

An outline is an example of a structure that allows students to break down parts and see the whole in an organized way. Some students, even though they are able to construct an outline, do not see the purpose of it; the outline makes no sense to them because they see only the parts existing in isolation, rather than perceiving the relationships between them. Other students find outlining helpful to organize their ideas.

Attributing involves the process of ascertaining a communicator's perspective. An example of this might be analyzing a character's disposition in a work of fiction, or analyzing opposing views presented on an issue. A classroom example might be to provide students with statements from elected officials and representatives of OPEC about why fuel prices are so high, and ask them to analyze the arguments. In this instance, students are expected to differentiate the points of view expressed by the spokespersons by analyzing their statements.

Anderson and Krathwohl (2001, p. 80) provide other examples of analysis:

- Distinguish fact from opinion.
- Distinguish reality from fantasy.
- Connect conclusions with supporting statements.
- Distinguish relevant from extraneous material.
- Determine how ideas are related to one another.
- Ascertain the unstated assumptions involved in what is said.
- Distinguish dominant from subordinate ideas or themes in poetry or music.
- Find evidence in support of the author's purpose.

These examples of analysis can help teachers create a variety of analysis prompts. Certain prompts may be assigned to students or the teacher may provide two or three prompts and let students choose which one they want to respond to. Either way all students are doing analysis and all students can be challenged.

PURPOSE

We cannot assume students will make an accurate analysis unless they know how to analyze as well as understand the content they are analyzing. Teachers spend time introducing, reviewing, or extending content, but sometimes students need specific direction in understanding how to process the verb along with the content. The steps on the graphic organizer help students to process the verb and reinforce the procedural language in a visual format. The language and the steps on the graphic organizer provide students with tools to be successful when analyzing information, a task, a point of view, a situation, or a problem.

When students analyze, they look for patterns and chunk information. The brain naturally seeks to make meaning by forming patterns (Willis, 2006). The procedure in the graphic organizer reminds students to look for categories and patterns so that they can break information down into manageable sections. Then students clarify meaning by analyzing each section to make sure it relates to the prompt. Students check to make sure they have not listed interesting but extraneous information. As students review their responses on the graphic organizer, their answers or responses become more precise.

BENEFITS

Analytical thinking helps us to determine what is consistent or inconsistent, relevant or irrelevant, positive or negative, significant or insignificant, sophisticated or simplistic, or even rational or irrational. As such, an analytical question is a thought-provoking question; it provides an opportunity for the teacher to ask a complex question that targets in-depth thinking. We want all our students to go beyond the basic level of knowing the content, and analysis provides us with a tool to get there.

When students know how to analyze information, they can determine what is important and therefore narrow down what they want to remember. They make decisions about how important the parts are and connect them to the whole. For example, understanding how to break down the components of a text passage and determine their relationships to one another are skills that can be learned and practiced. Knowing that parts can be broken down in terms of characteristics, actions, events, details, causes/effects, and so forth helps students grasp the potential of listing parts to form connections. Through such an analysis, students are able to make logical conclusions. When students do not use a thoughtful process, their analysis can miss the mark.

With primary students, the purpose of teaching analysis is simpler, namely to create an awareness that things are composed of parts and can be broken down. A concrete example shows the benefit of using the process. When talking about the human body, it is helpful to have a skeleton or model that can be taken apart. Tell students they can analyze the human body by looking at all the parts of it and understanding the role of each part. As students put together the body, they realize it is important to know what goes where so the body functions properly.

For older students, the ability to execute effective analysis is critical to their academic work across the curriculum and to their performance on standardized tests. Students will experience more success with an "analyze" prompt on a state assessment if they have been provided with the relevant tools.

APPLICATIONS

Analysis is a skill that can be used in classrooms at all grade levels and across content areas, from elementary students analyzing simple math patterns to high school students writing analytical essays. High school teachers often complain that their students cannot write an essay and have difficulty with thesis statements. This suggests that we need to do a better job of teaching analysis and building skills in this area.

As with any other skill, it takes practice to become good at analysis. Students must understand the process and be able to reflect on what they have done. Students may not see the value in spending time focusing on both the content *and* the thinking skill. The teacher can help change this by pointing out every time students use analysis. Bringing the verb to the forefront will encourage students to pay attention to it.

Let's take a look at some prompts teachers can use with the graphic organizer when they ask students to analyze content (adapted from Connecticut Standards, Georgia's Quality Core Curriculum, Maine Learning Results, National Council of Teachers of Mathematics Standards, National English Language Arts Standards, National Science Standards, National Social Studies Standards, New Hampshire Curriculum and Proficiency Standards, and Texas Essential Knowledge and Skills).

In the Elementary Grades

Language Arts

- o Analyze the character in the story. The students are given different characters to analyze.
- o Analyze the characteristics of various types of texts. For example, the teacher introduces a genre unit. She gives some students a nonfiction book, some students a mystery book, and some students a science fiction book. Students analyze the characteristics of their genre and compare their findings.

Writing

- o Analyze your writing piece for descriptive language.
- o Analyze your writing piece for sentence variety.

Math

- o Analyze your bar graph information. The teacher wants to make sure students can make sense of the information on the bar graph.
- o Analyze when to use different problem-solving strategies. The teacher gives students three word problems, and students determine which strategy to use.

Science

- o Analyze the different motions of an object (up, down, fast, slow, etc.). Students are given objects to experiment with prior to responding to the prompt.
- o Analyze the changes in weather over time. Students collect data and complete their analysis.

Social Studies

- o Analyze a problem that currently exists in your state. The teacher brainstorms a list with the students, and the students choose which problem they want to analyze.
- o Analyze your classroom rights and responsibilities. The teacher generates a list with the students and then they break into groups to analyze them.

In the Middle Grades

Language Arts

- o Analyze the author's point of view. The teacher suggests possible points of view, and the students analyze them.
- o Analyze specific devices that the author uses to involve readers. Students identify the devices, such as foreshadowing and irony, and then analyze them.

Writing

- o Analyze the significance of visual images and messages. The teacher uses this prompt in a whole group lesson and then asks students to find examples to demonstrate their points.
- o Analyze your writing for significant and insignificant information.

Math

- o Analyze data to construct convincing arguments. Pick a side on the question, "Should students be allowed to wear hats in school?" Students break the information into parts such as types of hats, how often they should be able to wear them, and concerns such as health issues. The students collect data by conducting a survey or doing random interviews. They look at what the data say and their relationship to their point of view and present their conclusion.
- o Analyze two-dimensional shapes and three-dimensional solids using geometric vocabulary. The class brainstorms ideas, and students work in pairs to create their analysis.

Science

- o Analyze the use of fossil fuels, solar power, and wind power and compare their practicality. After students complete their analysis, have them compare their responses.
- o Analyze the interactions between matter and energy. This could be a follow-up prompt based on a homework assignment.

Social Studies

o Analyze the social factors that led to the growth of sectionalism and the Civil War. The students brainstorm a list of social factors and break into groups. Each group analyzes a different social factor.

o Analyze the components of effective leadership in a democratic society. The students discuss what makes an effective leader and why they think so before using the graphic organizer.

In the High School Grades

English

o Analyze how story elements affect the meaning of a work. The teacher discusses the meaning of the work before asking students to respond to this prompt.

o Analyze an author's perspective. Students work in small groups to identify the author's perspective, analyze it, and then compare their analysis with other students.

Writing

o Analyze your use of tone and voice in your written work.

o Analyze responses from varied audiences. Students share their writing with three audiences—their peers, their parents, and a third audience of their choice. They create a written response form for each audience and analyze the responses.

Math

o Analyze the effects of scale changes. The students are given a drawing of a bedroom using a scale of one inch equals one foot. The teacher asks them to change the scale to one-quarter inch equals one foot. The students analyze the effects of the change.

o Analyze properties of operations using a base eight number system. The teacher differentiates the lesson by giving some groups of students easier base number systems and targeting only one property that they have to analyze.

Science

o Analyze the properties of substances and their subatomic particles. Students work in groups to complete their analysis.

o Analyze the role of DNA in diseases. The teacher encourages the students to move beyond creating a list.

Social Studies

o Analyze the delivery of medical care in Canada. Students research the medical care system in Canada and fill out the graphic organizer prior to writing a formal analysis.

o Analyze how the physical characteristics of a region influence the development of technology. In this example, the teacher suggests that some people who live in remote areas like the Aleutian Islands in Alaska feel they have a need to develop technology because they want to have more access to the world.

GETTING STARTED IN THE CLASSROOM

Introduce the "analyze" graphic organizer by calling attention to what the verb means, and explain the steps the students will use when making a thoughtful analysis (Figure 5.1, the Framed Puzzle, and Figure 5.2, the linear format). It's often helpful to model the steps by referring to a previous lesson or by doing a sample lesson with the students. Students usually understand how to break the concept, issue, or problem into parts. Teachers may need to spend extra time explaining the analysis skill because students sometimes think that by making a list of the parts, they have completed an analysis. Students need practice at all grade levels on finding relationships and making connections to the whole. This is usually where the analysis breaks down. When this happens, the conclusion is weak or simplistic. There is no depth of learning taking place.

With primary students, analysis can and should be taught with content that is appropriate for this age group. Young students are often naturally good at forming connections. Of course, some of the connections are absurd or irrational. The goal at this age is for students to apply logical reasoning to the process. Their conclusions may restate the obvious, but that is appropriate for this age group. As students become more capable of reaching inferential conclusions, they should be encouraged to do so. Some advanced first and second graders may be ready to do this much earlier than their peers. By knowing the students' capabilities, the teacher can differentiate by encouraging more sophisticated answers from some students.

SAMPLE LESSON

Mr. Beam offers his fourth-grade students a choice in style when he does his analysis lesson. Although he understands some of his students like the Framed Puzzle format (Figure 5.1), he prefers the straightforward linear graphic organizer (Figure 5.2). He thinks it looks more organized and is easier for students to use. Mr. Beam usually uses the linear format when he does his model lessons with the class. The students know Mr. Beam prefers to use this graphic organizer rather than the Framed Picture format, but they also understand that Mr. Beam encourages them to use the one they prefer. Both graphic organizers have the same steps and use the same process, so it really does not matter which format the students choose.

Mr. Beam's students also have the opportunity to choose books at their reading level. Mr. Beam asks his students to read the book and analyze the events in the story. Mr. Beam has already demonstrated how to do this by reading a picture book and modeling the process and the expected level of response. One of Mr. Beam's students reads the story *The Witches* by Roald Dahl. She lists the events in the story in the boxes on the graphic organizer in sequential order (Figure 5.3). The student, however, draws a conclusion that is not based on analysis. She concludes, "Being a small mouse helps the boy into tricking the witches by eating poisoned pea soup which turns them into mice." Although this is what happens in the story, she does not demonstrate an ability to make a good analysis. What the student should have done was to look at the relationships between the events that she listed and come up with a conclusion based on those relationships. She might have said in her conclusion, "Many fantastic things happen in this story."

Figure 5.1   Framed Puzzle Graphic Organizer (Analyze)

Name: _____ **Date:** _____

Analyze

1. State the problem: What is to be analyzed? _____

_____

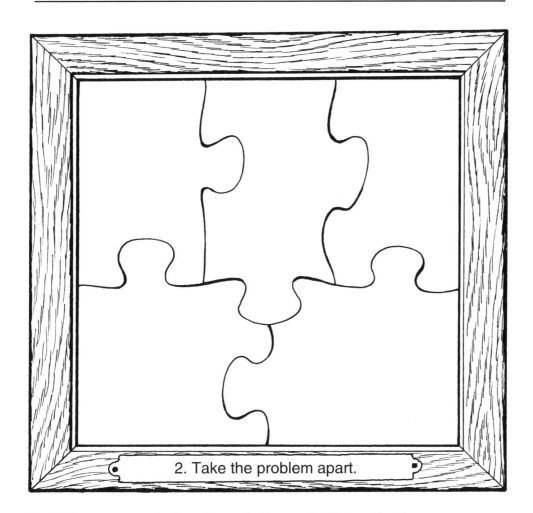

2. Take the problem apart.

3. State your conclusion: How do the parts fit together? _____

_____

Illustration by Bob Greisen.

Figure 5.2   Linear Graphic Organizer (Analyze)

Name: _____ Date: _____

Analyze

1. State the problem: What is to be analyzed?

2. Take the problem apart.

3. State your conclusion: How do the parts fit together?

Figure 5.3   Sample: *The Witches* Linear Graphic Organizer (Analyze)

Name:_____   Date:_____

Analyze

1. State the problem: What is to be analyzed?

Analyze the events in the story <u>The Witches</u>.

2. Take the problem apart.

1. The boy's grandmother tells him about witches and what they look like.	2. They go to a hotel where there is a witch training.	3. The boy goes into an empty room to train his mice.
4. The witches come in to have their meeting and take off their costumes.	5. The witches turn the boy into a mouse with a potion.	

3. State your conclusion: How do the parts fit together?

Being a small mouse helps the boy trick the witches into eating poisoned pea soup which turns them into mice.

ASSESSMENT

The rating scale can be used by either the teacher or the student. It can also be used with either graphic organizer format because both formats follow the same process.

Mr. Beam uses the rating scale (Figure 5.4) to score the student's analysis of the events in *The Witches*. Mr. Beam provided the opening statement (or prompt), so the student does not receive a score in this area. The events that are listed are important events in the story, and the parts all do support the analysis statement. The student receives a 5 in these two categories. Unfortunately, the student makes limited connections between the stated events and the stated conclusion. Therefore, Mr. Beam gives the student a 1 in the connections category. This assessment is useful, because the teacher can see exactly how he can help the student. It is clear the student understands the story and remembers details. With a little help from the teacher, this student will be able to make connections based on the analyzed elements in no time.

In the rubric version of the rating scale in Figure 5.5, the first row of boxes addresses the prompt statement. This is scored only when students generate their own analysis statement. Scoring in each criterion is indicated by an asterisk. Because Mr. Beam gave the

Figure 5.4 Sample: *The Witches* Critical Thinking Rating Scale (Analyze)

Criteria	Probing Question	Rating
Clarity	How clear is the analysis statement?	—
Importance	How important are the identified parts?	5
Consistency	Do the parts consistently support the analysis statement?	5
Connections	To what degree are connections apparent in the conclusion?	1

Figure 5.5 Sample: *The Witches* Critical Thinking Rubric (Analyze)

Beginning	Getting There	Arrived
Statement is inappropriate or irrelevant.	Statement is basic and predictable.	Statement is exceptional and targets depth.
Some parts identified but may not be important.	Main important parts are identified.	All important parts are identified. *
The parts do not relate to the statement.	Most parts relate to the statement.	All parts relate to the statement. *
Connection between the parts and the conclusion are unclear. *	Basic, obvious connections between parts and the conclusion.	Sophisticated, in-depth connections between parts and conclusion.

analysis statement, there is no score noted on the rubric in the first criterion. Also note that, instead of using a 1, 2, 3 scale on the rubric, the performance levels are named beginning, getting there, and arrived.

Although this graphic organizer, the rating scale, and rubric are basic tools, they do bring attention to the skill and describe a process to get students thinking about how to do a good analysis. The graphic organizer, the rating scale, and/or the rubric language can be modified as the level of student performance increases and the responses become more sophisticated. Use the graphic organizer to practice, practice, practice the skill of analysis while fostering critical thinking in the content area.

 ## KEY POINTS TO REMEMBER ABOUT ANALYZING

1. Analysis involves taking something apart, identifying the parts and their relationship to one another, and drawing conclusions or generalizations.

2. Analysis involves determining the importance of the parts of something and their relationship to the whole.

3. Analysis involves organizing the parts to fit within a structure or purpose.

4. Students can analyze information, a task, a point of view, a situation, or a problem.

5. Analysis allows students to make logical conclusions.

6. Analysis helps students understand the truth.

7. Analysis helps students determine consistency and relevance.

PAUSE FOR REFLECTION AND DISCUSSION

1. Think of many, varied lessons in which you could ask students to analyze something.

2. Why is it important to know how to do an analysis well?

3. What are some factors that contribute to a good analysis?

4. Why would knowledge of assumptions and inferences help to make an effective analysis?

5. What might differentiation look like in the classroom when we use the "analyze" graphic organizer?

6

"Prioritize"

Putting First Things First

Prioritize

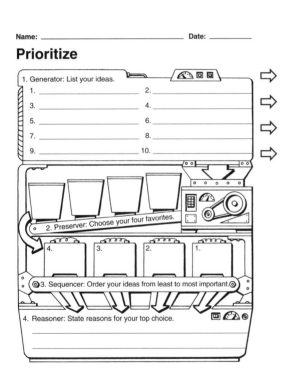

⇨ Graphic Organizer: Prioritizer

⇨ Verb: Prioritize

⇨ Synonyms: Order, sequence

⇨ Define the Steps:

1. Brainstorm ideas or facts.

2. Eliminate ideas or facts by narrowing down the list and choosing your top four preferences.

3. Sequence your ideas: Order your ideas from greatest to least.

4. Provide reasons: Give one or more reasons for your top choice.

DEFINITION

When we ask students to prioritize, we want them to arrange events, items, or ideas in relation to a factor of influence. These factors of influence are specific to the type of prioritizing that is going on. Depending on the context, students could consider such factors as time, importance, interest, appeal, practicality, and realism. The factors of influence affect the outcome of the prioritization. The most common factor people use to prioritize is importance. According to Levine (2002), students can fall behind in school when they have difficulty prioritizing useful information. All information, including useless trivia, seems important to students who have difficulty with this skill. Levine says this can occur with "those who focus on the right inputs but concentrate on the wrong aspects of those inputs" (p. 65). This is a very different learner from one who demonstrates an interpersonal style as described by Silver, Strong, and Perini (2000, p. 67). The interpersonal learner shows a style preference for doing prioritization as part of critical analysis.

Prioritization is part of the decision-making process. Let's look at a classroom example that shows the decision-making process when prioritization is not used (as depicted in Figure 6.1) and when it is used (Figure 6.2). Mrs. Coy's fourth-grade language arts students are studying the fairy tale genre. As a way to review the story *Jack and the Beanstalk*, the teacher asks students to use their decision-making skills to come up with a win/win solution where everyone ends up happy in the end. First, they identify the problems in the story. The students decide that one problem in the story is that Jack and his mom are poor. Another problem in the story is that the Giant does not appear to have any friends other than his wife.

The students come up with three solutions to solve both problems: (1) the Giant goes to anger therapy and he and Jack become friends, (2) the Giant opens up a theme park, and (3) the Giant gives Jack some golden eggs in return for some good public relations. These ideas are listed in a decision-making matrix in the first column of Figure 6.1. As part of the decision-making process, the students come up with four criteria to evaluate each solution—whether it is immediate, long lasting, practical, and it makes both happy. These ideas are listed across the first row. The students select a scale of 1 to 3 to rate each idea. Three is the top score. No solution under a given criterion may receive the same score.

The first criterion is "immediate" and refers to how quickly the solution can be accomplished. The Giant can quickly give Jack golden eggs in return for Jack doing some quality press releases. The press releases will explain to the world that the Giant is not evil, and this will result in people not being afraid of him. Then, people will dare to visit him and he will make friends. This is the most immediate solution so it receives a 3. After the Giant has a few therapy sessions, Jack can visit him. Then, they can become friends, and perhaps the Giant will loan Jack some money. This takes longer than the other solution, so it receives a 2. The students decide it will take a long time to put a theme park up in Beanstalk Land. This solution receives a 1.

The students go through the rest of the criteria measuring each against each solution. They add up the scores and discover that eggs in return for good public relations would be the best solution because it received the most points. Students complain, however, that each criterion is not of equal value. They want to prioritize their criteria.

In the new matrix in Figure 6.2, the criteria have been prioritized. The factor of influence that students decide to use to prioritize is importance. They decide that making both Jack and the Giant happy is the top priority, or the most important. That criterion now has a weighted value of four. The four is based on the number of criteria that are used to evaluate solutions. All the scores in that column (in Figure 6.1) are multiplied by 4 and recorded in Figure 6.2. The next important criterion is practicality and refers to how practical this solution is. Students give it a value of 3 because this is still very important. The scores in that column are multiplied by three. Students decide the immediate criterion is more important than the long-lasting one, because if the solution doesn't last, they can come up with something else. So they multiply all the numbers in the immediate column by two. The long-lasting column is multiplied by one, or the scores remain the same. When the new numbers are added together in each row, the students are surprised that the results are the same. Be aware, however, that sometimes, when students prioritize their criteria, it does change the outcome.

Figure 6.1   Making Decisions Without Prioritizing

	Immediate	Long-lasting	Practical	Makes Both Happy	Total
Giant goes to anger therapy and Jack visits him.	2	1	2	2	7
Giant opens up a theme park.	1	3	1	3	8
Giant gives Jack some eggs in return for some good PR.	3	2	3	1	9

Figure 6.2   Making Decisions With Prioritizing

	Immediate x 2	Long-lasting x 1	Practical x 3	Makes Both Happy x 4	Total
Giant goes to anger therapy and Jack visits him.	4	1	6	8	19
Giant opens up a theme park.	2	3	3	12	20
Giant gives Jack some eggs in return for some good PR.	6	2	9	4	21

PURPOSE

The purpose of teaching prioritization is to help students sort through ideas, organize them, and arrange them in order. In the twenty-first century, students are exposed to enormous amounts of data on the Internet. When doing research, it is important for students to prioritize the sites they visit. All sites are not of equal value, and students do not have unlimited time to wander through a laundry list of Web sites. Once they settle upon a site, students need to prioritize the information they find. Downloading all the pages and highlighting most of the words is not practical or useful; they need to learn how to differentiate between what is and is not important.

We prioritize as a part of daily life. We prioritize our shopping lists, our budgets, and our free-time activities. Not all prioritization requires a graphic organizer. When the prioritizing gets tough, however, it's nice to have a tool to fall back on. The graphic organizer is helpful when students need to write out the process to sort out large amounts of information or information with layers of complexity.

Prioritizing is an easy skill for students to understand. Young students may not use the word prioritize, but they practice it all the time in primary classrooms when teachers teach sequence. (Some sequences do not involve prioritizing, but all prioritizing involves sequences.) This can be a problem, however, for students who have difficulty prioritizing through sequential ordering. There are, for example, students who may have difficulties differentiating between before and after (Levine, 2002). Factual sequential memory issues may affect such a student's ability to hand in long-term assignments on time, or even to arrive at school on time. For students whose sequential memory and sequential organization are weak, the prioritization tool can be an effective strategy to compensate and address such problems.

BENEFITS

The benefits of teaching students how to prioritize are many. First, this skill is particularly important to the creative learner because prioritizing helps students sort through information. When students brainstorm, they come up with many ideas. Some creative learners do not know what to do with all their ideas. They are unable to sort through them to determine what is most important. They may think all of the ideas are important. By using the graphic organizer, the students can follow the steps to narrow down the field of ideas and focus on key ones.

Narrowing down a list of ideas is not a problem solely for creative learners. Teachers encounter this problem with many students. Sternberg and Grigorenko (1993) help us to understand the reasons for this problem. They connect goal setting and task completion to what they call forms of mental self-government. They identify these forms as monarchic, hierarchical, oligarchic, and anarchic. With the monarchic form of self-government, students are goal oriented and do not allow distractions to interfere with achieving their goals. With the hierarchical form of self-government, students have multiple goals and know that goals are accomplished by degrees. They are able to prioritize and problem-solve in an organized fashion. Sternberg and Grigorenko continue, "The oligarchic form [of self-government] allows for multiple goals, all of which are equally important. These individuals experience conflict and tension when they have to assign priorities to various tasks. Competing goals keep oligarchic individuals from completing tasks, because everything seems equally important" (1993, pp. 123–124). With the anarchic form of self-government, students have difficulty following rules and procedures. These students like to march to their own drum and create their own procedures. They do not like to be told what to do.

From this description, it is clear that oligarchic thinkers in particular need help prioritizing, because they think everything is important and have difficulty making decisions. They cannot decide what to do first. For these students, prioritizing is not just a "school" skill; it is a life skill. The more students practice this skill, the more effective they will be at prioritizing both in and out of school. By learning about the factors of influence and relying on a set structure, the oligarchic learner as well as other types of learners can become more productive when prioritizing content information, making decisions, and completing tasks.

APPLICATIONS

Prioritizing is a type of evaluative activity. According to the steps noted on the graphic organizer, students break a task or problem into parts, and then order the parts and evaluate them according to the factors of influence or criteria. Although they use analysis in the process of prioritizing, the focus of this skill is evaluation.

One way to teach prioritizing to young students is to help them to see what the process means. Go around and collect various classroom materials and ask a student to arrange them according to how much they like them. Begin with just three things and build to four or five. Then, ask the student to arrange them according to how important they are. Is the arrangement the same or different? Teachers build from these concrete learning experiences to more abstract applications such as asking prioritizing questions based on a read-aloud story. If the teacher stays with the main influences, such as importance and appeal, it does not take long for primary grade students to know how to apply the prioritizing skill with content. They understand that how we prioritize affects the outcome.

Prioritizing can help students effectively sort through options. The graphic organizer can be used whenever there is a listing of ideas, events, circumstances, or situations that need to be evaluated. It is easy to use with any course content. The following prompts can be used along with the "prioritize" graphic organizers. They are drawn from Connecticut Standards, Georgia's Quality Core Curriculum, Maine Learning Results, National Council of Teachers of Mathematics Standards, National English Language Arts Standards, National Science Standards, National Social Studies Standards, New Hampshire Curriculum and Proficiency Standards, and Texas Essential Knowledge and Skills.

In the Elementary Grades

Language Arts

o Prioritize the events in the story. The teacher asks one group of students to order the events in terms of the biggest impact on the main character and another group to order the events in terms of how interesting they are to the reader.

o Prioritize a list of questions you might ask the main character in the story. The teacher uses this prompt as a post-reading activity to see how well the students "know" the main character.

Writing

o In the rough draft stage of your fictional writing piece, list sentences to describe the setting. Prioritize the list in terms of the effectiveness of each sentence in creating a picture of the place. The teacher hopes, by using this prompt, that students recognize which sentences are extraneous and can be eliminated or minimized and which sentences should be maximized or emphasized.

o In the final draft stage in your persuasive writing assignment, list all the sentences in a paragraph that support the main idea and prioritize them in terms of which contain the strongest arguments. The teacher hopes students will discover sentences that do not belong in the paragraph.

Math

o Make a list of where you see right angles in your world and prioritize them in terms of importance. This is a fun way for students to see right angles in the world as well as to think about their applications.

o List four ways to solve a particular math word problem. Prioritize the list according to your preference. The teacher hopes students will see the difference between being comfortable with a preferred problem-solving strategy and being efficient by using the fastest problem-solving strategy.

Science

o Prioritize a list of characteristics that allow plants to survive in different environments. The teacher uses this prompt as an extension activity. The teacher wants students to understand how particular characteristics, such as deeper root systems or the thick leaves of succulent plants, allow plants to live in places with little available water.

o Prioritize a list of seasonal changes. The teacher wants students to make a list of changes in the season and prioritize the list according to which changes they like the best.

Social Studies

o Prioritize a list of conclusions about the impact of geographic features on people. Students are divided into groups identified as various U.S. regions and asked to discuss the geographic features of their region. They fill out the graphic organizer together as they prioritize conclusions about the impact of these features.

o Prioritize a list of significant events in our state's history. The teacher records a brainstormed list of state events as students call out their ideas. Individually, students fill out the graphic organizer.

In the Middle Grades

Language Arts

o Prioritize opinions presented in the story *Regarding the Fountain: A Tale in Letters of Liars and Leaks* by Kate Klise in terms of how realistic they are. Students work in pairs to identify the opinions of a particular character in the story. They prioritize the character's opinions and choose the opinion they feel is the most realistic and defend it with multiple reasons.

o Generate conclusions about the main character's personality based on a prioritized list of behaviors that support your conclusion. Students can choose from a list of four characters in the story. They identify examples of how the character behaves and prioritize which behavior most represents the character's true personality. They draw conclusions about the character's personality.

Writing

o Prioritize the information you collect when doing the research project. The students write facts and ideas on note cards. The students keep some cards and discard others because, although interesting, they do not answer their research questions. The students order the cards in terms of relevance.

o Prioritize writing problems that you want to focus on. The teacher wants students to identify areas in which their writing needs improvement and list them. Students should limit themselves to four areas. These should be prioritized according to where their writing abilities are the weakest. Students tell their partner what area they need to focus on the most and why.

Math

- Prioritize the information stated in this multiple-step word problem. The teacher uses this prompt to help students figure out which information to deal with first and which information is useless.
- Prioritize the information you deduce from these data. The teacher uses this prompt to help students figure out which information is the most important.

Science

- Prioritize a list of factors that can cause long-term changes to the earth. The teacher divides students into groups. The groups list factors that cause long-term changes. The group decides which four are to be "saved" for further evaluation. Individuals then prioritize their answers and give reasons. The groups compare answers and reasons in a class discussion.
- Evaluate how the environment responds to natural and human-initiated changes by making a prioritized list. The teacher uses this prompt as a follow-up to a reading assignment.

Social Studies

- Prioritize historical information from a variety of sources to identify and support the point of view of those involved in the Boston Tea Party. The teacher wants students to practice prioritizing information from multiple sources.
- Prioritize a list of effects on a community caused by population growth. The teacher has students complete this on their own as homework toward the end of the unit.

In the High School Grades

English

- In *Macbeth,* prioritize a list of decisions made by Lady Macbeth that affect the outcome of the play. In this example, the teacher expects students to consider the degree of impact she has on other characters in the play.
- Prioritize the importance of instances of the author's use of symbolism in the story. After reading the story, the teacher expects the students to find elements of symbolism in the story and to prioritize and evaluate them.

Writing

- Prioritize assumptions you made in your editorial. The teacher uses this as a way for students to reflect on how their assumptions affect their message in their writing piece.
- Prioritize various styles of writing to determine which style best suits you. The teacher shows samples of student writing on the overhead. The teacher asks students to prioritize which style might work best for them and explain why.

Math

o Prioritize a list of situations of conditional probability and independent events. The teacher uses the prompt as a way for students to apply their knowledge of probability.

o Prioritize from easiest to hardest linear equations with two bits of given information. The teacher provides various types of given information, such as two points, a point and a slope, a slope and an intercept, a point and a parallel or perpendicular line, and so on.

Science

o Prioritize a list of factors that affect the process of respiration. The teacher uses this prompt after students have an understanding of human body systems.

o Quantitatively investigate the effects of different reactants in chemical reactions and prioritize them. The teacher uses this prompt as a way for students to review the effects of reactants.

Social Studies

o Make a prioritized list of the powers of the Supreme Court according to what you think is important. This can generate a heated discussion as students support their ideas about power.

o Prioritize a list of cultural, geographic, and religious factors that have contributed to historical conflicts. This prompt is used to create a motivational discussion regarding students' points of view.

GETTING STARTED IN THE CLASSROOM

First, introduce students to the meaning of prioritizing. Show them that it means to arrange items according to factors of influence, and discuss the types of factors that might apply to different situations. Young students will need to practice this idea through concrete activities, with you modeling lessons.

The graphic organizer used with this skill is called the Prioritizer (Figure 6.3; concept by Leonard Drapeau). The name implies that this graphic can be associated with a machine that prioritizes. The format actually gives machine-like names to the steps. The first step is the generator, where items or ideas are listed. The next step is the preserver. Here students narrow down the items or ideas and decide which ones they want to preserve. There is room for four ideas to be saved. Most students, even oligarchic learners can narrow down options to four. It is from this point on that some students have difficulty. The items move from the preserver to the sequencer. In the sequencer, items or ideas are ordered according to a factor of influence. These factors are either specified in the prompt, that is, the teacher tells the students the factor to consider, or the students determine an appropriate factor themselves. In the final step, students are expected to justify their top choice in the reasoner.

An alternate form identifies the steps as list, choose, order, and justify rather than using the words generator, preserver, sequencer, and reasoner (Figure 6.4). For some students, the straightforward language helps them to remember what they are supposed to do in each step. You might, however, guess what the more popular form is. Both forms use only four steps, so that it is easy for students to remember the process. Either structure gives students something to rely on when they have difficulty prioritizing.

Figure 6.3 Prioritizer Graphic Organizer (Prioritize)

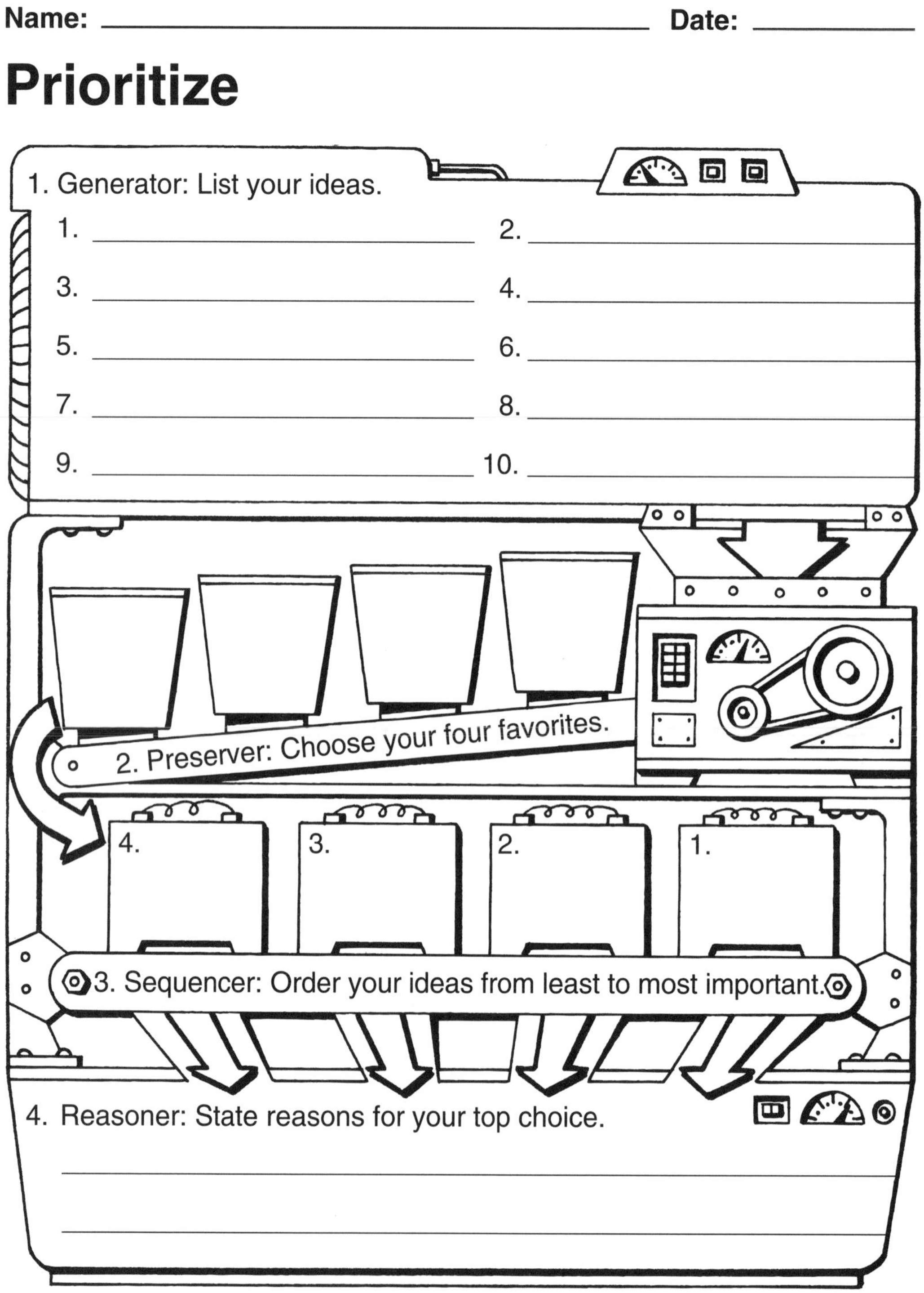

Name: _____ Date: _____

Prioritize

1. Generator: List your ideas.

   1. _____   2. _____

   3. _____   4. _____

   5. _____   6. _____

   7. _____   8. _____

   9. _____   10. _____

2. Preserver: Choose your four favorites.

   4.   3.   2.   1.

3. Sequencer: Order your ideas from least to most important.

4. Reasoner: State reasons for your top choice.

_____

_____

Concept by Leonard Drapeau, illustration by Bob Greisen.

Figure 6.4 Linear Graphic Organizer (Prioritize)

Name: _____ **Date:** _____

Prioritize

List your ideas. Choose four of your ideas.
Order your ideas with one being your top choice. State
reasons to justify your top choice.

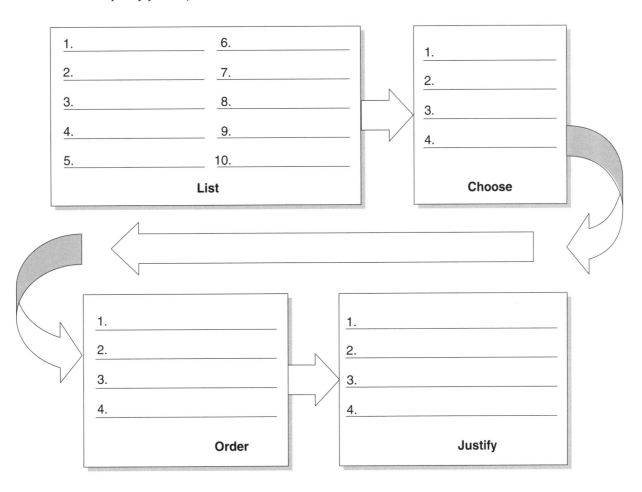

SAMPLE LESSONS

Let's look at two language arts examples from Mrs. Coy's fourth-grade fairy tale unit. Mrs. Coy begins the unit by reading *Cinderella* to the class. The teacher asks students to prioritize the events in the story in terms of importance. Because this class already knows how to fill out a "prioritize" graphic organizer, Mrs. Coy uses this open-ended prompt and the students complete the organizer on their own. In Brian's example (Figure 6.5), he lists five events in the story. He eliminates slave life and chooses the other four events as more important. He orders from greatest to least importance marrying the prince, no mother, twelve o'clock, and the fairy godmother. He justifies his top answer, marrying the prince, because of its future implications. He thinks she will have a big future, be treated better, have no chores to do, wear no rags, and not have to deal with "dumb" step-mom/sisters. Compare this to Cassandra's response (Figure 6.6). After she lists events and chooses four of them to save, she identifies from least to greatest importance losing the glass slipper, going to the ball, mother dying, and having a fairy godmother. She justifies her top idea by saying that without a fairy godmother, "Cinderella never would have gone to the ball or met the prince."

Figure 6.5   Sample: Brian's *Cinderella* Linear Graphic Organizer (Prioritize)

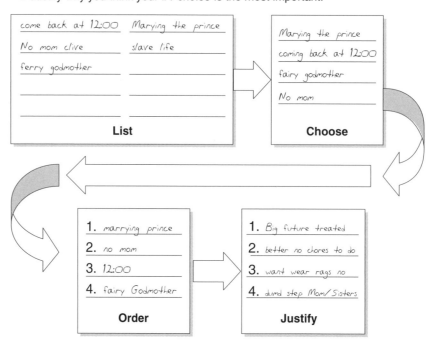

Figure 6.6   Sample: Cassandra's *Cinderella* Linear Graphic Organizer (Prioritize)

Name: _____   **Date:** _____

Prioritize

1. List many things you know about the story.
2. Choose four things that you think are the most important things from the list you made in #1.
3. Order the four things from least to greatest importance in the story.
4. Justify why you think your #1 choice is the most important.

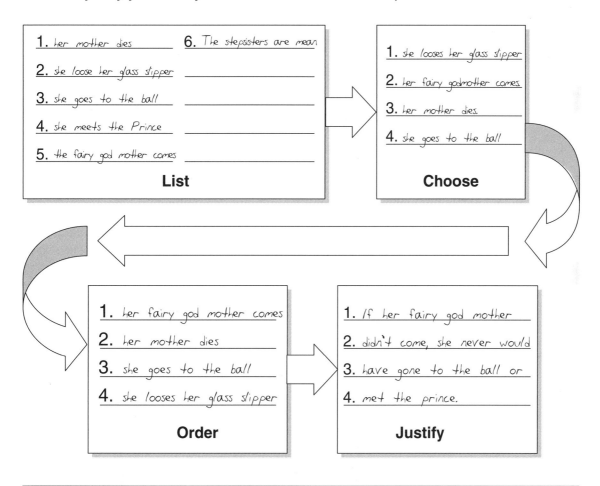

With this type of an activity, some students will want to know which answer is correct. It is hard for them to understand that answers can be different and correct. This is an excellent way to show point of view. We know that different points of view exist and more than one can be correct. As long as the facts are correct and the process is used correctly, there can be more than one way to look at something. Teachers need to help students to understand it is the reasoning behind the process that makes the answer correct or incorrect, relevant or irrelevant, or basic or sophisticated.

ASSESSMENT

The "prioritize" rating scale is meant to be a guide for improving student performance. It is designed generically so that it will work with most prompts in most content areas. At least one criterion relates to each of the steps in the graphic organizer. Each criterion has a probing question to help students determine their scores. Sometimes, students want to know how these scores relate to a grade. Parents want to know, too. Teachers can always correlate the numbers on the rating scale to a grade score.

Take, for example, how a teacher rated Brian's *Cinderella* "prioritize" graphic organizer (Figure 6.7). Because he listed an average number of relevant events, Brian receives a 3 on the rating scale. In the next step on the graphic organizer, Brian eliminates one choice from his list because he can save only four of his five ideas. He receives a 5. When Brian orders his responses according to what he thinks is most important in the story, he places the midnight deadline above the fairy godmother. This does not seem reasonable, because the midnight deadline would not have been important if there had been no fairy godmother. Because of this, his rating is a 3. In the last step, he does justify his top priority with many good reasons for his choice. He receives a 5. By analyzing Brian's responses, the teacher can see that he needs to work on generating events and ordering ideas.

If this rating scale was turned into a grade score, the teacher might say that each criterion is of equal value. The teacher adds up Brian's score, which consists of two 3's and two 5's for a total of 16 out of a possible 20 points. If a total score of 1–4 = F, 5–8 = D, 9–12 = C, 13–16 = B, and 17–20 = A, then Brian's total score of 16 means he receives a B+. If the teacher feels each criterion is worth a different value, then she can assign a different numerical value to each criterion.

The letter grade is not that valuable in helping students improve performance. Yet, sometimes it is helpful as a motivational technique. Brian might keep track of the 16 or B+ that he scored on this prioritizing activity. At the end of the semester, Brian can look through all of his prioritizing scores. If he sees improvement, he should be pleased that he has learned how to apply prioritization well. The letter or number grade only serves to confirm his achievement.

Figure 6.8 shows the ratings (asterisks) Brian would receive had the rubric been used in the lesson. This rubric uses "partially meets," "meets," and "exceeds" to describe the levels of performance.

Prioritizing can be used as a tool for pre-writing. It can be used to help with decisions when doing research. It can be used as a summarizer or a way to make evaluations. There are so many uses for this skill that its application in the classroom is truly limitless. By

Figure 6.7   Sample: Brian's *Cinderella* Critical Thinking Rating Scale (Prioritize)

Criteria	Probing Question	Rating
Relevancy	Are a number of relevant ideas listed?	3
Logic	Is it logical to preserve the saved ideas?	5
Appropriateness	Are the criteria or factors of influence applied or ordered appropriately?	3
Justification	Is the top choice justifiable?	5

Figure 6.8 Sample: Brian's Cinderella Critical Thinking Rubric (Prioritize)

Partially Meets	Meets	Exceeds
Generates few relevant ideas.	Generates some relevant ideas. *	Generates many, varied relevant ideas.
Logical reasoning not applied when preserving ideas.	Logical reasoning applied when preserving some ideas.	Logical reasoning when preserving all ideas. *
Difficulty using criteria to order ideas.	Mostly assigns criteria appropriately and sequence makes some sense. *	Applies criteria to all ideas and sequences appropriately.
Justification makes no sense.	Justification is obvious.	Justification is sophisticated, in-depth and reflects criteria. *

providing lessons that target the content with the skill of prioritizing, students will become better thinkers and improve their logical reasoning.

KEY POINTS TO REMEMBER ABOUT PRIORITIZING

1. Arrange events, items, or ideas in relation to factors of influence.
2. Factors may include time, importance, interest, appeal, and practicality.
3. Prioritization may be part of a decision-making process.
4. Not all criteria are of equal importance and can be prioritized.
5. Prioritizing may be a skill we use when we make an evaluation.
6. Some sequences do not involve prioritizing, but all prioritizing involves sequencing.
7. Prioritizing is a life skill.

PAUSE FOR REFLECTION AND DISCUSSION

1. What lesson might you use when you introduce the "prioritize" graphic organizer to a class?
2. Should you teach this skill before or after assume, infer, and analyze?
3. How can you help your students understand that prioritization is an important skill for them to use in their daily lives?
4. When does a lesson warrant using a "prioritize" graphic organizer?
5. How might you use the Prioritizer as a tool for differentiation?

7

"Judge"

Making Accurate Evaluations

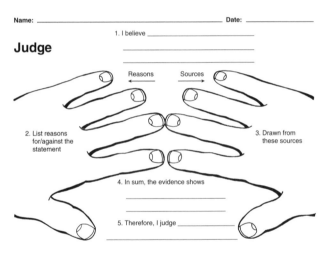

Name: _____ Date: _____

Judge

1. I believe _____

Reasons ← → Sources

2. List reasons for/against the statement

3. Drawn from these sources

4. In sum, the evidence shows _____

5. Therefore, I judge _____

➡ Graphic Organizer: Hands On

➡ Verb: Judge

➡ Synonyms: Form an opinion, decide, evaluate, criticize

➡ Define the Steps:
1. Make a belief statement.
2. List reasons or evidence for/against the statement.
3. Cite sources for the reasons or evidence.
4. Summarize the reasons or evidence.
5. Verify or modify the belief statement.

DEFINITION

When we judge, we evaluate. When we use criteria to formulate a judgment, we use critical thinking. According to Bloom et al. (1956), "The judgments may be either quantitative or qualitative and the criteria may be either those determined by the student or those which are given to him" (p. 185). Marzano and Kendall (2007) talk about both internal and external criteria. They say that, "Bloom refers to decision making as opinions, as opposed to judgments which by definition involve evaluation" (p. 8). Regardless of the type of judgment, sound judgment involves the use of criteria and evidence.

Do we expect students to use criteria in all situations when they judge something? They actually do consciously or unconsciously use criteria. Students make judgments all the time. They judge when they settle an argument, when they criticize, and when they make a decision about something. In these instances, do they apply criteria and evidence? Is their judgment based on conscious, sound reasoning?

Mr. Rose, a high school English teacher, wants his students to apply criteria when they make judgments about content. He asks his students, in their study of American Romantic literature, to decide the most significant problem relating to the practice of individualism in a structured society and to judge its impact on society. After pairs of students determine the most significant problem, Mr. Rose asks his students to use criteria when judging the impact of the problem on society.

It is difficult for many students to use criteria because they cannot think of any. Mr. Rose tells students, if they cannot come up with their own criteria, then ask questions about what they will be judging. The questions usually have criteria in them. For example, a student might ask how the problem they have identified caused changes in society. In the question, the idea of changes leads to the idea of positive/negative effects, which can be added to the list of criteria. Mr. Rose also gives students a list of generic criteria that they can use as prompts to create their own criteria. As a result of looking at the list, students can think of how the problem has impacted society in terms of money or safety. This is a working list, and students add to it throughout the year when they discover other criteria that are common in many situations (Drapeau, 1998). As students become used to generating their own criteria, they can add to the list without teacher prompting.

Common Criteria Used in Making Judgments

- Effectiveness
- Time
- Money
- Safety
- Fairness
- Resources
- Ease of use
- Enjoyment
- Usefulness
- Suitable
- Legal
- Appeal
- Improvements

Students can use criteria to form judgments based on either inductive or deductive reasoning. The inductive reasoning approach works well for students who process information from the specific to the general. For example, a student uses the criteria "interesting," "exciting," "fast paced," and "a page turner" to determine her judgment about a book she's reading, then concludes, "I think this is the best book I ever read."

Students use a deductive approach when their thinking moves from the general to the specific. For example, the student who says, "I think this is the best book I ever read," justifies her judgment based on specific examples from the story. She may use examples rather than criteria to support her judgment. The examples, however, are applications of criteria. The "judge" graphic organizer in this chapter uses a deductive approach.

Judgment does not function in isolation; that is, to make a judgment, you need something to think about. The output or application of ideas allows students to make judgments (Costa, 1991, p. 49). Huitt's (1998, p. 3) definition of critical thinking is "the disciplined mental activity of evaluating arguments or positions and making judgments that can guide the development of beliefs and taking action." Teachers can help students use critical thinking to understand how opinion, bias, and fact influence judgment. Because assumption, inference, analysis, and prioritization are all elements that affect judgments, these skills should be practiced in a disciplined way so they can be applied to a judgment or justification. Students can use a rating scale, rubric or, Richard Paul's (1999, pp. 3–30) universal intellectual standards—such as clear, accurate, precise, logical, significant, and fair—to evaluate a judgment. According to Paul, these standards can be applied to any question.

PURPOSE

The purpose of using a process to make conscious, logical judgments is to help keep students from becoming victims of faulty judgments based on little or unconscious thought. It is necessary for students to make judgments when they make decisions, solve problems, or analyze information. We ask them to judge something by checking out an assumption or conducting an experiment. When conducting an activity, we ask students to check or judge whether something is effective or not. Teachers also ask students to judge work based on criteria. The graphic organizer allows students to use a conscious structured process to ensure that they apply critical thinking when they judge and justify.

Primary students can use this process to learn how to make good judgments just like anyone else. They will, however, need to learn the process of making a judgment by practicing the steps in a variety of situations with age-appropriate content. For example, Mrs. Jones asks her first-grade students to judge the wolf's actions in the story *The Three Little Pigs* by Steven Kellogg. The students respond by saying they judge the wolf as mean. When encouraged to give reasons for their judgment, the students say, "He looks mean." This may be true, but looking mean may be different from acting mean. Mrs. Jones addresses this point and prompts the students even further. Another student gives the reason, "He blew the pigs' houses down." Mrs. Jones helps the students make the connection by asking, "How do you know destroying the pig's house is a mean thing to do?" The students' answer, "Because nobody is supposed to wreck your house." Mrs. Jones says, "I think the wolf destroying the house is a better reason why you think the wolf is mean rather than how he looks." The purpose of this activity is to help the students understand the steps in making a good judgment and to help them understand how the reasons support the judgment statement. The teacher asks them to cite the page where the wolf destroys the house. At this young age, they are already learning to back up their statements with cited sources!

BENEFITS

By practicing making quality judgments, students become more effective evaluators. At this point, if you have used the other critical thinking graphic organizers, some students begin to see that all these critical reasoning skills work in tandem. They can analyze an assumption, an inference, or even a judgment. They can judge an assumption or an inference. Students can prioritize when judging or assuming. In order to judge, they assume, infer, prioritize, analyze, and justify. Many of these skills can be used as alternatives with the same lesson, to give a different emphasis to the lesson or make it more complex. By substituting the verb in a question or prompt, teachers can easily differentiate the prompt within a single lesson.

With middle and high school students, you can double up the verbs and create more complex questions. For example, the teacher can ask students to analyze how religious and cultural beliefs affected the witch trials in *The Crucible* by Arthur Miller and make a judgment statement about Abigail Williams, Judge Danforth, or Mary Warren. Students will be more successful with such a multifaceted question now that they can use the graphic organizers to process each part of the question.

APPLICATIONS

Be sure to consider where in the unit the "judge" graphic organizer will be most effective. Because judge falls under the evaluation category, you want students to go beyond analyzing something. Your students need to have enough information to make an informed judgment. Therefore, once a teacher is midway through a unit or toward the end of a unit or book, the judge skill can be used effectively. At this point, students have the information to go beyond, "I like it and why."

The following are examples of prompts that can be used with the "judge" graphic organizer. These have been adapted from Connecticut Standards, Georgia's Quality Core Curriculum, Maine Learning Results, National Council of Teachers of Mathematics Standards, National English Language Arts Standards, National Science Standards, National Social Studies Standards, New Hampshire Curriculum and Proficiency Standards, and Texas Essential Knowledge and Skills.

In the Elementary Grades

Language Arts

o Judge what you think about the ending of the story. The teacher provides the following criteria for the students to use when they justify their judgment: appeal—how much you like the ending; resolution—how well the problem is solved; and predictability—how predictable is the ending. The students can add their own criteria. The criteria should be reflected in the reasons on the graphic organizer.

o Judge the character in the story. The teacher asks students to make a judgment statement about the main character and support their statement with reasons and evidence. This activity serves as a summary activity as well as an activity focusing on character development.

Writing

- Judge your own writing piece. The teacher provides the criteria and helps the students turn them into reasons on the graphic organizer. For example, "makes sense" can be a criterion and "is interesting" and "few spelling mistakes" are reasons to support a judgment.
- Judge how interesting your writing piece is. The teacher uses this example as a way to help students understand that more words do not necessarily mean more interesting.

Math

- Judge whether this math problem has enough information in it to solve it. The teacher divides the class into three groups. She gives an easy word problem with the right information in it to her struggling math students. She gives another group of students a more difficult math word problem with the right information and a third group a problem with missing information.
- Judge whether $2 + 3 = 3 + 2$. The teacher gives this example to students who are being introduced to the commutative property of addition.

Science

- Judge whether it is true that living things are made up of different parts. The teacher uses this introductory prompt to point out what "different parts" means.
- Justify why a fossilized animal might not be alive now. The teacher gives a fossil lesson and uses this prompt as a follow-up activity.

Social Studies

- Justify the statement that people learn about themselves through family customs and traditions. The teacher gives the students categories to help them get started. These categories are celebrations/holidays, superstitions, and dress.
- Judge the important ideas stated in the Declaration of Independence. The class lists the ideas as a whole and students work in pairs to create judgment statements and justify them.

In the Middle Grades

Language Arts

- Judge the effect of conflict on the plot. The teacher generates a list of criteria with students such as fairness, appeals to the audience, and supports a universal message. Given these criteria, students judge if the effect of the conflict in the plot is strong or weak and give reasons for their judgment based on the criteria. They find evidence in the story to exemplify their reasons. This is an advanced prompt, and only some students do this activity while others are asked to judge whether they like the plot or not and why.
- Judge the major influence of one character on another. Students work in groups as they identify the influences. Then they prioritize to determine the major influence and judge why. Students use both the "prioritize" and "judge" graphic organizers.

Writing

- o Judge whether your ideas are presented in an orderly way so that others can understand them. This graphic organizer activity is given to some students who are still having trouble with organization. The teacher works with a small group to list criteria such as sequential order, sentences that don't belong, message is confusing, and so on. The teacher uses the graphic organizer as a way for students to find specific examples of their weak organization.
- o Judge how your research affects your writing. The teacher uses this graphic organizer activity as a way for students to judge and then correct their writing before handing it in.

Math

- o Judge how useful variables are in mathematical expressions. The teacher uses this prompt as a way for students to understand the importance of variables.
- o Judge the relationship between a probability and a stated fraction. The teacher uses this prompt as a way for students to rehearse or practice understanding how a fraction can serve as a form of expression for probability.

Science

- o Judge whether all matter consists of particles called atoms that are made up of certain smaller particles. The teacher provides students with an opportunity to provide evidence or reasons for the definition of matter.
- o Judge whether objects will float or sink based on your understanding of density and buoyancy. The teacher uses the prompt to help students understand this vocabulary.

Social Studies

- o Judge whether you feel people were really forced to migrate (e.g., Irish, Ethiopians, Cherokees). The teacher asks students to use primary and secondary sources to defend their judgment.
- o Judge the impact that major events and technological advancements have had on the state's economy. Toward the end of the unit, the teacher generates a list on the board that identifies major events and technological advancements that the state has experienced. At this point, the students break into groups to judge the impact of these developments.

In the High School Grades

English

- o Judge whether a novel or film version of a story is more informative. The teacher has students fill out the graphic organizer and debate their positions.
- o Judge whether the use of symbolism in the novel impacts the reader's understanding of the characters. The teacher conducts a whole class discussion about the use of symbolism in the story. Then students fill out the organizer as a follow-up activity.

Writing

- o Judge the effectiveness of tone in your writing. The teacher uses this prompt to ensure that students are aware of how they use tone in their writing. It works well because they must cite examples to support their judgment.
- o Judge whether your use of intentional ambiguity in your writing helps the reader to understand the character's personality or confuses the reader. The teacher has the student fill out the graphic organizer. Then the students trade and read someone else's paper. The reader confirms or refutes the author's position.

Math

- o Judge whether the simulation demonstrates probability. The teacher sets up two simulations. Both demonstrate probability, but the numbers in one are incorrect. The students make their judgments and compare responses.
- o Judge whether the Fibonacci sequence is or is not arithmetic. The teacher uses this prompt as a way for students to demonstrate their level of understanding of the Fibonacci sequence and the definition of arithmetic.

Science

- o Judge whether the causes of chemical reactions are sped up more by catalysts or slowed down more by inhibitors. The teacher uses this prompt as a follow-up activity. Students work in groups to support their judgments based on their readings and lab activities.
- o Judge whether an electromagnetic wave needs matter to transfer energy. The teacher uses this prompt as a way for students to engage in discussion on the topic.

Social Studies

- o Judge whether urban growth is necessary. The teacher states the prompt and asks students to defend their judgment.
- o Judge why you think the New Deal was a success or a failure. The teacher uses this to lead into a review for a test. Students fill out their graphic organizers and share their responses. Then they are asked to synthesize the ideas in a three-paragraph essay.

GETTING STARTED IN THE CLASSROOM

Tell the students that when they give their opinion about something, they are making a judgment. Their opinion reflects their point of view, and they can quickly and casually make spontaneous judgments. Students use the steps on the "judge" graphic organizer, however, to make a more calculated, informed judgment. Students can use the Hands On graphic organizer (Figure 7.1) or the more linear boxed version (Figure 7.2) to judge a belief statement. The Hands On graphic organizer is an easy visual for students to associate with judging, because people often make points by holding up fingers.

Figure 7.1 Hands On Graphic Organizer (Judge)

Name: _____   Date: _____

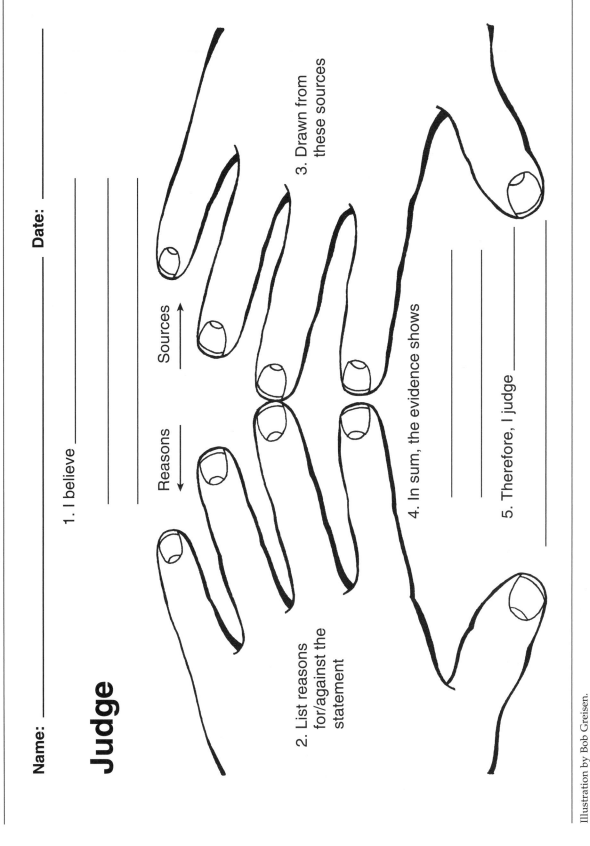

Judge

1. I believe _____

Reasons   Sources

2. List reasons for/against the statement

3. Drawn from these sources

4. In sum, the evidence shows _____

5. Therefore, I judge _____

Illustration by Bob Greisen.

Figure 7.2   Linear Graphic Organizer (Judge)

Name: _____   **Date:** _____

Judge

I believe _____

_____

Reasons:

[four square boxes, each above a triangle]

Sources:

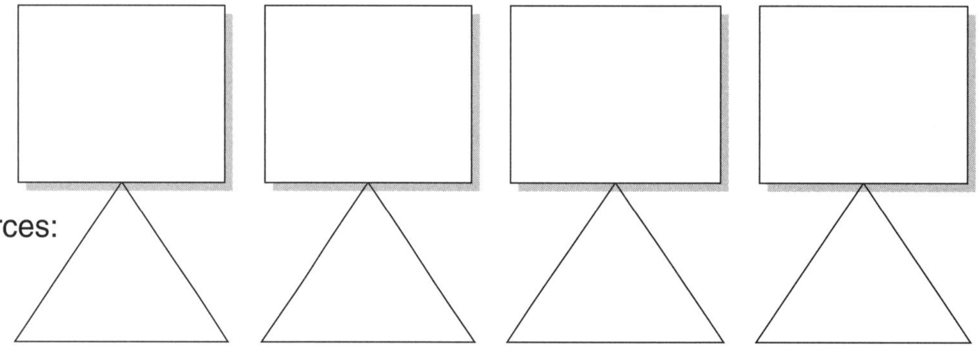

In summary, the reasons or evidence show _____

_____

_____

Therefore, I judge

[large empty rectangular box]

Introduce the lesson by showing students a sample of a completed organizer, by doing a sample lesson together, or by reviewing a "judge" lesson from a previous class. In the Hands On graphic organizer (Figure 7.1), students write above the hands in Step 1 what they believe to be true and make a belief statement. On the fingers of the left hand in Step 2, they list reasons or evidence for or against the statement. In this step, students generally write reasons or provide evidence to support the statement. To make a quality judgment, however, students do need to consider reasons to refute the statement as well. On the fingers of the right hand in Step 3, students cite the source for each reason or piece of evidence.

In the area below the index fingers next in Step 4, students reevaluate their reasons. This step should include considering such things as the reliability of the sources, ambiguities in the information collected, and biases and assumptions. Students should not just restate the reasons. They should analyze and reevaluate them and then make a summary statement based on the reasons or evidence.

On the bottom of the paper next in Step 5, students have the opportunity to revise their belief statement or elaborate on it. This may be difficult for some students because they just want to restate their original belief or they may have trouble reflecting on the reasons. This process actually requires students to evaluate or judge their original belief statement and form a conclusion. By connecting information and determining its relevance, the student response in Step 5 will confirm the original statement or revise it so that it is more focused and specific. This process will help students improve their comprehension, as well as increase their ability to make logical judgments.

SAMPLE LESSONS

In this example, Mr. Baylor, a third-grade teacher, reads *Rollo Bones Canine Hypnotist* by Marshall M. Moyer to his class. He uses the short picture book to model how to fill out the Hands On graphic organizer. After he finishes reading the story, rather than ask students to summarize it, he tells them that they are going to complete a Hands On graphic organizer to make a judgment about the story.

Mr. Baylor says, "Since it is usually unbelievable that a dog could hypnotize people, we are going to make a judgment about the dog Rollo Bones." In the space above the hands (Figure 7.3), Mr. Baylor writes what they believe to be true from the story, which is that Rollo Bones, the dog, can hypnotize people. The next step is to give reasons or evidence to support or refute the belief. Mr. Baylor tells the students that evidence can come from a variety of sources. Evidence can be verbal or nonverbal, implicit or explicit (hidden or obvious), an emotional outburst or a gesture.

After Mr. Baylor describes different types of evidence, the students cite four examples from the story that demonstrate the dog's ability to hypnotize people. They place each example on a finger on the left hand. The students must verify their information. They tell Mr. Baylor on what page each example occurs. Mr. Baylor writes the pages on the fingers of the right hand. The students reevaluate the evidence in the space between the hands and verify the original statement. On the bottom of the paper, they make a judgment, which Mr. Baylor says must go beyond just restating the original belief. The students judge Rollo Bones to be an extremely intelligent dog that has an unusual ability. As students become more sophisticated in their thinking, they will move from a summary concluding statement to one that integrates more specific and elaborative language.

Figure 7.3 Sample: *Rollo Bones Canine Hypnotist* Hands On Graphic Organizer (Judge)

Name: _____ Date: _____

Judge

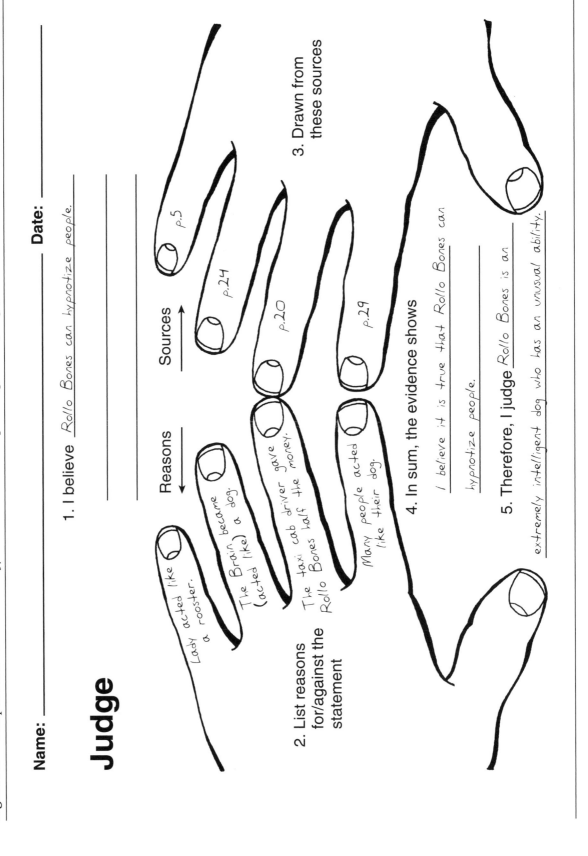

1. I believe _Rollo Bones can hypnotize people._ _____

Reasons → ← Sources

- Lady acted like a rooster.
- The Brain became a dog. (acted like) a dog. p.5
- The taxi cab driver gave Rollo Bones half the money. p.24
- Many people acted like their dog. p.20

  p.29

2. List reasons for/against the statement

3. Drawn from these sources

4. In sum, the evidence shows

I believe it is true that Rollo Bones can hypnotize people. _____

5. Therefore, I judge _Rollo Bones is an_ extremely intelligent dog who has an unusual ability.

100

In Mrs. Coy's fourth-grade language arts fairy tale unit, she gives all students the same prompt to work with. The belief statement is, "Things work out for the best" (Figure 7.4). Since happily ever after is an element of fairy tales, the teacher knows this prompt should work with any fairy tale book. In this lesson, students read different fairy tale books but they all use the same prompt and the "judge" graphic organizer. Meg judges the validity of the statement after she reads the story *Cinderella's Rat* by Susan Meddaugh. Meg finds four examples of things that happened in the story that might have appeared to be bad but were actually good. Because of the evidence, she thinks the rat was happier as a rat than as a boy. In her final judgment, Meg focuses on the changes the rat's sister went through. By judging the original statement to be true and finding supportive evidence, Meg discovers how the author, through a variety of twists in the plot, chooses to solve the overriding problem in the story.

Figure 7.4   Sample: Meg's *Cinderella's Rat* Linear Graphic Organizer (Judge)

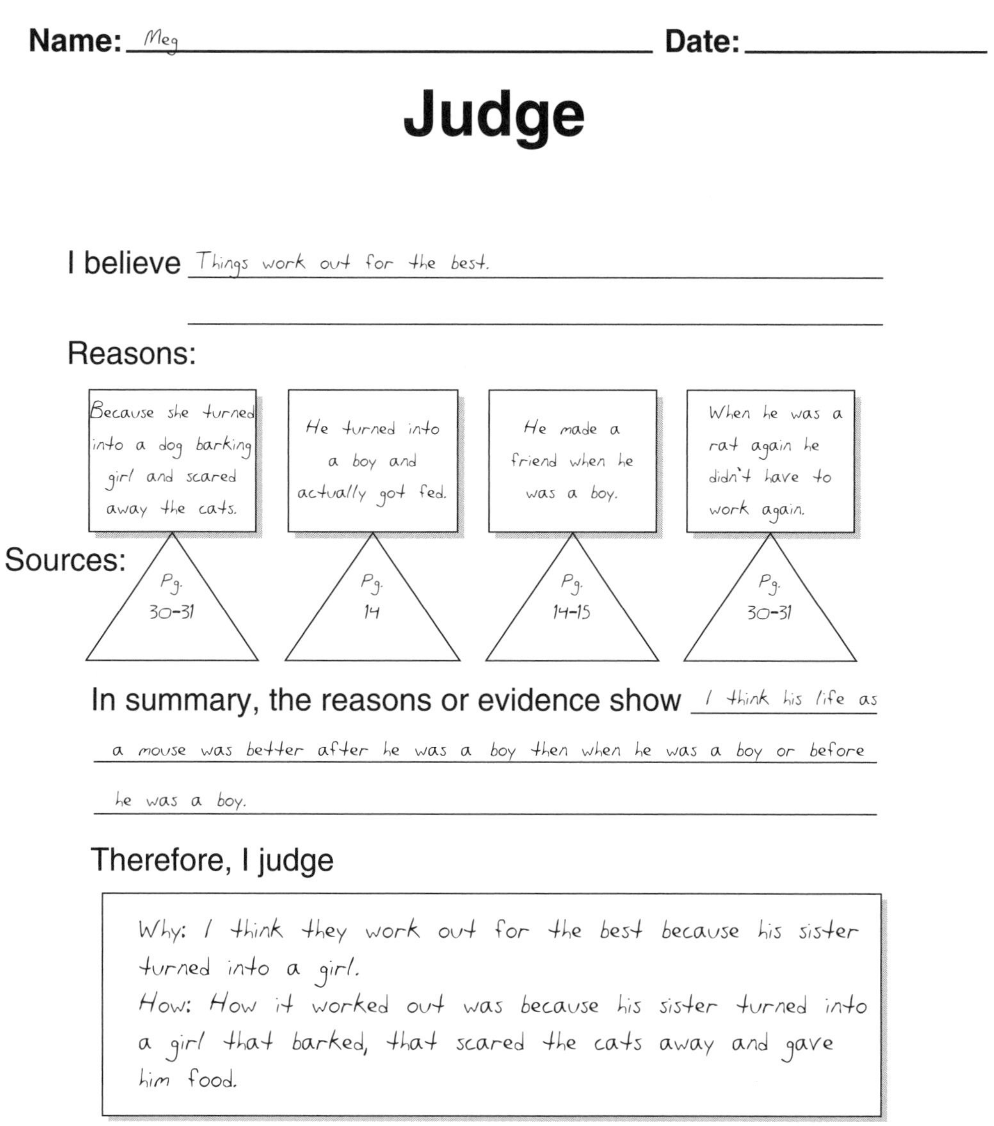

Name: _Meg_____ **Date:** _____

Judge

I believe _Things work out for the best._

_____

Reasons:

| Because she turned into a dog barking girl and scared away the cats. | He turned into a boy and actually got fed. | He made a friend when he was a boy. | When he was a rat again he didn't have to work again. |

Sources:
Pg. 30–31   Pg. 14   Pg. 14–15   Pg. 30–31

In summary, the reasons or evidence show _I think his life as a mouse was better after he was a boy then when he was a boy or before he was a boy._

Therefore, I judge

Why: I think they work out for the best because his sister turned into a girl.
How: How it worked out was because his sister turned into a girl that barked, that scared the cats away and gave him food.

Some students draw conclusions that are not supported by their evidence, even though they make a correct judgment. These students make jumps in their thinking. They have difficulty processing sequentially and making connections. Other students do not see the need to verify their answer if their answer is the "right" one. Teachers can help students understand that they do not always have to use this process when they make a judgment, but when they want to use it, they should know how to do so successfully.

Highly able learners often make leaps in their thinking and do not see the need to write down every little step. When this happens, it may be because the prompt or assignment is too easy. If the reading material is at a high level and the information is sophisticated and complex, they will see more of a need to use a tool to process their judgment.

ASSESSMENT

Let's take a look at Meg's example again and see how her work was rated using the completed rating scale in Figure 7.5. This rating scale evaluates each step of the judgment process with a score of 1 to 5. Key qualifying words identify the focus of each step. First, if the student comes up with the belief statement, the most important characteristic is that it is clear. If it is unclear, the rest of the judgment will be less than effective. Second, the reasons that support or refute the belief statement must be relevant. If they are true but not relevant, it doesn't contribute to the evaluation process. Third, sources must be accurate and credible. If the reasons are relevant but the source is questionable, the judgment is weak. Fourth, the reasons or evidence, must be analyzed and synthesized in a summary statement. If the evidence cannot be synthesized, then verification may also be weak. The last step in the graphic organizer asks for a concluding statement that indicates a final judgment. This judgment must be logically justified based on the presented information.

The teacher gives the original statement to the class in Meg's example. Therefore, the student is not rated for clarity. Meg's reasons are very relevant to the story. She receives the top rating, a 5. In fact, she receives a 5 in all of the areas. For a fourth grader, Meg demonstrates strong evaluative reasoning.

Meg's scores on the rubric version of the rating scale in Figure 7.6 are marked with an asterisk. Because the belief statement was provided by the teacher, there is no asterisk for the first criterion.

Figure 7.5   Sample: Meg's *Cinderella's Rat* Critical Thinking Rating Scale (Judge)

Criteria	Probing Question	Rating
Clarity	How clear is the statement?	–
Relevancy	How relevant are the reasons?	5
Accuracy	How accurate are the sources?	5
Application	To what degree are the reasons analyzed and then summarized?	5
Logic	How logical is the conclusion based on the stated information?	5

Figure 7.6 Sample: Meg's *Cinderella's Rat* Critical Thinking Rubric (Judge)

1	2	3
Unable to generate a statement.	Statement is vague or unclear.	Statement is clear and concise.
Determines few relevant reasons.	Determines some relevant reasons.	Determines many relevant and unobvious reasons. *
Drawn from few reliable sources.	Drawn from mostly reliable sources.	Drawn from reliable and varied sources. *
Summary statement is vague.	Summary statement reflects reasons.	Summary statement reflects inferential reasoning and informs judgment. *
Obvious judgment reflects partial evidence.	Literal judgment supported by most of the evidence.	Sophisticated judgment supported by evidence. *

When teachers ask students to judge something, students will learn that they are expected to go beyond saying something like "I like it." By applying critical thinking when using the graphic organizer, they are asked to process the information through a logical procedure. As students learn to analyze the evidence or reasons as part of the judgment process, they practice looking for inconsistencies, biases, and logical lines of reasoning. The graphic organizer format allows teachers to see just where they can help students improve their thinking and create more accurate responses.

KEY POINTS TO REMEMBER ABOUT JUDGING

1. Judgment is based on criteria and standards.
2. Criteria are used to assess accuracy, effectiveness, efficiency, and sound reasoning.
3. Criteria are used when students give reasons or justify their judgment.
4. Judgments may be reasonable or unreasonable based on the justifications or reasons given to support them.
5. The purpose of making judgments is to evaluate something.
6. To judge, one might also do any of the following: assume, infer, analyze, prioritize, and/or justify.

PAUSE FOR REFLECTION AND DISCUSSION

1. How can learning to make good judgments improve student achievement in your content area?
2. Why is it useful to know how to make conscious judgments using critical thinking?
3. What might the expectations for making a quality judgment look like in the third grade, compared to the eighth or tenth grade?
4. What steps can you add or subtract from the graphic organizer to better suit your needs?
5. How might you differentiate for students in your classroom using the "judge" graphic organizer?

PART III

Four Creative Thinking Verbs and the Graphic Organizers to Use With Them

Brainstorm

Connect

Create

Elaborate

8

"Brainstorm"

Generating Multiple Ideas

Brainstorm

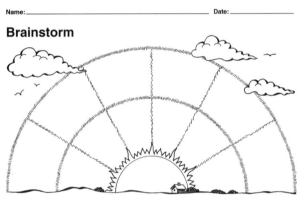

1. State the idea, issue, or problem in the sun.
2. Write two related ideas in the spaces above, and pass it to the next student.
3. Write two ideas on another rainbow and pass it on until all the rainbows are complete.

⇨ Graphic Organizer: Rainbow of Ideas

⇨ Verb: Brainstorming (fluency)

⇨ Synonyms: Generate, list

⇨ Define the Steps:

1. List ideas in response to a specific prompt.

2. List more ideas by piggybacking on the responses of others.

3. Continue to list ideas until all possibilities are exhausted.

DEFINITION

Paul Torrance (1987) identified four skills of creativity that are validated and used widely: fluency, flexibility, originality, and elaboration. These four skill areas are derived from the work of Guilford (1967, 1977), who characterized creative thinking as divergent thinking. Divergent thinking means coming up with more than one idea as opposed to convergent thinking, which means coming up with the one right answer. In this section of the book, each chapter targets one of the four creative thinking skill areas identified by Torrance. A graphic organizer is provided for each skill. In this chapter, fluency is targeted through non-verbal brainstorming.

In the beginning of any brainstorming session, it is helpful to remind students about the rules of brainstorming (Davis, 1992; Treffinger, Isaksen, & Firestien, 1983). Alex

Osborn (1963), an advertising executive who was looking for new ways to generate ideas in traditional business meetings, described four ground rules for brainstorming. He found that these rules helped participants express new ideas and improved their ability to build on one another's ideas. Teachers use these rules in the classroom to increase the productivity of brainstorming sessions.

1. The first rule is that *criticism is not allowed.* Teachers ask students to refrain from saying, "That's a stupid idea" or "That will never work." Teachers can help students to learn that what may seem "stupid" or "useless" can sometimes turn out to be useful. Therefore, during brainstorming, ideas shouldn't be evaluated. Teachers must also maintain an accepting environment during brainstorming so students will feel comfortable sharing ideas.

2. The second rule of brainstorming is that *quantity is encouraged.* The purpose of brainstorming is to create a long list of ideas (Davis, 1992). If we digress from brainstorming and start deciding which ideas are acceptable, we're interrupting the flow of ideas resulting in fewer ideas generated. The more ideas students generate the more likely they are to come up with an original one.

3. The third rule is that *piggybacking is allowed;* students may come up with an idea based on someone else's idea. It's often easier for students to adapt an idea than to come up with a completely original one. For example, if students are brainstorming what factors might be involved in taking a sea voyage in the 1500s, and one student comes up with a storm, then another student might come up with other weather conditions that could affect a ship's progress. In this third step, students may piggyback by combining ideas or elaborating on ideas based on another student's response.

4. The last rule of brainstorming is that *wild and exaggerated ideas are accepted.* Crazy and zany ideas can suggest more realistic or really good ideas. Sometimes it is easier to reign in an idea than it is to come up with a new one. "Osborn said the wilder the idea the better," according to Davis (1992, p. 162). Because we want a lot of ideas, even outrageous ones are welcome—within the parameters of the prompt, of course. Wild ideas help students think outside the box. The acceptance of freewheeling thinking helps students feel comfortable sharing all of their ideas, regardless of how ridiculous or absurd they may sound at first.

Rules of Brainstorming

1. Criticism is not allowed.

2. Quantity is encouraged.

3. Piggybacking is allowed.

4. Wild and exaggerated ideas are accepted.

Using creative thinking graphic organizers resembles using critical thinking graphic organizers in that students need to understand what the prompt is asking. If students are asked to brainstorm ideas for things they could do outside during lunch recess, a student might say, "snowball fights." This is an acceptable response unless the teacher says, "What are some things we could do outside during lunch recess that follow our school rules?" In this case, snowball fighting is not an acceptable answer. It is perfectly appropriate for the teacher to use brainstorming prompts that have conditions attached. In such an instance, student responses must fall within those conditions or they are not acceptable responses. Although brainstorming promotes freedom of thought, it is not "free for all" thinking.

PURPOSE

It is important for students to know why they are using this strategy and what it can do for them. The purpose of brainstorming in school is to call on content knowledge, generate many ideas about the content, and extend what is known. This ability is contextual. Certain students may not be creative in math because they cannot come up with different problem-solving ideas. Yet, the same students may be able to come up with different ways to test a hypothesis in science. Thus, idea generation is dependent upon the context of the situation and the content information that is needed by students to produce responses. As students practice brainstorming in a variety of contexts, they increase their overall ability to generate many ideas, and begin to extend the skill to different content areas.

The creative-adaptive person, according to Parnes (1988), modifies or adapts information or ideas to come up with solutions, whereas the conforming person relies on past experience as a guide and doesn't consider new possibilities. According to Parnes, "The visionizer sees what might be, the conformist sees only what is" (p. 21). For conforming students, who may think there's a hidden agenda or that the teacher is looking for a particular answer, brainstorming is difficult; they don't trust the process. By practicing brainstorming, however, students begin to see its value. This can help eliminate the idea of functional fixedness—that there is only one way to do something—and allow these students greater fluency in their thinking.

Brainstorming is not meant to be just a regurgitation of facts, but a projection of possibilities as well. If teachers want students to simply recall information, they should just ask students to make a list of what is known. This does not promote creative thinking. Brainstorming goes beyond listing literal information and includes the consideration of possibilities.

BENEFITS

The foremost benefit of either verbal or nonverbal brainstorming is being able to see possibilities and options. We need not feel limited by the first idea that comes to mind. Because first ideas are usually obvious ones, and more unusual ideas occur after the first three minutes of brainstorming, teachers need to allow more than a few minutes to get the most out of a brainstorming session. When using the nonverbal Rainbow of Ideas graphic organizer, students need time to write responses. This is something to consider when you think about the amount of time needed for a nonverbal activity versus a verbal activity.

As students begin to recognize the value of brainstorming, they see that the ridiculous idea can actually be helpful. The ridiculous idea may help students connect to more realistic or practical ideas. It is helpful to describe to the students how crazy ideas have led to good or even great ideas. For example, when the idea of talking movies was proposed in 1927, Harry Warner, president of Warner Pictures, said, "Who the hell wants to hear actors talk?" When the idea of flying machines was introduced to Lord Kevin in 1895, he said, "Heavier than air flying machines are impossible." When students are aware of such reactions, they may be less quick to dismiss ideas as wild, crazy, or unusable. There will be times when a student suggests a ridiculous idea just to elicit a reaction from the class. Because we are not judging ideas at this point, I recommend recording the idea, making little response, and moving on. The student's idea, although ridiculous, becomes just one of many ideas.

Research indicates that students become more fluent in their thinking if they practice brainstorming. Student improvement in fluency supports the notion that creativity can be taught. How will you know if your students' ability to brainstorm improves? First, just listen to their responses. In their classroom performance, you will notice students will begin to generate more responses. They will be able to consider more than one or two ideas, and they will understand that more than one idea can be correct.

Teachers who want quantitative evidence of student improvement use the *Torrance Tests of Creative Thinking*. Paul Torrance (1974) created these tests to assess fluency, flexibility, originality, and elaboration. Teachers can pre- and post-test students' fluency to show growth over time. The Talents Unlimited model (1995) fosters fluency through brainstorming in a strand called productive thinking, and offers a criterion-referenced test for teachers to use. This test provides quantitative data, and teachers can extrapolate fluency, flexibility, and elaboration scores. Teachers can also use the rating scale and rubric described later in this chapter to conduct informal assessments of brainstormed responses.

APPLICATIONS

Brainstorming may not be most effective as an introductory activity for a unit. At this point, students can't provide a quantity of ideas because their content knowledge is limited. The activity would not last long, and students would not get much out of it other than fun. Brainstorming should be more than fun—it should be an effective tool for reinforcing, reviewing, and extending content. As such, it is better to brainstorm midway or toward the end of a unit when students have more information.

For example, in a simple machines unit, students might be expected to brainstorm the effects of different types of force before they decide how to create an invention. If students have limited knowledge about types of force, brainstorming will not be particularly productive. Allowing time for research prior to brainstorming may help. Students need content information to come up with different combinations of ideas. In this sense, brainstorming is not just a motivational strategy but also an important instructional tool.

Brainstorming as a class or in groups is usually more effective than brainstorming alone, and students often prefer this social way of learning. Those students who have a strong interpersonal style of learning (Armstrong, 1994; Gregory & Chapman, 2002; Silver, Strong, & Perini, 2000) particularly prefer the interaction of peers. They have the support of one another when they are searching for answers. They do not have to worry about coming up with all the answers by themselves. They can feed off of one another's ideas.

With the use of brainstorming rules, small groups of three or four students usually function well. We all know, however, that personalities within small groups affect productivity. As with any other activity, teachers need to be aware of which students work well together. Teachers might want to consider whether to mix introverts with extroverts, highly verbal students with nonverbal, or mix types of intelligences, such as interpersonal with intrapersonal. Students who have a large knowledge base often feel resentful when placed in a group with struggling students. They feel they're doing all the work. The struggling students quickly learn that if they only know a little bit about the topic, they will not have many ideas to share. This feeling certainly doesn't help their self-esteem. One answer to the grouping problem in your classroom is to make sure to use flexible groups. This means that groupings change from activity to activity or from project to project. When grouping by ability level, teachers can work with the struggling learner group while the other groups work independently. When grouping heterogeneously, teachers need to make sure that all students can contribute to the group successfully.

Brainstorming is very effective as an oral activity because students hear one another's answers and that gives them ideas. The verbal students are quick to share their answers, either in whole class or small group activities. When it is a whole class activity, try recording the ideas on a white board or chart paper so as not to interrupt the flow of ideas. Although there are benefits if students take on this role, they may write so slowly that the class becomes frustrated. You can remedy this situation by having two or three student recorders at a time. Having to record a large number of responses is a great problem to have, because it means the students are becoming fluent thinkers.

Verbal brainstorming is a problem for nonverbal students who are either unwilling to respond out loud or unable to due to language delays or limited language ability. The highly verbal learners can take over and quickly overpower the nonverbal students, who end up saying nothing. We want all students to feel comfortable participating in the lesson so that they can share what they know. If this is a problem, here's one solution to ensure all students participate. This strategy is used with Odyssey of The Mind teams that compete at solving problems. The strategy is easily transferable to the classroom.

> Students can work in groups of six to do their brainstorming. In each group, one student acts as the recorder. The other students are assigned numbers between 1 and 5. The students are given a deck of cards with the numbers 1–5 on them. The top card is turned over. Whoever has the number on the top card makes a response, turns the next card over, and the next person responds. The students continue to respond until they run out of time or run out of cards. In this way, all students have a chance to participate. The students can use dice rather than cards. One thing that I like about using dice or cards is that students cannot anticipate when their turn will be. When students make responses in order, they tend to "space out" when their turn is over because they know they won't have another turn for a while. With dice or cards, students may end up with two or more turns in a row. The element of chance helps keep students focused.

When using dice or cards, make sure you supply specific rules. For example, you have thirty seconds to respond; you may pass only one time; you can ask a friend for help; you may not repeat an answer; and if you were the recorder during the last brainstorming lesson, you may not be the recorder for this lesson. At the end of the brainstorming time, the groups share their ideas with the rest of the class.

Another solution is to use the Rainbow of Ideas graphic organizer. This graphic organizer is designed to be a nonverbal activity. Students who do not speak in class are provided the opportunity to generate ideas because they write their responses rather than speak them. The "talkers" will not overpower the "nontalkers." Individual brainstorming is preferable when students feel pressure to keep up with other students. Students who need more time to process information do not feel so rushed. Students who are more pensive and reflective write their ideas at their own pace. Individual brainstorming may also be desirable when teachers want students to generate ideas specific to a personal problem, issue, or concern. It is important to consider the needs of the learner in a differentiated classroom. Working individually can alleviate stressful situations that might diminish some students' achievement.

Brainstorming fits naturally with almost any content. In a textbook or on a worksheet, for example, students might encounter a knowledge or comprehension question. The worksheet question might ask students to list elements of tall tales. If the teacher wants to encourage creative thinking, she can change the question and ask students to brainstorm the many ways a character could have an extraordinary ability. Both prompts address aspects of tall tales, but the second prompt demands a creative response whereas the first prompt draws on recall.

How else can you foster more creative thinking in your classroom, when your standards and texts target critical thinking verbs? Many times, a critical thinking verb can be use in conjunction with a creative thinking verb. For example, a Maine state standard says, "Compare how different economies meet basic wants and needs over time." Some groups can focus on critical thinking with a compare and contrast chart to target the standard. Other groups can brainstorm how different economies meet basic wants and needs over time. The class emerges from their groups to discuss their findings. From the lists of generated information, the students individually make comparisons and then formulate generalizations in an essay. The brainstormed lists serve as the first part of the lesson.

Here are a few examples of prompts to get your students to brainstorm (adapted from Connecticut Standards, Georgia's Quality Core Curriculum, Maine Learning Results, National Council of Teachers of Mathematics Standards, National English Language Arts Standards, National Science Standards, National Social Studies Standards, New Hampshire Curriculum and Proficiency Standards, and Texas Essential Knowledge and Skills).

In the Elementary Grades

Language Arts

o Generate ideas about what the main characters wish for or should have wished for in *The Fisherman and His Wife* by Freya Littledale. The teacher hopes to extend recall by allowing students the opportunity to think of other possible wishes.

o Generate ideas about talent based on the ideas in *Abel's Island* by William Steig. The teacher provides students with an opportunity to think beyond the literal examples of talent in the story.

Writing

o Brainstorm exciting events for a creative writing project. This is an opportunity for students to generate ideas and then choose one to write about. It is easier for students to begin writing a story using this prompt rather than saying to students, "Write a story about anything."

o Brainstorm a list of things you see, hear, smell, and taste. The teacher places students in groups and gives them one category to brainstorm. The students pool their lists and then individually choose one word from each list to include in their story.

Math

o Brainstorm things that come in sets. The teacher uses this prompt to reinforce the definition of set.

o Brainstorm types of measurement. The teacher tries to reinforce the notion of standard and nonstandard measurement through this prompt.

Science

o Generate ideas on what simple machines can do. The teacher hopes students will expand their conception of what constitutes a simple machine.

o Brainstorm ideas about seeds. The teacher gives this prompt to her students as a pre-assessment in the plant unit. Students are encouraged to write down anything they know or think they know about seeds.

Social Studies

o Generate many ways you can help a friend. As part of the "our community" unit, the teacher talks about roles people play in the community. A friend is an important role that we all share. The teacher builds on the idea of friendship with this prompt.

o Generate ideas about the Vikings. Students list everything they know and think they know about the topic. This is a good way to spark interest in an upcoming lesson.

In the Middle Grades

Language Arts

o Brainstorm different ways equality is portrayed in *Harrison Bergeron* by Kurt Vonnegut. The teacher wants students to identify the obvious and the more abstract ways equality is presented in the story.

o Based on the story *The Outsiders* by S. E. Hinton, brainstorm ideas related to gangs. The teacher has students work in pairs to brainstorm what they have read about gangs as well as what they know about gangs.

Writing

o Brainstorm all the possible writing mistakes you could make. After students complete a writing assignment, and it is corrected, they go back and circle the mistakes they made that are listed on their brainstormed list. The teacher uses this lesson as a way to help students recognize mistakes they make while writing or editing.

o Brainstorm situations in which you might use a persuasive argument. The teacher uses this lesson to introduce students to why it is important to learn how to make a good persuasive argument.

Math

o Brainstorm ideas, words, or uses for platonic solids. This playful way to reinforce a definition can turn silly. Students, however, can also generate some powerful imagery.
o Brainstorm what would happen if fractions did not exist. The teacher uses this lesson as a way for students to think about how fractions are used.

Science

o Generate reasons for concern about radioactive decay. The teacher uses this prompt as a follow-up to a reading assignment. The teacher hopes students will add their own concerns to those mentioned in the text.
o Brainstorm uses of electricity. The teacher uses this prompt to help students realize how dependent we are on "power."

Social Studies

o Brainstorm what would happen if our American rights were suddenly overturned. The teacher uses this negative tactic to encourage students to think about how important our rights are. The students, of course, must know the Bill of Rights.
o Brainstorm goods and services that are currently produced in our state as well as possible new goods and services that might be produced in the near future. The teacher uses this prompt to review information, and it allows students to predict future possibilities.

In the High School Grades

English

o Brainstorm ways the literature written by American authors explores the human condition. The teacher first asks the class to brainstorm a list of American authors. The students then discuss what is meant by the human condition by citing examples. Finally, students nonverbally brainstorm their responses to the prompt.
o Brainstorm ways that complex elements of plot affect the overall quality of the work. The teacher discusses the meaning of the prompt with the students. The students brainstorm a few ideas as examples and then work in small groups to complete the "brainstorm" graphic organizer.

Writing

o Brainstorm how language usage may depend upon the situation. The teacher uses this lesson as a way to show how dialect, grammar, and slang influence people and their interactions.

      o Brainstorm a list of questions you might use at a writing conference between the teacher and yourself. The teacher uses the students' ideas to create a writing conference checklist.

Math

      o Brainstorm a variety of simulations related to probability. The teacher uses this prompt as a review and extension activity toward the end of the unit.
      o Brainstorm relationships among geometric figures. The teacher gives the students a picture with geometric figures on it. Some figures overlap and other are connected by one side. Groups of students brainstorm relationships.

Science

      o Generate explanations for phenomena such as black holes and quasars. Students list explanations based on a reading and add their own ideas.
      o Brainstorm issues that illustrate the effects of technological imbalances. The teacher reviews the definition of "issue" and breaks the class into groups to respond to the prompt.

Social Studies

      o Brainstorm reasons for imperialism. The teacher gives students this prompt after they read an article that gives four reasons for imperialism. The teacher hopes students will take the four reasons and use them to come up with their own ideas to add to the list.
      o Brainstorm the obvious and not so obvious causes of the American Revolution. The teacher encourages the students to use recall to cite causes and hopes students will use reasoning to come up with other plausible explanations.

GETTING STARTED IN THE CLASSROOM

Once students have done a lot of verbal brainstorming in the class, they will be more adept at transferring this ability to a written format. The Rainbow of Ideas graphic organizer (Figure 8.1) is used to engage students in a nonverbal brainstorming activity (adapted from Davis, 1992; Treffinger, 1995). In this chapter, only one graphic organizer is provided and it appears in a pictorial format. If teachers want their students to use a linear format, lined paper works fine for listing ideas.

Explain to students that what they'll be doing is the same as verbal brainstorming, except that they will write their answers instead of speaking them. Begin by placing students in groups of no more than four. All students in the group need to be able to write. Each person receives a Rainbow of Ideas graphic organizer, reads the prompt in the center of the rainbow, and responds to the prompt by writing down two ideas in any space on the rainbow. When students finish writing the two ideas, the paper is placed in the center of the group. Each student then takes a different paper from the center pile and adds two more ideas. Students will only be allowed to speak to one another when they can't read the student's writing or they don't understand the response. Students just keep adding ideas and trading papers until they either run out of ideas or they run out of time. If students cannot think of any more ideas, they should be encouraged to keep reading the responses on different papers. By reading the responses of others, the teacher hopes students will engage in piggybacking and come up with new ideas. When time is up, the papers are returned to the original owners.

When the Rainbow of Ideas graphic organizer is used as a tool to generate ideas, the discussion that follows the activity is deeper because students have had time to process the ideas. The extra time spent on doing a written activity rather than a verbal brainstorm may result in more active involvement by more of the students. If verbal brainstorming is the only type of brainstorming you practice in your classroom, please consider this variation.

SAMPLE LESSON

The Rainbow of Ideas graphic organizer activity allows teachers to gain insights they might not otherwise obtain if they use only oral brainstorming over and over again. Take, for example, a lesson involving a story called *Kio and Gus* by Matthew Lipman. The teacher asks her students to brainstorm many different events that happened in the story (see Figure 8.2). Small groups of second-grade students sit together to fill out their rainbows. They write about whatever they remember from the story, feelings they have about events in the story, or any associations derived from the events in the story. You can see from the responses that this group is very literal. They write down facts that they remember from the story. This is generally what will happen with this type of activity with young students, but the fact that they fill out all the sections is quite an accomplishment. Because students in this group clearly remember and understand quite a bit about the story, the teacher can begin to introduce them to inferential reasoning. They are ready to move beyond the literal. The teacher gained valuable information about the students from the written activity.

In deciding when to use a graphic organizer, you must ask yourself: What is the purpose of the activity? What do I want my students to know and understand as a result of this activity? For example, the teacher asks students to brainstorm a list of all the ways Cinderella could have gone to the ball if she had no fairy godmother. Students would need to know and understand the story to come up with a list. After students brainstorm the list, the teacher might ask students to judge which idea they like best. They may use this idea to do a story rewrite. Most often, brainstorming is not a stand-alone activity, but is used to generate ideas that become the basis for the next lesson or activity.

ASSESSMENT

Grading creative thinking is always a difficult task. Some teachers do not like to grade creative responses because they feel they are too subjective. Teachers are "correct in that there is some sacrifice of objectivity; however, research shows that evaluators are remarkably consistent in their assessments of creativity" (Amabile, 1983; Sternberg & Lubart, 1995, cited in Sternberg & Williams, 1996, p. 23). Is it necessary to assess or grade a brainstorm activity? Giving specific feedback seems more in keeping with the creative process. Because brainstorming is asking students to come up with many ideas, the rating scale may only be appropriate some of the time.

In the *Kio and Gus* example, we can use the rating scale (Figure 8.3) to assess the group's responses. The first criterion targets the word "generate." Because the group

Figure 8.1 Rainbow of Ideas Graphic Organizer (Brainstorm)

Name: _____   Date: _____

Brainstorm

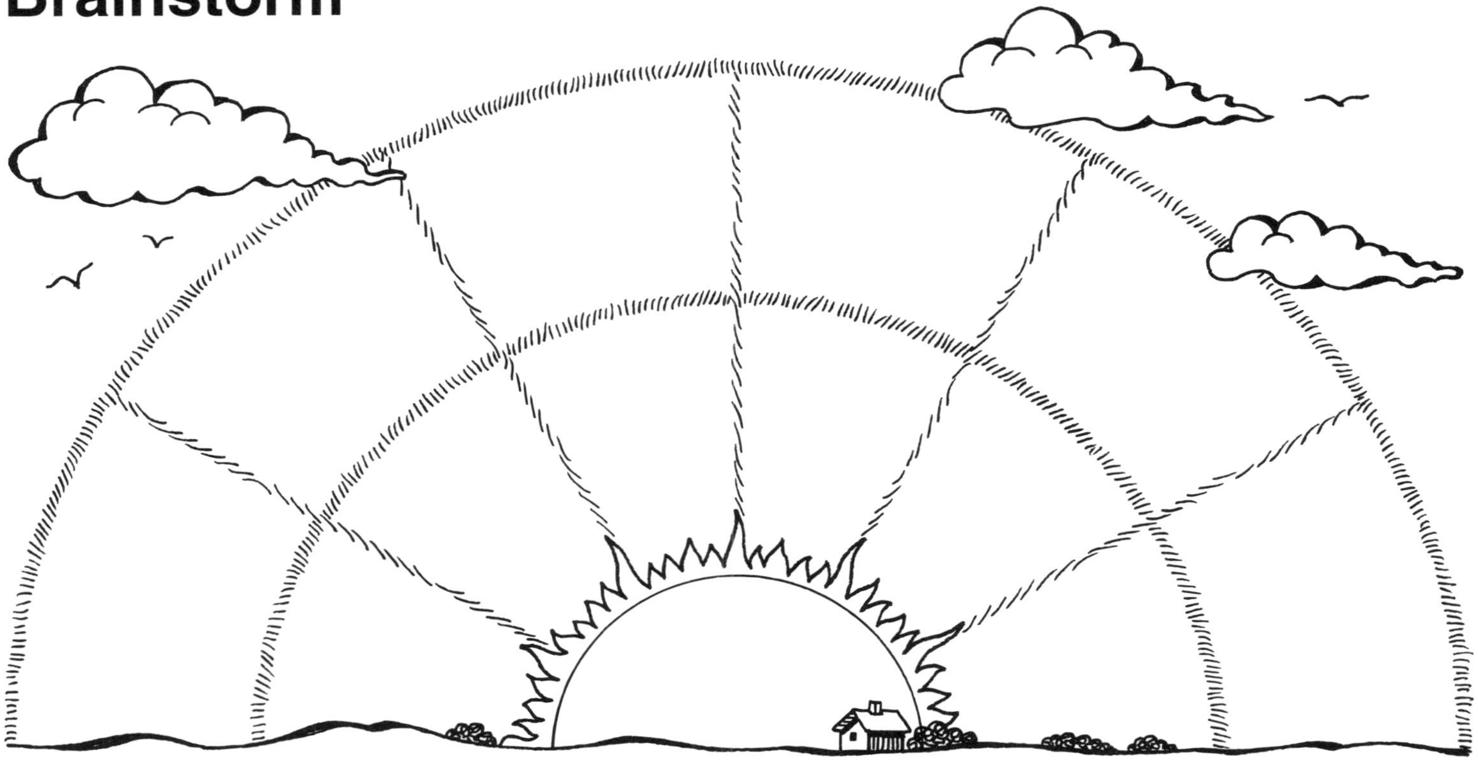

1. State the idea, issue, or problem in the sun.

2. Write two related ideas in the spaces above, and pass it to the next student.

3. Write two ideas on another rainbow and pass it on until all the rainbows are complete.

Illustration by Bob Greisen.

Figure 8.2 Sample: *Kio and Gus* Rainbow of Ideas Graphic Organizer (Brainstorm)

Name: _____   Date: _____

Brainstorm

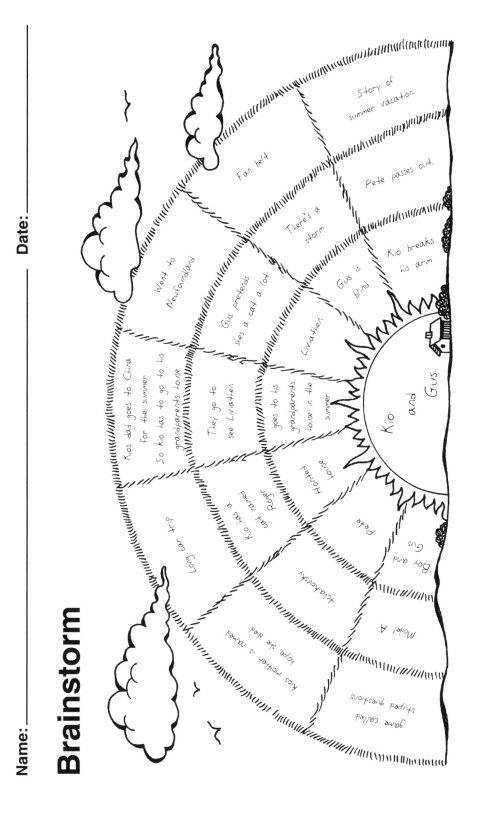

1. State the idea, issue, or problem in the sun.

2. Write two related ideas in the spaces above, and pass it to the next student.

3. Write two ideas on another rainbow and pass it on until all the rainbows are complete.

generated many answers and filled up the whole rainbow in the given amount of time, they score a 5 in this category. The next criterion is relevancy. Students should not stop the flow of brainstorming to assess for relevancy, but they should check their answers before handing them in to the teacher. If their answers do not fit within the parameters of the prompt, they may need to edit their list after they finish brainstorming. The student responses listed in the example are all relevant. The ideas they listed actually occurred in the story. The students receive a 5 in this category.

The group also receives a 5 in listing uncommon ideas because they write both main and subordinate ideas on the graphic organizer. Responses such as "She pretends she is a cat a lot" and "Game called Stupid Questions" are less obvious events in the story. For second graders, these types of answers indicate an attention to detail and are considered uncommon responses.

The probing questions on the rating scale help students to understand what quality brainstorming looks like and therefore they can become more fluent at doing it. In this way, students are encouraged not only to think about content, but about their thinking about the content—in other words, to engage in metacognitive thinking.

The rubric can also be used with the Rainbow of Ideas graphic organizer. The specific language on the rubric can help students review their brainstorming responses or the teacher can use it to assess the responses. The rubric translation (Figure 8.4) of the *Kio and Gus* rating scale shows what the language should look like, and scores are marked with asterisks.

Naturally, the teacher uses the assessment tools to provide feedback to the groups, but the graphic organizers can also be used to gain information about individual students. The teacher can tell by the handwriting if all the students in the group participated. An

Figure 8.3   Sample: *Kio and Gus* Creative Thinking Rating Scale (Brainstorm)

Criteria	Probing Question	Rating
Generation	How many ideas were generated?	5
Relevance	To what degree do the responses relate to the prompt?	5
Uncommon	To what degree are the responses less obvious or unusual?	5

Figure 8.4   Sample: *Kio and Gus* Creative Thinking Rubric (Brainstorm)

1	2	3	
Few Ideas	Some Ideas	Many Ideas	*
Responses have little to do with the prompt or may be inaccurate.	Most of the responses relate to the prompt and all are accurate.	All responses relate to the prompt and are accurate.	*
Responses include main ideas only.	Responses include literal or common ideas.	Responses include less obvious and unusual ideas.	*

informal assessment can help the teacher see whether a student is having trouble brainstorming, remembering the story, or understanding the story. Later, the teacher can meet with the student to try to sift out why the responses were weak. If it's a brainstorming problem, then additional creative activities can help the student build these skills. If the student doesn't remember the story, then helping the student with memory strategies is beneficial. If the student doesn't understand the story, then helping the student with comprehension strategies works best.

 ## KEY POINTS TO REMEMBER ABOUT BRAINSTORMING

1. Brainstorming provides a deliberate way to generate many ideas.

2. Brainstorming can accommodate different styles of learning.

3. Brainstorming fits in a variety of contexts.

4. By practicing brainstorming, we can improve our fluency, a creative thinking skill. To improve fluency, practice is necessary.

5. To improve at brainstorming, feedback is essential.

6. Because brainstorming is not strictly recall, it is a creative thinking activity.

PAUSE FOR REFLECTION AND DISCUSSION

1. What makes a good brainstorming lesson?

2. Why do we need rules when we brainstorm?

3. What are the advantages to using the Rainbow of Ideas graphic organizer over verbal brainstorming?

4. How can you foster more brainstorming in your units of study?

5. In what ways might you differentiate your brainstorming lesson?

9

"Connect"

Making Unlikely Associations

Connect

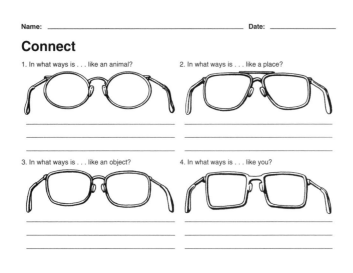

1. In what ways is . . . like an animal?

2. In what ways is . . . like a place?

3. In what ways is . . . like an object?

4. In what ways is . . . like you?

⇨ Graphic Organizer: Rose-Colored Glasses

⇨ Verb: Connect (flexibility)

⇨ Synonyms: Associate, relate

⇨ Define the Steps:

1. State your focus or problem: word, idea, situation.

2. Make analogies between the given word, idea, or situation and an animal, place, thing, and yourself.

3. Determine how the connections help you to better understand the given word, idea, or situation or help you to solve a problem.

DEFINITION

The second creative skill area identified by Paul Torrance (1987) is flexibility. Flexibility means not just generating many things but different kinds of things. For example, if students are asked to think of many different effects of disastrous weather and they list ten ideas relating to damage to structures, then their ideas are all basically the same. Flexibility is a skill that allows them to consider all different types of effects of severe weather, such as what can happen to roads, vehicles, public services, people, and so on.

Flexibility requires an open mind. Flexible thinkers are able to look at options, consider different points of view, and are willing to change their minds. As Costa and Garmston (2001, p. 18) write, "They are open and comfortable with ambiguity."

Flexible thinking helps us to make unlikely connections. For example, it's easy to connect the idea of planets with the solar system. Students know and understand there are different planets that make up our solar system. But this does not involve depth of knowledge. If we ask how Mars is like a dog, however, students might say they both experience gravitational pull, both can be destroyed, and certain atmospheric conditions must be present for them both to exist. These responses show, through a forced association technique, "Creative thinkers connect the unconnected, especially to seemingly unrelated ideas" (Maxwell, 2003, p. 102).

Active student involvement results from hooking students through prior knowledge, interests, and enjoyment. Making unlikely connections can draw in students as they encounter new topics, by connecting the new content with their existing knowledge or interests. According to Davis (1992, p. 120), "When we think analogically or metaphorically, we take ideas from one context and apply them in a new context, producing the new idea combination, new transformation, new theoretical perspective, or more colorful literary passage." When teachers help students learn how to make associations between unrelated things, students learn that they can connect anything (Michalko, 1998). Students become more engaged in part because it's fun to make absurd, forced associations, but also because they begin to see the power of the connections.

As students practice flexible thinking in content areas, it becomes more natural for them to form associations. It is a way for students to discover that deep meaning gives content substance, and students often find that deep learning is more interesting than surface-level learning. Flexible thinking may not come as easily or as quickly as brainstorming, but it is worth the time and effort.

PURPOSE

Flexible thinking helps students to solve problems, consider a range of ideas, and understand different perspectives. It is an especially important skill for those who are very black and white in their thinking. It enables students to explore multiple aspects and characteristics of a problem or situation.

All teachers are concerned with their students doing well on state tests. Some states use analogies on their tests, and making unlikely connections or forced associations will help students with analogies. Most state tests also ask analytical questions. For example, a prompt in a reading section might ask students to analyze a character at the beginning, middle, and end of a story. While it would seem in this instance that an "analyze" graphic organizer might be helpful, the "connect" graphic organizer could help students to think of ideas that never would have come up with the Framed Puzzle graphic organizer (see Chapter 5, "Analyze"). Both graphic organizers, critical and creative, require that students review the story and examine the character's attributes.

When answering a question on a test, some students can only think of one or two obvious answers, which is not enough for a high score. Students can use a flexibility tool such as the Rose-Colored Glasses graphic organizer to stimulate their thinking. With a little practice, students become adept at the process of forced association. By combining critical and creative thinking, their answers can become more articulate, thoughtful, and creative.

BENEFITS

Flexible thinking helps students become more creative in their thinking, and the more creative the better! Often, it feels more comfortable to ask for connections between closely related items. For example, the teacher might ask students to relate a planet to an asteroid. Although this works, students will search deeper in their knowledge if they compare a planet to a shoe. Don't be afraid to push the far out associations.

Certain students will not see the benefit of making unusual connections. Students who are weak in this area might generate limited responses. This only confirms to them that this kind of activity is meaningless. Students who prefer analytical thinking sometimes feel this type of lesson is a waste of time because it is too fanciful or silly. These students need to understand that stepping aside to take a skewed view of something they think they know—a word, a person, an event—might uncover hidden attributes and insights. Through group discussions that generate many responses, reluctant participants will see unusual connections that would not have surfaced otherwise.

Remember, the overall purpose of flexible thinking is to promote increased academic achievement. If students can work in their preferred style, learning is increased. Most students, however, don't even know what their cognitive style is. If teachers challenge students to venture outside of their comfort zone, previously unsuccessful students may become more successful, when they discover that a mode of instruction matches their cognitive style of learning. According to Sternberg (1996), we need to accommodate all our thinkers—analytical thinkers, creative thinkers, and practical thinkers.

Finally, most students enjoy connecting content to the absurd or the ridiculous. They think it's funny to compare the U.S. Constitution to a duck. They might come up with answers like, "They both exist over time," "People look at them," "There is order to both," "They can seem complex to some people," and so on. Students begin to understand components of the U.S. Constitution they might not have otherwise thought about. This can spark in-depth discussion about the physical nature of the Constitution, why its structure is effective, or how its authors came up with such a complex document that has endured over time. These ideas might not have emerged had the students not been encouraged to think outside the box.

APPLICATION

Flexibility is a creative thinking skill that is used to reinforce or extend knowledge in content areas. When deciding if and when to use this type of thinking, you might want to think about the answers to these questions: What do you want your students to know and understand? What state standard are you addressing? What is the essential question? What is the learning objective? What activities will you ask your students to do that will achieve the objective? Will it be measured? Although flexibility may not be addressed in the actual learning objective, it may be used in the activity to reach the objective.

So, what does an instructional learning objective that uses flexible thinking look like? Let's take an example from a Texas state standard in reading that states, "The student uses a variety of strategies to comprehend selections read aloud and selections read independently." Your instructional objective might be, "The student will change the ending of the story to reach a different solution to the central problem, while still maintaining the original storyline." You can then use the Rose-Colored Glasses graphic organizer to help students come up with many different solutions.

For example, in the story of *Jack and the Beanstalk,* one problem is that Jack steals the Giant's favorite things. The students might decide the solution to the Giant's problem is to have Jack sent to jail. The students relate the idea of sending Jack to jail to a person, a place, a thing, and themselves. They consider the solution in an unconventional way. The students use the ideas generated from the "connect" graphic organizer to recreate the story with a new ending.

When doing such an activity, ask, "Does this activity achieve the objective and state standard?" The instructional objective stated above uses the word "change," which directly relates to flexibility. It is appropriate for students to use a graphic organizer that supports changing the solution by connecting it to unrelated ideas. When playing around with different associations and then rewriting the ending, students address the second part of the objective, which is to demonstrate an understanding of the original story. The changed version reflects the responses from the graphic organizer, which must make sense within the framework of the original version. This instructional objective also addresses the state standard, which asks students to use a strategy to demonstrate an understanding of the story.

Prompts that focus on flexible thinking through forced associations begin with words such as "connect" or phrases such as "In what ways is (something) like (something else)?" In the examples below, some prompts follow the graphic organizer format, where the content is compared to several things. Other prompts connect the content to just one or two things. Teachers can modify the graphic organizer if fewer connections are required. The examples that follow are adapted from Connecticut Standards, Georgia's Quality Core Curriculum, Maine Learning Results, National Council of Teachers of Mathematics Standards, National English Language Arts Standards, National Science Standards, National Social Studies Standards, New Hampshire Curriculum and Proficiency Standards, and Texas Essential Knowledge and Skills.

In the Elementary Grades

Language Arts

o In what ways is the main character like a rope? The teacher uses this activity to encourage students to consider the protagonist's characteristics.
o Generate predictions about the story and connect them to unrelated objects. Halfway through the story, have the class make predictions about how the story will end. The students choose their favorite prediction and work with a partner who has chosen the same prediction. They fill out the graphic organizer and then the whole class shares responses.

Writing

o In what ways is creative writing like an animal, place, object, and you? The teacher uses this activity to find out what students think about creative writing. Their personal impressions are sure to find their way into their responses.
o In what ways are the rules of spelling like a menu? The teacher tries to highlight the usefulness and shortcomings of spelling rules.

Math

o In what ways are fractions like an apple, a dog, and Martin Luther King, Jr.? The teacher wants students to apply their conceptual understanding of fractions. After they complete the graphic organizer, the students take their favorite connection and draw a picture of the association.

- Connect properties of shapes and figures to a mountain, a river, and the ocean. The teacher uses this prompt to review the properties rather than ask students to "Define the properties of shapes and figures."

Science

- In what ways are plants like jelly beans? The teacher asks this at the end of a unit. She tells students they should think about everything they know about plants when they connect them to jelly beans.
- In what ways is the classification system like a holiday and a doctor's appointment? Any broad concept such as a classification system works well in a prompt like this one, because the concept is multifaceted and lends itself to a variety of connections.

Social Studies

- Relate how recreation affects the state economy to the president, the beach, and toast? The students list different ways recreation affects the state economy. They connect items on their list to unrelated things. They use their ideas to develop a persuasive agreement in support of keeping the town's recreation area open to the public.
- In what ways is this artifact like Bart Simpson, a river, and a bird? When studying regions, the teacher brings in an artifact (in this case, a metal lobster measurer) and does not tell students what it is. Students list ways this artifact (from what they can see) connects to the unrelated things. After the activity, the teacher tells them what the artifact is, how it is used, and what region it comes from. The teacher uses the lesson to build on the idea that tools may be specific to regions.

In the Middle Grades

Language Arts

- In what ways is this significant moment in the story like a frog? The teacher leads the discussion as students review the story and identify a significant moment. Students work on their own to form their associations. When students share their responses, the teacher helps them to see the impact of the significant moment in the story.
- Connect the main character's perspective on the issue posed in the story to unrelated things. The teacher uses this activity to teach about perspective and point of view.

Writing

- In what ways are editorials like kangaroos? The teacher wants to make sure students know and understand what an editorial really is before she has them write one.
- Connect vivid language to three words that you randomly choose from the dictionary. The teacher hopes the students will use what they know about vivid language to make connections to unrelated words. The students are expected to use vivid language in their writing piece.

Math

- o In what ways are abstract representations like a phone call? The teacher uses this prompt as an introductory activity to reinforce the meaning of representations.
- o In what ways is the area of an irregular shape like a nightmare, an ice cream, and a tree? The teacher uses this activity to help students remember that they must use a variety of strategies to find the area of irregular shapes.

Science

- o In what ways is the food chain like a visit from a friend, a traffic jam, and a lollipop? The students use their responses to talk about the relationship between predator and prey.
- o Connect ways that natural and artificial selection affect species over time to a hurricane, an A on your report card, and new shoes. The teacher uses this prompt after students have read an article on evolution. Students brainstorm the different ways, choose one, and make their connections.

Social Studies

- o In what ways is the United Nations like a peanut butter and jelly sandwich? The teacher uses this prompt after students have studied the roles and responsibilities of the United Nations.
- o Generate connections between the Boston Tea Party and a lion, the desert, a leaf, and you. The teacher uses this as a prompt for students to connect what they know and then use three of their associations in a summary about the political climate at the time of the Boston Tea Party.

In the High School Grades

English

- o In what ways is the stylistic effect of dialogue in a story like a noun, a verb, and an adjective? With this prompt, the teacher hopes to help students understand that dialogue reflects the representation of character, time, and location.
- o Connect the universal theme to your best friend. This lesson reinforces the importance of universal themes in literature. Students discuss the theme in class and fill out the Rose-Colored Glasses graphic organizer in small groups as a follow-up to the discussion.

Writing

- o In what ways is the imagery in your writing piece like a person, place, thing, and you? The teacher uses this activity as a way for students to check their use of imagery in their writing. After students fill out the graphic organizer, the teacher asks the students to reflect on their responses and adjust their writing.
- o Connect a particular point of view to a person, place, and thing of your choice. The teacher tells students to write a fictional story from any point of view other than a person's (i.e., the cat's point of view, the chair's point of view, etc.). The teacher asks students to identify a point of view and fill out the Rose-Colored Glasses organizer. Through this activity the students will gain a better understanding of a particular point of view before they begin their writing.

Math

o In what ways are complex numbers like the principal, your house, and a box? For some students, vocabulary such as "complex numbers" is hard to learn. When connecting the new word with a variety of unrelated associations, it is easier to remember its meaning.

o In what ways is random sampling like a sunny day, a vacation, and a notebook? The teacher uses the graphic organizer to reinforce the definition and uses of random sampling.

Science

o In what ways is the role of DNA in evolutionary change like Shakespeare, the pyramids in Egypt, and chocolate? The students work in groups to respond to the prompt after they read about DNA in a handout.

o Connect ways that atoms are joined by chemical bonding to a rattlesnake, a computer, and an apple. The teacher uses this prompt to find out if students really understand chemical bonding.

Social Studies

o In what ways is U.S. foreign policy like Bill Gates, New York City, and popcorn? The teacher uses this prompt with small groups of students to discuss what they know about foreign policy. The responses are shared with the class and discussed in terms of accuracy and originality.

o Relate the concept of cost-benefit analysis to Rosa Parks, woods, and a pen. Students break into groups and connect the topic to one of the unrelated ideas. The teacher writes Rosa Parks, woods, and pen on different sections of the blackboard. When the time is up, students in each group choose their favorite association and write it under the correct heading on the board. The students look at the ideas and synthesize their own definition of cost-benefit analysis.

GETTING STARTED IN THE CLASSROOM

The Rose-Colored Glasses graphic organizer (Figure 9.1) and its complementary linear format (Figure 9.2) focus on making unlikely connections. These organizers use forced association to help students think more deeply about a topic, problem, or situation. Both promote flexible thinking because students connect the content to a variety of things—animals, places, objects, and themselves. Students can use the completed graphic organizer as a pre-writing tool to create ideas or to develop more depth in a writing piece they're working on. Teachers can use the graphic organizers to generate a discussion or to find out what students know by examining their connections.

Be sure to bear in mind that before students can make unlikely connections, they must understand that we define and compare things according to characteristics or attributes. A good place to start, especially with young children, is to show them how to identify common characteristics in things. Attribute blocks are a concrete way to demonstrate this skill. Primary teachers often introduce these small colored blocks by pointing out their attributes. For example, the teacher places blocks in sets by color (all reds together), and pattern (one blue, one red, one blue, one red). The blocks can also be characterized by their size and number of edges. This helps students understand what characteristics and attributes are.

Figure 9.1 Rose-Colored Glasses Graphic Organizer (Connect)

Name: _____   Date: _____

Connect

1. In what ways is . . . like an animal?

_____

_____

2. In what ways is . . . like a place?

_____

_____

3. In what ways is . . . like an object?

_____

_____

4. In what ways is . . . like you?

_____

_____

Illustration by Bob Greisen.

Figure 9.2   Linear Graphic Organizer (Connect)

Name: _____ **Date:** _____

Connect

In what way(s) is _____ like _____ ?

an animal

In what way(s) is _____ like _____ ?

a place

In what way(s) is _____ like _____ ?

an object

In what way(s) is _____ like _____ ?

you

It may be too much for young students to connect a concept to four different things, as called for in the Rose-Colored Glasses or the "connect" linear format. In this case, you might ask them to connect a character to just one thing, such as an animal or a place. It is much harder to connect a character to an object, such as a doorknob. Many young students have an easier time connecting a character to themselves.

There are times when teachers at all grade levels will want to modify these graphic organizers and only ask students to make one or two connections. The greater the number of different ways students make connections, however, the more deeply the students will need to analyze the content. Once your students start making connections, you will be amazed at how fluent they become. They will surprise you with their unlikely connections. It's fun and refreshing for students to discuss concepts this way—often a relief from the constant analytical and evaluative questions we usually ask.

SAMPLE LESSONS

In this first lesson, the teacher reads the story *Holes* by Louis Sachar to her whole sixth-grade class. Students individually choose random words by category (animal, place, object, themselves) to associate with Stanley, a character in the story, and fill out their own graphic organizers. This doesn't really constitute differentiation, aside from the fact that students are not all using the same words to make associations.

One student, Brian, chooses the words "wolf," "desert," "ball," and "me" (see Figure 9.3). He thinks Stanley is like a wolf because both are cunning and observant and both know how to survive. The next connection, to a place, is more abstract, and students really need to dig deep for answers. Brian associates Stanley with a desert; apparently, he feels both need nurturing. The next association is between Stanley and a ball, and Brian says they both go "round and round" (Stanley's life seems to go around in circles), Stanley's life and balls are both colorful, they both bounce back, and they both go with other children. In the last section, in which Brian associates himself with Stanley, the common characteristics he identifies are that they both have determination and a positive attitude and both are boys.

It is evident that Brian is able to apply abstract associations and demonstrates a full understanding of the character in the story. If the teacher had simply asked students to "describe" Stanley's character, she might not have received answers of this depth.

Once students understand the process of making connections, they will often choose words that make it easy to find correspondences, resulting in answers that are more common and that require less creative thinking. To minimize this tendency, tell the students they will be making unlikely connections and ask them for an animal, place, and object. Do not tell them what word or concept they will be connecting these to. That way, students will have less of a chance to control the associations. You can also have students choose words randomly from the dictionary or from a word wall (if you have one in your classroom).

A second lesson example involves a fourth-grade fairy tale unit, in which students all read the story of *Cinderella*. They are then asked to make unlikely connections to animals, places, objects, and themselves to see what they can discover about Cinderella.

In her graphic organizer, Julie compares Cinderella to a dog (Figure 9.4). She says both eat, are dirty, and have faces. In the place category, Julie compares Cinderella to a zoo; they both like animals. (Of course, a zoo cannot like animals, but the people at zoos do. Therefore, the answer is accepted.) In the object category, Julie compares Cinderella to a tree; she says they are both tall and drink water. In the final category, Julie says she and Cinderella are both people, like to dance, have chores, eat, drink, and wear clothes.

Figure 9.3 Sample: Brian's *Holes* Rose-Colored Glasses Graphic Organizer (Connect)

Name: _____   **Date:** _____

Connect

1. In what ways is . . . like an animal?

Stanley   like a   wolf

They know how to survive.

They are cunning.

They are observant.

2. In what ways is . . . like a place?

Stanley   like a   desert

They both need nurturing.

3. In what ways is . . . like an object?

Stanley   like a   ball

Life goes round and round.

Comes in colors

Bounces back

Goes with other children.

4. In what ways is . . . like you?

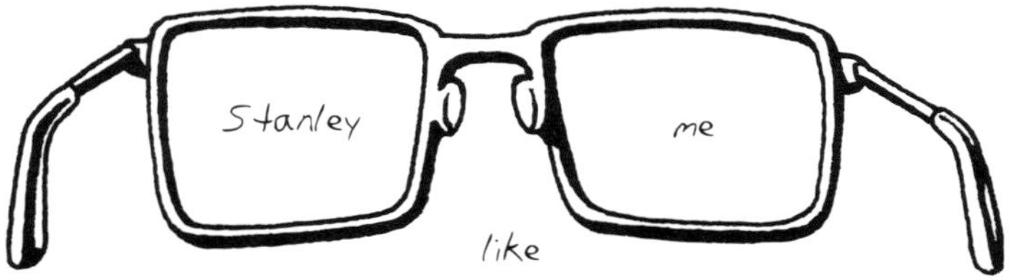

Stanley   like   me

determined

Sees the positive side

boys

Figure 9.4 Sample: Julie's *Cinderella* Linear Graphic Organizer (Connect)

Name: _Julie_ **Date:** _____

Connect

In what way(s) is _____Cinderella_____ like _____a dog_____?
an animal

both eat
both dirty
both have a face

In what way(s) is _____Cinderella_____ like _____a zoo_____?
a place

she likes animals

In what way(s) is _____Cinderella_____ like _____a tree_____?
an object

both tall
both drink water

In what way(s) is _____Cinderella_____ like _____Julie_____?
you

both people   both eat
both like to dance,   both wear clothes,
both have chores,   both drink

In Julie's set of responses, no answers really stand out. In fact, the teacher notices that Julie has trouble making associations to anything that is not alive. The abstract associations of place and object are very difficult for her. The teacher is going to work on this skill with her because Julie does not enjoy school and the teacher feels that this type of activity could be motivating for her if she were successful at it. She also wants to move Julie from the concrete to the abstract.

In such a situation, you can encourage students like Julie to build their answers in a single category rather than taking on multiple categories at the same time. For instance, Julie's teacher could encourage her to come up with more answers in the "object" category before attempting to build up the "places" category. Once Julie is comfortable with the object category, the teacher can start to piggyback this strategy with the idea of personification.

ASSESSMENT

The rating scale for making unlikely connections addresses four areas (Figure 9.5). The first criterion addresses how much the connections make sense. Julie's responses do make sense so she receives a 5 in this category. The next area looks at flexibility. That means we want to consider whether students demonstrate flexible thinking and make connections with all of the associations, not just in one or two areas. Julie's flexibility score is a 3, because she has only one response for two of the analogies. The third criterion takes into account how original the student responses are. We want to encourage unusual connections. Julie makes fairly obvious connections and receives a 3 in the originality category. Finally, teachers really want to encourage independence in this skill area. This is a hard skill for many students, and they will easily become teacher dependent. By placing independence as a criterion, students know from the start that depending on the teacher for help is not a goal. Because Julie did not receive any help filling out the graphic organizer, she scores a 5 for independence.

The rating scale is transposed into a rubric in Figure 9.6. Julie's performance level is indicated on the rubric with asterisks.

Classroom activities that promote creative thought foster a deep joy in students; yet, for some teachers they will have to step out of their comfort zone to conduct such lessons.

Figure 9.5 Sample: Julie's *Cinderella* Creative Thinking Rating Scale (Connect)

Criteria	Probing Question	Rating
Logic	To what degree do the connections make sense?	5
Flexibility	To what degree are analogies made with all associations?	3
Originality	To what degree are the connections creative or unusual?	3
Independence	To what degree were the associations made independently?	5

Figure 9.6   Sample: Julie's *Cinderella* Creative Thinking Rubric (Connect)

Beginning	Getting It	Got It
Connections make little sense.	Connections mostly make sense.	Connections are logical and based on sound reasoning. *
Analogies made with some of random words.	Some analogies made with most random words. *	Many analogies made with all random words.
Connections are obvious.	Connections are common. *	Some connections are unusual or creative.
Some teacher help is needed.	Minor teacher or peer prompting.	Independent work. *

Because some teachers do not think they are creative, they shy away from such activities. To differentiate, however, it may be beneficial for teachers to conduct lessons that promote flexibility to meet the needs of students. Teachers must trust that these lessons will enhance student learning. When using this graphic organizer, teachers foster insight into the content, while nourishing the creativity in their students.

KEY POINTS TO REMEMBER ABOUT CONNECTING

1. Forced association allows us to connect ideas, sometimes in surprising ways.
2. Flexible thinking promotes creative analysis of ideas, concepts, issues, themes, and problems.
3. Analogical or metaphorical thinking can be used in any content area.
4. We can think flexibly when we consider options, make choices, solve problems, and engage with different points of view.
5. Some verbs that focus on flexible thinking are "change," "modify," and "correct."
6. Connecting two unrelated words is more likely to stimulate creative thinking than connecting two related words.

PAUSE FOR REFLECTION AND DISCUSSION

1. In what ways is flexible thinking like a lollipop?
2. Why are metaphorical and analogical thinking useful tools when targeting flexible thinking?
3. How can we help students see the benefits of using this kind of thinking?
4. Why is making unlikely connections a fun way to learn?
5. How might you apply this strategy in your classroom?
6. How might you differentiate the lesson using the graphic organizer?

10

"Create"

Making Something New

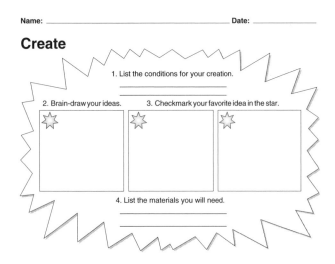

Name: _____ Date: _____

Create

1. List the conditions for your creation.
_____

2. Brain-draw your ideas.   3. Checkmark your favorite idea in the star.

4. List the materials you will need.
_____

⇨ Graphic Organizer: Idea Burst

⇨ Verb: Create

⇨ Synonyms: Design, produce, construct

⇨ Define the Steps:

1. State the limiting conditions for your product.

2. Draw your ideas, creating more than one design.

3. Choose your favorite idea or design.

4. List the materials you will need.

5. Construct your final product.

6. Review construction or choice against conditions in number one.

7. Test, adapt, rehearse.

8. Present your creation to an audience.

DEFINITION

The third creative thinking skill area that Paul Torrance (1987) identified is originality. We often associate originality with the "Oh Wow" product or idea. This type of creativity, sometimes referred to as the Big C (Goleman, Kaufman, & Ray, 1992), tends to put creativity on a pedestal. It is an exalted but limited notion of originality and creativity that targets the exceptional few and is unattainable for most students.

According to Webster's *New World Dictionary of the American Language* (1964), *original* is defined as

1. having to do with an origin, initial, first, earliest; 2. never having occurred or existed before, not copied, fresh, new, novel; 3. capable of or given to inventing or creating something new, or thinking or acting in an independent, individual, fresh way; 4. coming from someone as the originator, maker, author. (p. 1033)

The first two definitions support the "Oh Wow" or "Big C" way of thinking about originality, but the third and the fourth definitions allow for a more inclusive interpretation. They imply a more individualistic approach to originality, in which the way of thinking or doing is particular to the person. This is what Goleman, Kaufman, and Ray (1992) and Csikszentmihalyi (1998) refer to as the "little c." It is new to the individual. That does not mean it is necessarily new to everyone else.

If we define this aspect of creativity this way, everyone can see themselves as original thinkers at least part of the time. It occurs when a student "never thought of something like that before." It occurs when students try to do something different. It occurs when teachers modify an instructional strategy in their classroom or when cooks use their own version of a recipe. In thinking about it this way, originality becomes a teachable and attainable skill.

The verb that is used in this section to target originality is "create" (or design). According to Daniel Pink (2006), in his book *A Whole New Mind,* we must all become designers because we are moving from the Information Age to the Conceptual Age. Design is a significant way to create solutions, and it can be an authentic way for students to learn to use both sides of their brain (not just their left side).

To create, quite simply, means to produce something. Anderson & Krathwohl say, "In create, the student must draw upon elements from many sources and put them together into a novel structure or pattern relative to his or her own prior knowledge. Create results in a new product, that is something that can be observed and that is more than the student's beginning materials" (2001, p. 85). In this definition, creating is seen as more of a synthesis and takes into account many levels of thinking. Students may need to brainstorm ideas, analyze them, evaluate them, modify them, and elaborate on them before creating a product.

There are many inhibiting factors that prevent students from creating an original product. Not all students have enough self-esteem and self-confidence to share or use their ideas. Some students may be creative thinkers but not creative producers. They lack the skills to bring an idea to fruition. A student's lack of independence can also affect the student's ability to create an original product. Distractibility can also be a factor that affects performance. According to Levine (2002), students can have issues with visual, auditory, or tactile distractibility.

Conceptual knowledge is a critical element of creative production (Alexander, Schallert, & Hare, 1991, cited in Alexander, Parsons, & Nash, 1996). If the student lacks confidence, has distractibility issues, lacks organizational skills, or does not know content at a conceptual level, then the student's creativity is inhibited. In any one of these situations, the student's ability to create an innovative product is minimized and often the student is unable or chooses to be unproductive.

Students sometimes do not take the time or have the patience to follow through on the product. An older student may not have time because of a work schedule or home responsibilities. We know that children of poverty often have difficulty focusing on schoolwork. Students may be in the habit of not turning in homework. These are all disabling conditions that do not support creative production.

There are other students who do not demonstrate the ability to come up with creative ideas, but whose products nevertheless end up looking great. The key word here is "looks"—the ideas are ordinary, yet the product looks fantastic. Teachers should make sure the finished look of a project does not affect their judgment unless the look of the project is part of the assignment to be assessed. Conversely, the originality can be present in the content and not in the product itself. Teachers need to make it clear if they are looking for original thinking, original design, and/or original presentation style.

PURPOSE

To create something, students move from generating ideas (brainstorming) to implementing those ideas in product form, whether it be a popsicle-stick character, a math word problem, a brochure of a location, an invention, and so on. Therefore, the purpose of the Idea Burst graphic organizer and the "create" graphic organizer, its linear counterpart, is to help students move through the process to create original products.

The purpose of creating something in the school setting is for the student to demonstrate an understanding of content information in a product form. Although this seems obvious, it is surprising how many shoe box dioramas are produced to demonstrate the student's understanding of a story. The diorama may very well be original and creative, but how can a teacher tell what a student knows and understands about a story by looking at a diorama? Without a written summary to go with the diorama or without an audiotape description, the teacher really does not know to what degree the student understands the story. Students may need to be reminded that the purpose of creating a product is to show what they know. The product is a vehicle for expression.

The purpose of promoting originality when creating something is to encourage students to try to push themselves beyond their status quo. Originality may refer to the unusual look of something, or the use of something, or the solution to a problem, or the composition of something. By practicing fluency and flexibility activities, students will gain tools to help them recognize originality and be more original in their thinking. They learn to hear and see uncommon ideas. They realize that the idea that exists alone in a category is original because it is different from the others (Talents Unlimited, 1995). They begin to think creatively as a habit of mind.

BENEFITS

The practice of original thinking encourages students to think beyond a regurgitated list of facts about content. To use original thinking, students really need to know and understand content. If not, their creative product won't demonstrate original thought. Teachers don't have to feel that letting students go "out there" in their thinking is compromising content. It's difficult to be creative about that which we know little. Depth of content truly comes into play when we ask students to apply original thinking to a creative product.

Another benefit of original thinking is that students must practice other thinking skills to accomplish this task. Creative thinkers use their fluency and flexibility skills to generate many different original ideas. They use their evaluation skill to decide which idea they want to use. They analyze what they will need to do to turn the idea into a product. In this regard, both critical and creative thinking are working hand and hand.

The benefit of using the Idea Burst graphic organizer is to guide students through the creative process so that they can be successful. It is a procedural tool that helps students plan and organize their ideas. They use many processes in this one graphic organizer. Students brainstorm, consider options, and make decisions. As such, the skills of critical thinking and creative thinking are included in the steps. The form itself seems more like a critical thinking process, and it might seem odd to some why a creative process graphic organizer looks like an analytical tool. In the revised Bloom's Taxonomy, the highest level of the taxonomy is identified as create and within the category are the verbs generate, plan, and produce (Anderson & Krathwohl, 2001, pp. 84–88). These three cognitive processes are the basis for the "create" graphic organizer.

APPLICATIONS

Many classroom opportunities for students to use original thinking can be found in oral, visual, written, or kinesthetic activities. As a result of the activities, students create products that tend to be some sort of display, invention, or performance. Teachers show examples of what original products look like by sharing examples of work done by other students. You can use these tools, citing examples and showing examples, to help students understand your expectation when you ask them to create something. The graphic organizers in this chapter are another kind of tool to help guide students through the process of creative expression.

The Idea Burst graphic organizer allows students to brainstorm in images and make decisions before creating a product. It can also be used to generate and test a hypothesis as part of the inventing process. Invention is one type of task that "engages students in generating and testing hypotheses" (Marzano, Norford, Paynter, Pickering, & Gaddy, 2001, p. 197), which is one of the nine categories of instructional strategies proven to improve achievement.

Here are just a few prompts that can be used along with the graphic organizer in the classroom (adapted from Connecticut Standards, Georgia's Quality Core Curriculum, Maine Learning Results, National Council of Teachers of Mathematics Standards, National English Language Arts Standards, National Science Standards, National Social Studies Standards, New Hampshire Curriculum and Proficiency Standards, and Texas Essential Knowledge and Skills).

In the Elementary Grades

Language Arts

○ Create a square for a story quilt that illustrates a scene in the story. The students are all reading different books. Students fill out the organizer before they decide which scene they want to illustrate on their piece of cloth. When the students complete their square, the teacher uses fabric glue to fasten all the pieces together and hangs the quilt in the room.

    o Create a word bank to record all your new illustrated vocabulary words. The teacher shows examples of word banks that students have done in the past. The students fill out the organizer and create their own word bank.

Writing

    o Create a writing piece that has sound effects to go along with it. The teacher asks students to choose two out of the three musical instruments they have drawn on their graphic organizer to use when they read their writing piece. Students will need to work in pairs so that one student does the sound effects while the other reads the written work.

    o Create a box of writing tips for yourself. The teacher asks students to bring a small box to school. The students use the graphic organizer to create designs to decorate their box. This box holds their personal writing tips.

Math

    o Create a picture that uses lines that are 3½ inches, 4¼ inches, 1 foot, $\frac{1}{3}$ of a yard, and include two parallel lines. Students draw the lines on a piece of paper in three different configurations. They decide which one they like best and elaborate on it. The teacher uses this lesson to provide an opportunity for students to use measurement in a creative, original way.

    o Create a display for our 100th Day of School celebration. Remember your display must show one hundred of something. The primary teacher goes over the conditions with the students: It must be small enough that you can carry it to school (or someone can carry it for you), one hundred things must fit on it, it won't fall apart, and so forth. The teacher has students brainstorm ideas and then draw them in the boxes on the graphic organizer. Students choose which idea they like the best and list the materials they will need. Students are expected to make the item and bring it to school for their celebration at the end of the week.

Science

    o Create an original invention that improves quality of life. The teacher shows the students inventions that have helped people. The teacher asks students to brainstorm problems they know people have. The students are asked to think of many different ways these problems can be solved before they decide on their invention.

    o Create a model of the solar system. This lesson reinforces the order of the planets and the size of them. This is a homework assignment.

Social Studies

    o Create a mobile that shows our five senses. The teacher asks students to think of unusual ways we use our senses and show them on their mobile.

    o Create a picture book about wellness. The teacher says the book must include nutrition, exercise, safety, and relaxation. Use the graphic organizer to plan and create the book.

In the Middle Grades

Language Arts

- o Create props to go along with an oral presentation based on the summary of your story. The students in each literature circle will summarize the story they just read and present the information to the class. The presentation will be enhanced with the use of props. The students decide which props they will make. The teacher asks them to fill out a graphic organizer on their prop and emphasizes the importance of originality when designing the prop.
- o Create a "3D" symbol to demonstrate the antagonist's point of view. The teacher provides the students with an example of a symbol that could be used to represent point of view. For example, in the story *Regarding the Fountain: A Tale in Letters, of Liars, and Leaks* by Kate Klise, the main character Ms. Florence Waters's point of view might be symbolized by a light bulb because she is definitely an idea person. The principal, Mr. Walter Russ, might be symbolized by a black cloud, which represents his point of view. The students fill out the graphic organizer before they create their "3D" symbol.

Writing

- o Create a grammar board game. The teacher wants a creative way to review grammar. She lists the grammar skills the students need to cover in their board game. Students create three board designs and choose their favorite one. They plan out their original game.
- o Create a newsletter with editorials expressing multiple points of view. Students use the graphic organizer to decide on a layout design for the newsletter. Different students take on different roles to write and print the newsletter.

Math

- o Create a playground with the given dimensions and the given amount of money. The math teacher wants students to make a scale drawing and do a cost projection. The students use the organizer to consider different playground layouts before they actually do the drawing and cost analysis.
- o Create a presentation on a mathematician. The students work in groups of four on the graphic organizer and create three ideas that take into consideration a ten-minute time limit. The presentation must be interesting for the other students to listen to and contain meaningful information about the mathematician that the teacher assigned to them.

Science

- o Create a display that illustrates the relationship among atoms, neutrons, and protons. Students work in a group to create the display. They brainstorm possible displays before they decide on the one that will best show the relationships.
- o Create a poster that demonstrates succession and other ways that ecosystems change over time. Students research succession. The teacher asks them to think of unusual ways ecosystems have changed over time. The students discover most changes are predictable and not unusual. They sketch out different layouts for the poster. After they choose their favorite, they collect the materials they need and complete the project.

Social Studies

○ Create a product of your choice to show how the exchange of goods and services around the world has created economic interdependence. The students use the graphic organizer to think about different product choices before they actually create their product.

○ Create a three-dimensional timeline that depicts the movements of pastoral peoples (Hebrews, Turks, Huns, Mongols) by examining references to them in the chronologies of other peoples. After reading some nonfiction accounts, the teacher has students work in groups to complete this project.

In the High School Grades

English

○ Create a journal with entries expressing the protagonist's thoughts. The teacher borrows a bookmaking guide from the art teacher. She shows students some ideas that they could adapt to make a journal. The teacher gives the following conditions about the journal: It has to be smaller than a piece of paper, it must be visually appealing, it must not fall apart, and it is due in a week.

○ Create a game that can be used to review the vocabulary in this story. The novel that the students are reading is laden with new vocabulary. The teacher uses this lesson to help students create a pleasurable way to keep track of all the new words. The teacher uses the graphic organizer so that students have to think of more than one game idea before they decide on what they want to create.

Writing

○ Create a bumper sticker that reflects the message in your writing piece. The teacher asks students to create a bumper sticker in keeping with the style of the writing, and the "mood and tone" of the writing. The bumper sticker must also address the theme that is conveyed in the writing.

○ Create a design for the cover of your trifold. The inside of the trifold will show examples of flashback and foreshadowing in relation to your writing piece. This is an activity that helps students extend their writing piece. In the middle section of the trifold, the student author summarizes her own writing piece. The student hands the trifold to another student. In the first section, this student explains what happened prior to the events in the writing piece. Then, this student passes the trifold to yet another student. In the third section, the student tells what happens after the events in the writing piece. The trifold goes back to the original student author who tries to integrate the new ideas into the writing piece through the use of foreshadowing and flashback.

Math

○ Design a jigsaw puzzle that demonstrates probability distributions. The class discusses what the prompt means. The teacher shows two- and three-dimensional jigsaw puzzles that have been done by previous classes. The students do this as a homework assignment.

○ Design a method to estimate the number of iPods in the school. Each team of four students must come up with multiple ways to address the assignment, decide on the most effective one, and carry it out. The results indicate to students the problems inherent in conducting research and validating results.

Science

o Create a poster describing the major functions of cells. The teacher uses this activity to reinforce content. It is given as a homework assignment.
o Construct a model that demonstrates which chemical elements make up molecules of substances found in living organisms. The teacher asks students to create the model out of construction paper. The students work in groups to discuss molecules, draw visual representations, and put them together in a drawing of a model. The group must come up with three designs for the model before they can actually choose one and move into the construction phase.

Social Studies

o Create a picture to go along with a magazine article that describes either the positive or negative impact of credit on an individual's financial life. The teacher describes the impact of media on the public. She shows students examples of propaganda techniques that are used to manipulate people. The teacher divides the class in two. Half of the students create a picture that represents the viewpoint that credit is good. The other half creates a picture that represents the viewpoint that credit can be bad. The teacher emphasizes the importance of the visual impact that the picture makes. The picture can be an original drawing or one found in a magazine. The magazine article selected to go along with the picture must reflect the negative or positive point of view. Students use the graphic organizer to plan and create the product.
o Create a product of your choice that describes the effects of World War II on the home front. The teacher asks students to fill out the graphic organizer and have the choice approved by the teacher before the student creates the product.

GETTING STARTED IN THE CLASSROOM

When you want your students to create or design something, use the Idea Burst graphic organizer (Figure 10.1) or its linear counterpart (Figure 10.2). Walk the students through the steps on the template so that they will know and understand what is expected and what each step means. Depending on your objectives, you can either tell the students what they need to create or design and have them fill in the task on the title line, or you can give students a choice about what to create. When given a choice, for example, they might be asked to create something that demonstrates their understanding of the U.S. Constitution. Explain to students that they may need to brainstorm ideas and decide what they want to create before they even begin to plan and organize their product. The graphic organizers take students through Steps 1–4 of the creative process: the planning stage.

In Step 1, students are asked to consider the conditions or parameters of what they are being asked to create. Students consider requirements, limitations, or restrictions in this step. Originality may or may not be a stated requirement. By listing conditions up front, students understand the confines of the assignment.

When students move into Step 2, they brainstorm different designs. This visual brainstorming forces students to think of many, different creative products. Just as it is important to foster verbal and written brainstorming, it is also important to foster visual brainstorming. Visual brainstorming is an attempt to use drawings and sketches to conceptualize and capture ideas. According to Michalko, "The sketches may be abstract, symbolic, or realistic" (1998, p. 80). It is important for students to understand that it is not

Figure 10.1   Idea Burst Graphic Organizer (Create)

Name: _____   Date: _____

Create

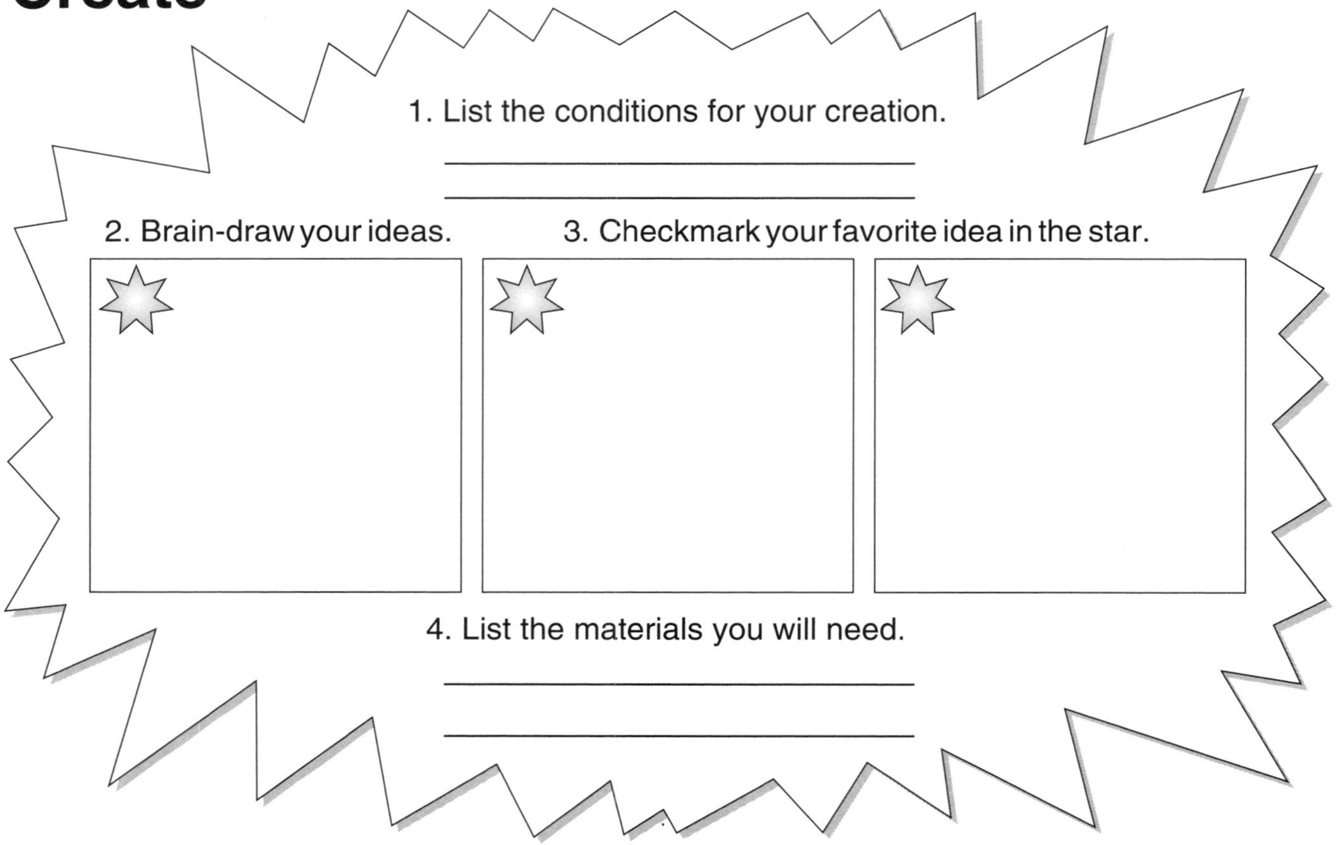

1. List the conditions for your creation.

2. Brain-draw your ideas.

3. Checkmark your favorite idea in the star.

4. List the materials you will need.

Illustration by Bob Greisen.

Figure 10.2 Linear Graphic Organizer (Create)

Name: _____ **Date:** _____

Create _____

1. Consider the requirements, limitations, conditions, or
   restrictions of whatever you are going to create. List them.

   _____

   _____

   _____

2. What does this thing that you are going to create look like?
   Consider more than one design. Draw your ideas in the boxes.

3. Choose one design you like the best and put a* in the little
   box to indicate your choice.

4. List the materials you will need to make your creation.

   _____

   _____

   _____

necessary to draw well. The intent is to sketch out the ideas to articulate and visualize their conception. Make sure students do not feel limited by the three boxes in Step 2. If they have more than three ideas, students can use additional paper. For visual learners and many English Language Learners, the visual images are easier to use than written ideas. The image allows the learner to go beyond the boundaries of written language.

In Step 3, students are asked to identify which idea they like the best by placing a check mark or asterisk in the box. Students may want to double-check each idea to make sure it meets with all the requirements stated in Step 1. If an option does not meet the requirements, students may want to adjust an idea or design option or not choose the idea. If this choice is a critical decision, teachers might want to extend this step by having students prioritize their choices by asking questions generated from factors of influence (for example, Do I have the skills to accomplish this? Can I complete it in the time allotted? Do I have the materials?). In some cases, a student might want to use the "prioritize" graphic organizer to help her make a decision. This is a perfect example of differentiation, where one or two students need to use an additional support strategy to make a decision but others in the class do not. Once the design is determined, in Step 4, the students list the materials that are necessary to create the product.

At this point, some students might need a support strategy before they are able to actually move from listing materials to the construction phase. The students list materials in Step 4 but now need a plan that organizes who will do what when so that they can be productive during the construction phase in Step 5. The teacher differentiates the lesson for these students by providing a planning tool such as the one that appears in Figure 10.3 (Drapeau, 1998). On the planning tool, students set a timeline for when each thing should be done, and they check off each task as it is completed. The bottom of the form provides a place for students to list "what ifs," such as what if I cannot get the material or what if I need more time. When they list the "what ifs," students are anticipating problems, which gives them an opportunity to go back and revise their plan before they begin working on their product.

Once students have listed all the materials needed in the "create" graphic organizer, they are ready to produce their product. The steps on the graphic organizer have guided them from idea generation to fruition. There are some teachers, however, who feel the creative process is not complete until the product is shared with an audience. At this point most students do not need to use a graphic organizer. However, another way for the teacher to differentiate a lesson is to give a checklist with written steps (Figure 10.4) to some students to help keep them on track. After they create their product in Step 5, Step 6 on the checklist reminds them to check to make sure they have met all the requirements.

For example, if a condition in Step 1 states that their model must fit on a desktop and the students have designed a model that takes more room, then the size of the model will obviously need to be modified or the student will need to negotiate for more space. In another example, students are asked to create a story and present it to first graders. In Step 1, a condition states that the story and presentation must appeal to a first-grade audience. If the students did not take this into account when they created the story and presentation, then they will need to think about perhaps adding some colorful objects, sound effects, or something else that will hold the young students' interest. If students did not accommodate all of the conditions stated in Step 1, then in Step 7, they will need to modify their product to match up with the conditions.

Step 7 also reminds students to practice or rehearse before presenting their product to an audience. Students know the benefits of rehearsing when they are getting ready to act in a play. They know the benefits of practicing a sport before a game. Teachers should remind students that this is the same thing. Whether they practice presenting their product in

Name: _____   Date: _____

Planning Chart Create

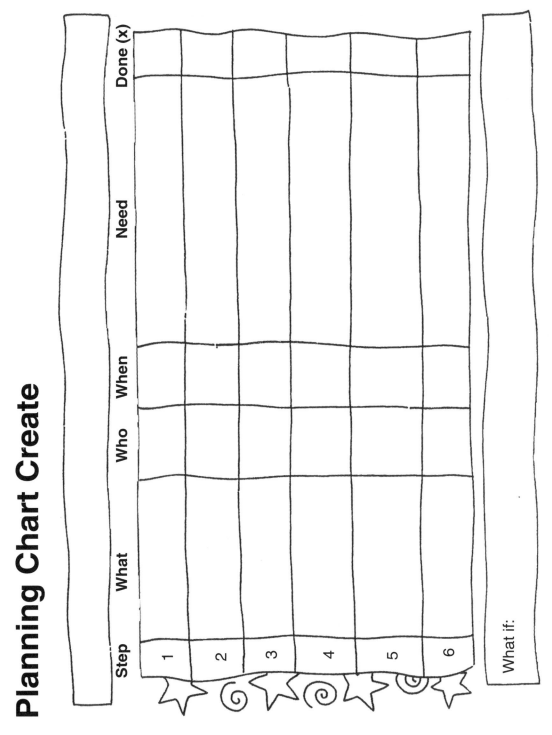

Step	What	Who	When	Need	Done (x)
1					
2					
3					
4					
5					
6					

What if:

Source: Drapeau. (1998). *Great Teaching with Graphic Organizers.* Scholastic.

Figure 10.4 Supplemental Checklist (Create)

Name _____ Date _____

Steps 6–8 Checklist

After you create your product:

☐ Check requirement or conditions.

☐ Test, rehearse, and adapt.

☐ Present to an audience.

front of a younger brother or sister or a dog, it really doesn't matter as long as they say it out loud. By doing so, students will hear themselves make mistakes and can make necessary adjustments.

Finally, students are asked to present their product to an audience. For some students, this is the hardest part because they do not like getting up in front of people. Here again, teachers may need to provide support for students who have this anxiety. Perhaps the teacher allows the student to present the product with a friend. The teacher may allow the student to give a short presentation or the teacher provides the student with written guidelines to describe how to make a presentation.

SAMPLE LESSON

In a sixth-grade language arts class, the teacher demonstrates the use of the Idea Burst graphic organizer to the students. They have not used this organizer before. After the class reads the story *Holes* by Louis Sachar, the teacher asks the students to identify problems in the story. One problem they identify is the amount of work it takes to keep digging all those holes. The teacher asks the students to come up with solutions to this problem. One suggested solution is that if the kids in the story had an automatic shovel, their work would be much easier. Capitalizing on the teachable moment, the teacher tells the students to fill out an Idea Burst graphic organizer on this idea of an automatic shovel (Figure 10.5). She tells the students that they will not actually make the automatic shovel, but they will create a drawing and identify what materials are needed to create this imaginary shovel.

The teacher gives the prompt, "Create an Automatic Shovel." As a class, the students list the conditions. They say it must not use electricity, and it must have renewable battery power, be soft on the hands, have a big scoop, and lift easily. In Step 2, three students go up to the board and draw an automatic shovel design. One looks like an automatic shovel that goes up and down, one draws a vacuum that sucks up dirt and throws it, and the final picture looks like a mini bulldozer. After much discussion, the class chooses the mini bulldozer as the best idea. The materials that are needed to create this are a pattern from the bulldozer company for bulldozer designs, a copier or computer to shrink down the pattern, and whatever tools it takes to build a bulldozer for digging small holes.

This application of the graphic organizer is different from using it to create an actual physical product. In this instance, the teacher uses the organizer as a follow-up activity, such as focusing on an event in the story. The graphic organizer is just a way for students to visualize an automatic shovel. After students complete the graphic organizer, the

Figure 10.5   Sample: Automatic Shovel Idea Burst Graphic Organizer (Create)

Name: _____   Date: _____

Create

an automatic shovel

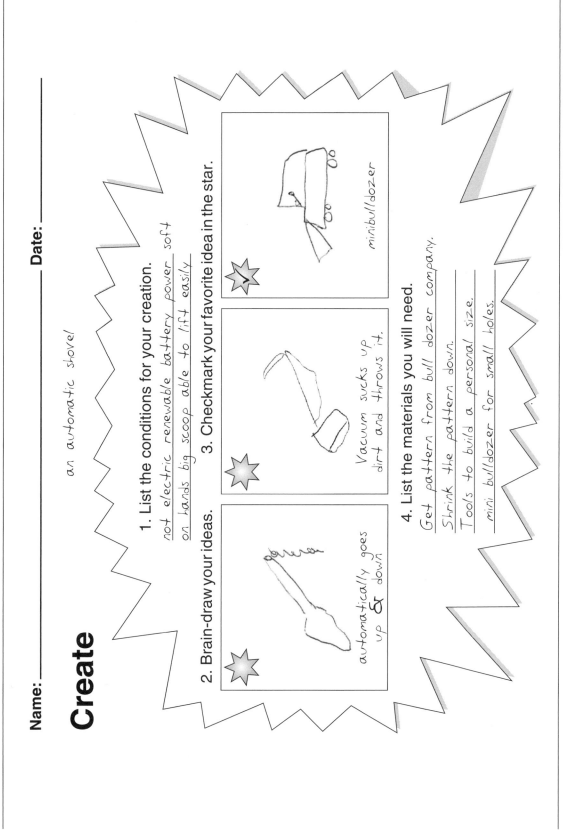

1. List the conditions for your creation.
not electric renewable battery power soft
on hands big scoop able to lift easily

2. Brain-draw your ideas.
automatically goes
up & down

Vacuum sucks up
dirt and throws it.

3. Checkmark your favorite idea in the star.
minibulldozer

4. List the materials you will need.
Get pattern from bull dozer company.
Shrink the pattern down.
Tools to build a personal size.
mini bulldozer for small holes.

teacher asks the students how the story would be different if someone had arrived with automatic shovels. They compare the new version of the story with the old one.

This graphic organizer format can be effective in helping students formulate their ideas, as in the *Holes* example, or in guiding students when they actually produce a product. Students can use it to plan out a project or the creation of any kind of product. It can also be used as a tool to find out what students really like or what they think others would like. For example, in terms of their own preferences, students might be asked to create an ideal home that fits in with their favorite region of the country. In terms of what someone else prefers, students might be asked to create a birthday present for a person who lives in a particular region of the country.

ASSESSMENT

The overall purpose of the Idea Burst graphic organizer is to guide students through the creative thinking process to produce original ideas and products. Assessment is an important part of the process and helps students increase their achievement by receiving specific feedback. The rating scale and rubric described in this section serve this purpose. They are not meant to be static in nature. The criteria in the rating scale and rubric reflect the objectives of the lesson and the intended use of this graphic organizer.

The rating scale criteria for the Idea Burst graphic organizer are explained to the students in generic terms before they apply them to the actual lesson. The teacher explains that fluency, the first criteria, is built into this process because students are expected to list not only the requirements or the nonnegotiable parts of the product, but they are also expected to list other limitations, conditions, or restrictions that they foresee. The number of ideas that the teacher expects to see will vary according to the content focus and product possibilities. For example, if there are no given conditions, the teacher might ask students to come up with at least five of their own conditions they need to consider for a possible design.

The Idea Burst organizer has three boxes in which students draw the designs they're considering. If they want to add more boxes, they can. In Step 2, the designs or creations should be different from one another because we want to see how well the student applies flexible thinking. Step 2 is also rated for originality. We are looking for not just different kinds of ideas, but also unusual ideas. In Step 3 on the graphic organizer, students are asked to make a choice. This choice must be consistent with the conditions stated in Step 1. Does the student's design choice address few or all of the conditions? Finally, the materials are considered in terms of relevancy.

Once the students understand how this rating tool works, they are ready to apply it to the example they generated together based on the story *Holes*. The teacher asks them to consider the number of responses they made on the Idea Burst graphic organizer. Although they think their five answers are really good, the students think they probably could have come up with more than five answers. They think five is probably average, so they decided to give themselves a 3 in the fluency category (see Figure 10.6). The students think the ideas they generated are all different. They give themselves a 5 for flexibility. They decide their creations are original. The automatic shovel is original, the vacuum cleaner is modified, and the bulldozer is shrunk down to become a mini bulldozer. They decide to give themselves a 5 in this category as well.

The students use logical reasoning to determine if their choice, the mini bulldozer, fits within the stated conditions. Since students designed this invention with the conditions in mind, they decide they deserve a 5 in consistency.

When looking at the materials they listed, the final step on the graphic organizer, they decide that the materials are not really listed for their choice. They actually created a plan, a "to do" list, rather than list materials. They give themselves a 3 and blame the teacher for not directing them. The teacher explains how important it is to learn from mistakes and what better way to see how something works than to test out the idea. The teacher also explains that it is important to understand how to fill out the graphic organizer before students are expected to complete one on their own. The students want to change their answers and of course the teacher lets them. Because the students do not know what the actual materials are for a mini bulldozer, the teacher agrees that, in this case, they can state, "Materials usual for a bulldozer but smaller." With this change, they all agree to change the rating score from a 3 to a 5. The rating scale in Figure 10.6 reflects the original score, before it was changed to a 5.

The rubric version of the rating scale is shown in Figure 10.7. The scores are marked with asterisks.

The Idea Burst graphic organizer helps students structure their creative production so that they can be successful. The nature of the format allows it to be used in a variety ways, both for the physical production of two- and three-dimensional products, and as a tool

Figure 10.6   Sample: Automatic Shovel Creative Thinking Rating Scale (Create)

Criteria	Probing Question	Rating
Fluency	How many ideas are generated?	3
Flexibility	To what degree are the ideas different from one another?	5
Originality	How original are the designs?	5
Consistency	To what degree does the choice address the conditions in #1?	5
Relevance	To what degree are the materials relevant?	3

Figure 10.7   Sample: Automatic Shovel Creative Thinking Rubric (Create)

It's a Start	You're Getting It	WOW!
Few ideas generated.	Some ideas generated. *	Many ideas generated
Ideas all seem similar.	Some different types of ideas.	Many different kinds of ideas. *
Designs are common.	Design/s may show some originality.	One or more designs are unique. *
Choice addresses some of the conditions listed.	Choice addresses most of the conditions listed.	Choice addresses all of the conditions listed. *
Some materials are relevant.	Materials are all relevant but some materials are missing. *	All materials are listed and are relevant.

for promoting originality in idea generating and visual brainstorming. The products or responses may be realistic, imaginary, or symbolic. Original thinking may be emphasized in a variety of the steps on the graphic organizer. The Idea Burst graphic organizer relates to Marzano, Norford, Paynter, Pickering, and Gaddy (2001) generating and testing hypothesis category, because students are generating designs and products and testing them against the stated conditions. There is room in Steps 6 and 7 to revise the design.

As we move on to the last area of creativity addressed in this book, we certainly do not leave the other areas behind. In the next chapter, teachers discover how elaboration is built upon fluent, flexible, and original thought.

KEY POINTS TO REMEMBER ABOUT CREATING

1. Create can mean producing an original, one-of-a-kind idea or product.

2. Creating can be the application of an idea that is new or original to the individual.

3. Originality moves beyond the status quo.

4. To use the creative process one must know the content.

5. Create can mean to synthesize ideas.

6. When one creates, it is observable.

7. Creating is a process that ends up being communicated.

? PAUSE FOR REFLECTION AND DISCUSSION

1. Is creativity synonymous with originality?

2. In what ways does the Idea Burst graphic organizer help students understand what it means when we ask them to create something?

3. How might you encourage original thinking?

4. What is the significance of visual brainstorming in Step 2 on the Idea Burst graphic organizer?

5. How does the rating scale help students create more effective products?

6. Does providing models of original thinking help students? Why or why not?

7. In what ways might you differentiate using the Idea Burst graphic organizer in your class?

11

"Elaborate"

Getting the Details Down

➡ Graphic Organizer: Wheel of Words

➡ Verb: Elaborate

➡ Synonyms: Add details, embellish

➡ Define the Steps:
1. State the topic, situation, or problem.
2. Surround the topic, situation, or problem with one-word or short phrase descriptors.
3. Combine two adjacent descriptors to create a sentence.
4. Classify the resulting sentences.

Name: _____ Date: _____

Elaborate

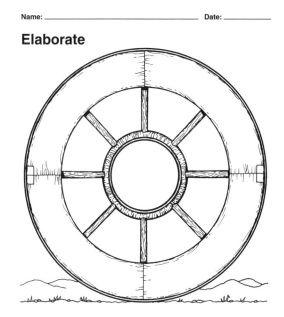

1. State the idea or topic in the center of the wheel.
2. List related ideas, vocabulary words, and so on in the inner circle.
3. Combine two words into an interesting sentence in the outer circle.
4. Classify the sentences and put a code in each small box.

DEFINITION

The fourth creativity skill area that Paul Torrance (1987)
identifies is elaboration, or to describe something in detail. Marzano identifies this skill in his four types of knowledge: "vocabulary terms and phrases, details, organizing ideas, and skills and processes. Details are specific pieces of information that include facts, time sequences, cause-and-effect sequences, and episodes." (Marzano, Norford Paynter, Pickering, & Gaddy, 2001, pp. 291, 305). When students elaborate on a topic, they give additional information that provides specificity and contributes to their depth of understanding.

To elaborate means to build upon existing information or ideas. It involves taking an idea and improving it, so that it is better in some way. Contrary to public belief, Thomas

Edison did not actually invent the light bulb. "He took an idea and elaborated on it" (Michalko, 1998, p. 94). He came up with a system that could light many bulbs. Rather than call Edison the inventor of the light bulb, perhaps we should call him the elaborator of the light bulb. Elaboration involves persistence, effort, and determination.

Students who are good at elaboration demonstrate persistence and willingness to explore concepts in more depth. They have learned that a merely correct response will suffice, but that if elaborated upon, their response will make a much more powerful statement. These students are often not satisfied with the status quo; they want to know more and will research more details.

Perhaps the strongest application of the elaborative skill occurs in writing assignments. Students who are good writers use vivid or descriptive language because they want their writing to sound alive and not flat. According to Michalko (1998), "Paul Valery, the French poet, asserted that stubborn elaboration was an important component of creativity and took great exception to the suggestion that poets receive the best part of their work from muses. He called that a concept of savages" (p. 94). Whether a piece of writing is prose or poetry, fiction or nonfiction, it is made more memorable by the use of rich, detailed language.

Elaborative writing is required by most state standards. The state writing prompts expect students to use detail and vivid language in their writing sample. The rubrics used to score state assessments identify this area and students are scored on it. This is a particular problem for students who use only basic vocabulary—often English Language Learners and special education students. Practicing the use of elaborative language in a variety of ways helps all students to understand what we are looking for and what is meant by vivid language. The Wheel of Words graphic organizer is just one tool that helps students express an idea more clearly and in a more interesting way.

PURPOSE

The purpose of engaging in elaborative thinking is to extend ideas, embellish details, make more expressive conclusions, promote depth of understanding, and foster communication skills. If this is accomplished, students' achievement is increased. If they know very little about a topic, students will be unable to elaborate; they must first gain a deep conceptual understanding of the content. We need to help students understand that adding one more sentence to their assignment does not constitute elaboration; the sentence must add depth, specificity, or a broader interpretation of the content.

Emphasizing elaboration in the classroom helps to promote language development. Some students actually do know the content but do not have the language to express well developed ideas. They can, however, draw their responses. All forms of elaboration should be encouraged in the classroom. Lessons promoting nonverbal modalities will hook the nonlinguistic learners and help them to practice elaboration in their area of strength. Then, the teacher can assist the students in converting their responses into words. Students will likely be much more successful with these types of activities and their understanding of the content will be enhanced through their preferred learning style.

Marzano (2004) states that one of the factors influencing achievement is background knowledge. For students who come from language-deprived homes to command enough language to elaborate, teachers should focus on vocabulary and language acquisition. Students need to build their vocabulary base as well as build their descriptive language vocabulary.

Jacobs (2006) encourages classroom teachers to promote lessons in which students use three types of vocabulary. These three types are high-frequency words, specialized terminology, and embellishments and refinements. As Jacobs writes, "Ask any teacher who has scored the written essays on the Advanced Placement examinations about the importance of vocabulary. Two student essays that fundamentally state the exact same premise with the exact same details and with accurate language mechanics and grammar are scored differently on the basis of the quality of the diction" (Jacobs, 2006, p. 35). Jacobs defines high-frequency words as words that are used across content areas. Verbs such as the ones targeted in the chapters of this book are examples of high-frequency words because they are often used with any content. Specialized vocabularies are words that are specific to content or subject area.

The graphic organizers in this chapter are specifically designed to allow for elaborative expression. Elaboration is a powerful tool for both nonfiction and fiction writing, to convey either expository or narrative information. It can also be used with other modes of expression, including verbal, visual, and kinesthetic activities. Teachers can encourage elaboration in the writing process by showing images without words. After looking at pictures with strong imagery, students are able to generate words and description. By using images to strengthen learning, the teacher can better reach the visual learner. If students need to use descriptive language when telling a story orally, or provide detailed information when discussing content information, the teacher can use the graphic organizers provided in this chapter as tools to help students generate description. In kinesthetic activities such as skits, students use the responses on the graphic organizer to demonstrate through their descriptive actions as well as their "elaborate" words the adjectives and adverbs that enhance the meaning of the play.

What do we need to think about when we place students in instructional groups that address the elaboration skill? All students have the potential to be elaborators. Some students by nature are already good at it. When grouping students it is important to think about each student's cognitive style. What will happen if a teacher groups all elaborators together? They don't complete the task. They carry on and on and tend to elaborate on certain points. They get stuck and do not move on. They have a tendency to run out of time and not finish the task. They may not be good time managers. With grouping considerations, it is best to have only one or two elaborators in a group. They will naturally take on the role of encouraging the group to go beyond the basics, while others in the group will keep these students realistically focused.

BENEFITS

One initial benefit of addressing elaboration in the classroom is that students become aware of the power of vivid language. At the most basic level, we know that it's important to provide a print-rich language environment with word walls and word banks at the elementary level, language-based visuals at the middle school level, and vocabulary word lists at the secondary level. These are concrete visual reminders that words and how we use them are important in the classroom. Encourage your students to be word collectors!

Elaboration is the skill that helps teachers to understand what students are trying to express. It is about effective communication. Sometimes students give so little information about a topic, it is difficult to assess their learning. Teachers often assume this is all the knowledge the student has about the topic, which may or may not be correct. She may simply not know what else to say, or may lack the language facility to express information. By practicing elaboration, students learn how to answer the question completely and go beyond the basic information. They know how to embed the vocabulary specific to the topic into their answers. They know to use adjectives and adverbs to give more description.

Students should also know that when a test question says "explain why" or "explain what," they can use details to elaborate on the who, what, when, where, why, and how. When students are asked for their opinion or for a logical reason, they can elaborate on their answers. The graphic organizer gives students a structure to encourage elaboration. The use of the visual format allows students to move from being stuck to generating more description.

APPLICATIONS

Elaboration can be used in many ways in the classroom. We want to encourage the use of rich vocabulary, and of vocabulary specific to content. For example, in a high school classroom, if the words "westward expansion" are placed in the center of the wheel on the Wheel of Words graphic organizer, the descriptors around the wheel could be Trail of Tears, Mormons, 49th parallel, "54-40 or fight," and so on. The graphic organizer provides a tool for students to create strong sentences and meaningful connections based on the descriptors.

Another way that elaboration can be used in the classroom is to help students understand the power of language. After students read the play *Romeo and Juliet*, the teacher passes out the graphic organizer with the word fate, death, or love in the center of the wheel. Students fill in their thoughts or ideas related to the central idea. They combine the words to create strong sentences. Students see how the power of the central word influences the responses.

Finally, words that appeal to emotion can also be used for elaboration. For example, when students are learning about propaganda techniques, they can take an issue such as animal rights, and place scare tactic type words around the topic to generate strong sentences. Students place animal testing in the center of the circle on the graphic organizer and surround the topic with words such as death, no exercise, no affection, and so forth.

Elaboration is a skill that can be applied in all content areas. Students use detailed language to describe vocabulary, facts, rules, concepts, themes, issues, problems, principles, and just about anything else one can imagine. Many of these applications are addressed below in the prompts that target the different content areas (adapted from Connecticut Standards, Georgia's Quality Core Curriculum, Maine Learning Results, National Council of Teachers of Mathematics Standards, National English Language Arts Standards, National Science Standards, National Social Studies Standards, New Hampshire Curriculum and Proficiency Standards, and Texas Essential Knowledge and Skills).

In the Elementary Grades

Language Arts

- o Elaborate on the character in the story. The teacher places the character's name in the center of the graphic organizer, and students generate adjectives to describe the character. The adjectives are combined to create sentences. The students are asked whether each statement is a main idea about the character (place "m" in the box) or a detail (place "d" in the box).
- o Elaborate on the problem in the story. The problem of the story is placed in the center of the circle. Descriptive words are placed around the circle and the students create their sentences. The students are asked to sequence the sentences in the order they appear in the story.

Writing

- ○ Choose random words to describe your topic. The teacher uses this as a pre-writing activity. After students generate sentences, they mark the boxes with "y" for yes, use this idea in the actual writing assignment, or "n" for no, don't want to use this idea.
- ○ Elaborate on the setting of your creative writing piece. All the students write their setting in the center on the graphic organizer. The teacher asks students to generate words for things they hear, smell, and/or feel in their setting. Students use the words to create sentences. The students order the sentences in the boxes according to their placement in their writing piece.

Math

- ○ Elaborate on the facts that define a quadrilateral. The teacher uses this as a vocabulary lesson in math class.
- ○ Elaborate on the math vocabulary/skills in the chapter by creating number sentences. In the center of the organizer, the students write the subject of the chapter, perhaps, fractions. They list key math words/skills around the circle. Then, individually, they combine the two words to come up with a number response. If the two words the students combine are "same" and "multiply," one student might create a number sentence by multiplying the same fraction, say, $1/3 \times 1/3$. Another student might create a number sentence by combining the two words using the same denominator, say, $1/3 \times 2/3$. Any response is acceptable so long as they combine the two words and turn them into a number sentence. Students trade papers and solve each other's problems. Students code the boxes with "h" for help if they need it.

Science

- ○ Elaborate on the parts of the solar system. The teacher uses this activity to review information. The class generates a list of words relating to parts of the solar system and the teacher places them on the graphic organizer. The students work in pairs to create sentences. They mark each sentence with "t" for true if they know their sentence is true and "u" for unsure if they don't know whether the sentence is true or not. The teacher uses this information to evaluate how much more she needs to review before the test.
- ○ Elaborate on plant structure. This activity builds on the typical "label the parts of a plant" worksheet. The graphic organizer helps to create descriptions to go along with the labels on the worksheet.

Social Studies

- ○ Elaborate on the jobs of the community helper. The teacher names the community helper and the students list the jobs that this helper does. The class combines the jobs to come up with interesting sentences.
- ○ Elaborate on the risk settlers took moving westward. The teacher uses this as a follow-up to a video that students see about a family who moves to the West. Rather than students summarizing the video, the teacher uses this activity as a way for students to process what they saw.

In the Middle Grades

Language Arts

- Elaborate on the effects of the mood of the story on the reader. Students work in groups to identify the mood. Then they generate effects. After they create sentences, they mark the boxes indicating the greatest to least effect. The class debates their answers.
- Elaborate on the element of risk in the story. The teacher uses this activity to show character development. The teacher defines the risk taken in the story with the class. The class generates words to describe the risk. Students work in pairs to place the descriptors wherever they want on the graphic organizer. After they create sentences, they code their ideas according to how elaborate the sentences are (on a 1 to 4 scale). Then the whole class talks about their best sentences and how the descriptions in the sentences relate to the risk in the story.

Writing

- Surround your noun with adjectives to create interesting sentences. This is a grammar lesson. Students are given a list of words of which only some are adjectives. They must choose adjectives and complete the organizer.
- Elaborate on your main character's wish or desire in your writing piece. This is a great way for students to address character development in their writing. They have to know and understand the character that they write about to come up with a wish or desire that makes sense. It also shows them characteristics of their character that they might not have included in their writing.

Math

- Elaborate on how to divide fractions. Students list things like flip the second fraction upside down, multiply numerators, convert mixed numbers, and so on. The teacher reminds students that each idea must be different. They code their boxes by indicating which sentence they like the best.
- Elaborate on ways you can remember the difference between LCM and GCF. The teacher uses this activity to help students create their own mnemonic to remember the difference between these two math concepts.

Science

- Elaborate on the qualities of a good environmentalist. This activity gets students to think like an environmentalist. The lesson encourages point of view along with the science content. It is a great introduction into a lesson about a well-known environmentalist and the contributions this person made.
- Elaborate on how different influences affect groundwater. The teacher encourages the students to incorporate what they know about the water table, water runoff, drainage, pollution, acid rain, amount of rainfall, weather disasters, and so on with groundwater. After the class brainstorms the influences and they talk about their effects on groundwater, the teacher divides students into groups. Each group takes a different influence and elaborates on it. After they create sentences, they note which sentence indicates the greatest influence on groundwater. The class shares their ideas.

Social Studies

- Elaborate on the Golden Age. After reading a chapter in a book about the Golden Age, the students list facts and elements of the era such as the great center for the arts, brought on by nobles, and so on, and combine ideas to make true sentences. The students will organize their ideas by indicating in the box on the organizer whether this is a main idea or detail and then use their ideas to write a summary.
- Elaborate on whether the stock market affects the U.S. economy or the U.S. economy affects the stock market. In this economics unit, students take a point of view and elaborate on it. After they create their descriptive sentences, students draw a picture demonstrating their main points.

In the High School Grades

English

- Elaborate on the use of colloquialisms in the story. Students work in pairs to generate descriptors and create sentences. The teacher asks the students to choose their favorite sentence and write it on a colored piece of paper and decorate or illustrate it. The teacher makes a bulletin board with the students' selections on it.
- Elaborate on the impact of the paradox in the story. The class identifies the paradox in the story. Individually, students elaborate on the impact. They generate descriptions. Then they trade papers and create sentences using another student's words. The teacher collects the graphic organizers and reviews the sentences. The next day, she puts sentences from their organizers on the overhead to show the best examples of the impact of paradox and the best examples of elaborative language.

Writing

- Elaborate on peer editing. The teacher uses this activity to help students move through issues they have with peer editing. The class brainstorms some descriptors. The teacher adds some descriptors if the students do not come up with the main problems. When it comes to coding the boxes, the teacher asks students to check any box that represents a problem they experience with peer editing.
- Identify the tone in your writing and surround it with descriptive words. The teacher uses this as a post-writing activity.

Maths

- Elaborate on the uses of scatter plots. The teacher uses this activity to create a conversation regarding the use of scatter plots as effective tools to demonstrate data. In their descriptors, students generate ideas about the limitations as well as the advantages of using scatter plots.
- Elaborate on the stated coordinate points. The teacher gives students coordinate points that they connect with lines. Students add their own coordinate points, draw more lines, and add to the lines to make a picture. They look at the four pictures they create and mark which one they like the best.

Science

o Elaborate on factors that affect our ability to extract oil from Alaska reserves within environmentally protected land. The teacher uses this activity as a way for students to generate discussion in their groups.
o Elaborate on how scientists gather data on the universe. Students conduct research as homework to learn about tools scientists use and data they collect when studying the universe. They synthesize their findings by identifying ways scientists collect data on the graphic organizer. Students create sentences and indicate how many sources they used.

Social Studies

o Elaborate on the changing conditions in Boston in the 1770s. The teacher gets the students started by brainstorming just two or three ideas about changing conditions. Students work in groups to generate the additional conditions and then combine ideas to come up with elaborative sentences. The teacher asks students to come up with one generalization based on the four sentences they created. Students share these generalizations and they are discussed by the class.
o Elaborate on the causes of World War II. Toward the end of the unit, the teacher uses this activity to begin the review process. After students brainstorm the many causes of World War II, each group takes a cause and elaborates on it. Then they write a diary entry about how this cause affected a fictional family. The teacher talks about the significance of realistic fiction.

GETTING STARTED IN THE CLASSROOM

The Wheel of Words graphic organizer (Figure 11.1) helps students combine flexible thinking with elaborative thinking. With this graphic organizer, students "synthesize two existing ideas and combine them into a third, new idea" (Harris, 1998). This is a similar strategy to the one in the Rose-Colored Glasses graphic organizer in Chapter 9. Even though both use a forced association technique, the Rose-Colored Glasses graphic organizer connects unrelated words to create analogies, similes, and metaphors that help build conceptual understanding. The Wheel of Words uses forced association to combine related ideas to come up with descriptive language.

This is how it works. Either you or a student places a word, idea, problem, or concept in the center of the wheel (Figure 11.1)—or in Step 1 in the corresponding linear graphic organizer (Figure 11.2). Descriptive words are placed between the spokes in the Wheel of Words or on the lines above each "v" in Step 2 in the linear graphic organizer. These can be single words or short phrases. The descriptive words can be vocabulary words, spelling words, subtopics, or any word associated with the topic. Then, two adjacent words are combined to form a sentence in the outer wheel or below the "v in Step 3."

Students are asked to combine these words without using the word "and." With young students, including the center word keeps the sentence focused on the original topic. Older students may combine the two words but not include the center, because we want to eliminate redundancy.

After the four sentences are created, the students fill in the little boxes on the linear format or the little boxes in each of the sections of the outer wheel. The boxes are used to classify the sentences according to criteria that fit the lesson. For example, students write in the box "m" for main idea and "s" for subordinate idea, or "m" for main idea and "d" if the sentence is a detailed sentence used to support the main idea. The boxes can also be used to number the sentences. This helps the students organize their writing by determining sentence order. Some other uses are listed in the examples in the application section.

SAMPLE LESSONS

In the fairy tale unit, Joyce places the title of the book, *Jack and the Beanstalk,* in the center of the wheel (Figure 11.3). She chooses words that have to do with the story—adjectives, characters, events, or whatever she chooses. The two adjacent words are combined to create a sentence. Joyce uses the words hen and selfish in the sentence, "The selfish Giant wanted his hen back." She combines giant and ugly to say, "The ugly Giant was treated unfairly." Joyce combines mother and shy to read, "Jack's mother was so shy she sent Jack to sell the cow." Finally, Joyce combines music and hunger to say, "The Giant hungered for music."

The teacher asks students to number their sentences in the order that they occurred in the story. Joyce has a hard time deciding on the order. It is hard for Joyce to order the sentence, "The Giant was treated unfairly" because it is a generalization, not a specific action in the story. She decides on identifying it as the third sentence and using "The selfish Giant wanted his hen back" as a supporting statement. By going through this process, Joyce has already thought about how she can organize a story summary. She has some good sentences to start a paragraph and she has supporting sentences.

The second classroom example is an autobiographical piece written by a boy named Bruce. In this lesson, the teacher asks the students to write about themselves and tells them they will be sharing their graphic organizers with their parents at conferences. On the top of the paper, all of the second-grade students write "me" (Figure 11.4). Then, they write words or short phrases describing themselves. In Step 2, Bruce writes hungry, smart, happy, hop, pet lover, clean, swimmer, and boy as his descriptors. The teacher highlights the blank areas next to Step 2 so that Bruce will know where to write his answers. Then the teacher asks the students to combine the words to make sentences.

Bruce combines hungry and smart to read, "I am smart when I am hungry." He combines happy and hop to say, "I'm happy when I hop." He then combines clean and pet lover in the sentence, "I'm a clean pet lover." In the last combination, he puts boy and swimmer together to say, "I am a swimmer boy."

The teacher does not ask students to do anything with the boxes. The teacher asks students to read their favorite sentence. She later shares the graphic organizer responses with their parents. The parents love to see what their child has said and the students are proud of their papers. They want to hang them up on the bulletin board and share them with the other students after parent conferences.

The teacher is pleased with Bruce's responses. This is the most he has written on any assignment. He is proud of his sentences and happy to share his ideas about himself. The teacher takes a moment to work with Bruce to point out the possibility of using a contraction for I am. She helps him identify spelling and grammar mistakes. The teacher expects the students to correct their grammatical errors.

In this example, the teacher uses the activity to begin to talk about what an autobiography is. She also wants to use it to break the ice for parent conference night. She uses the student's responses to build a classroom community environment.

Figure 11.1   Wheel of Words Graphic Organizer (Elaborate)

Name: _____   **Date:** _____

Elaborate

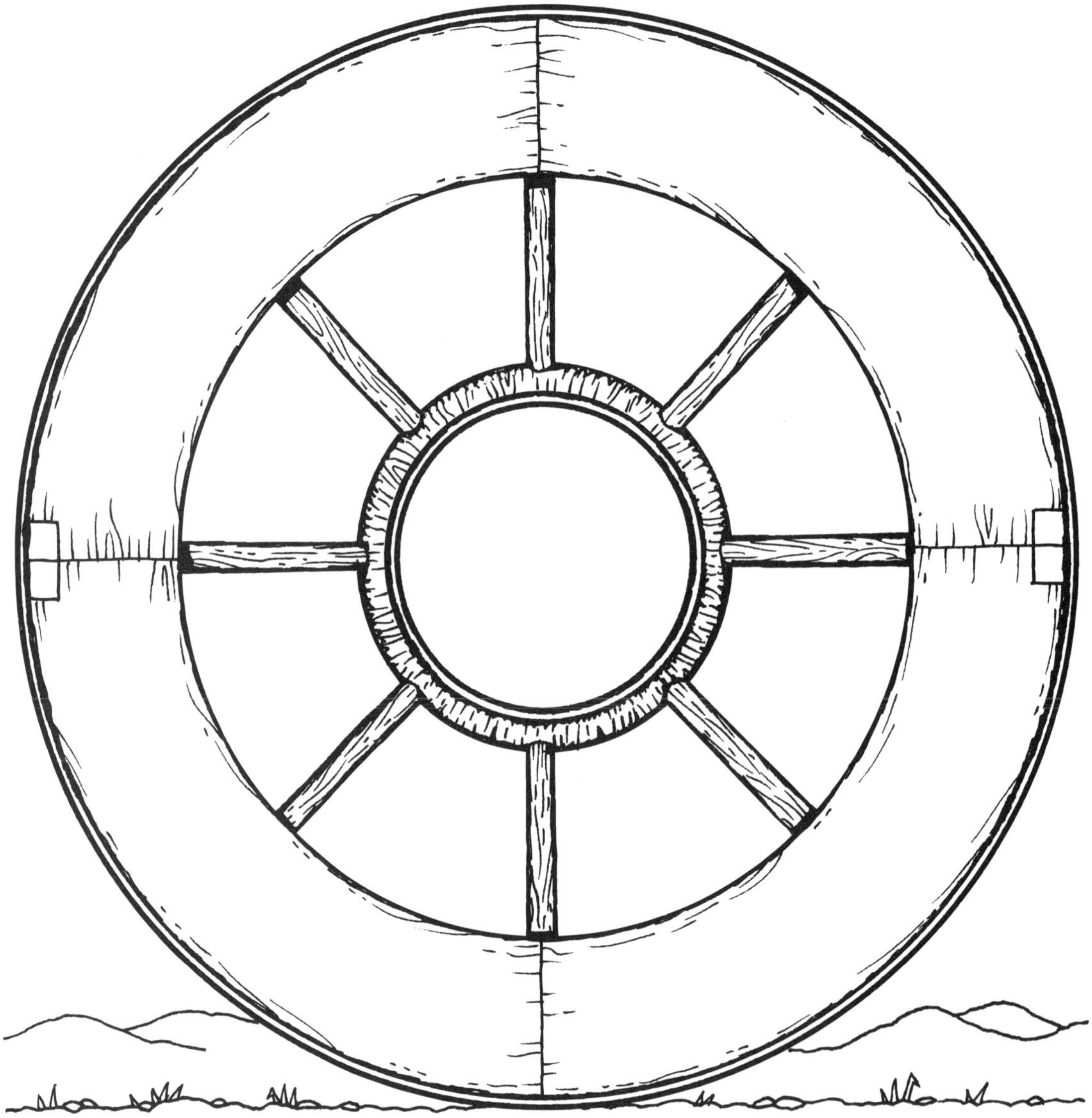

1. State the idea or topic in the center of the wheel.

2. List related ideas, vocabulary words, and so on in the inner circle.

3. Combine two words into an interesting sentence in the outer circle.

4. Classify the sentences and put a code in each small box.

Illustration by Bob Greisen.

Figure 11.2   Linear Graphic Organizer (Elaborate)

Name: _____   **Date:** _____

Elaborate

1. State the idea or topic.

2. List eight related ideas, vocabulary words, adjectives, problems, and so on next to each number 2.

3. On the lines below the V, combine the two words into an interesting sentence without using "and."

4. Put a code in each box according to order, main idea/detail, or supporting evidence.

1.   The topic _____

2. _____   2. _____

3. _____
   _____ ☐

2. _____   2. _____

3. _____
   _____ ☐

2. _____   2. _____

3. _____
   _____ ☐

2. _____   2. _____

3. _____
   _____ ☐

Figure 11.3   Sample: Joyce's *Jack and the Beanstalk* Wheel of Words Graphic Organizer (Elaborate)

Name: Joyce _____   **Date:** _____

Elaborate

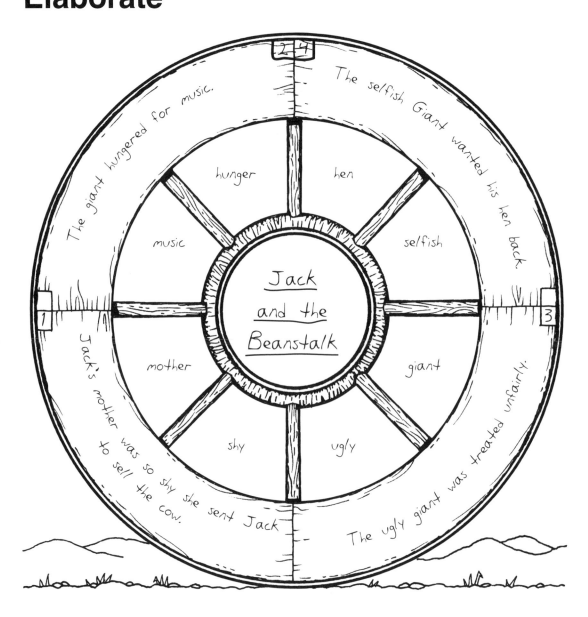

1. State the idea or topic in the center of the wheel.
2. List related ideas, vocabulary words, and so on (see p. 160) in the inner circle.
3. Combine two words into an interesting sentence in the outer circle.
4. Classify the sentences and put a code in each small box.

The teacher piggybacks on the lesson and asks students to bring in their baby pictures. They create a bulletin board that says, "All about us." This works well at the elementary level because the students are still at a young enough age to share personal pictures and stories about themselves. It is a good way for the teacher to find out their interests and strengths so that she can differentiate the curriculum. As students reach the preadolescent stage of development, they may become less willing to share personal information.

ASSESSMENT

An assessment tool for the Wheel of Words can be very helpful and effective to help students build elaborative language. It may not be necessary, however, to use an assessment tool in every single lesson. When the Wheel of Words is used as a pre-writing or pre-thinking tool for a discussion, it may not be necessary to have students rate themselves or for teachers to take the time to rate the students. If the graphic organizer is used to review vocabulary, then teachers might want to assess the graphic organizer to make sure the students have used the words in an appropriate, contextual way. If students have weak language skills, a teacher may want to use the rating scale or rubric to guide students in their language usage. In this way, the graphic organizer and the assessment tools can help to increase a student's ability to apply content-specific language.

The Wheel of Words rating scale lists six possible criteria, which are well suited to most content-area activities. The list of criteria, however, will change according to the focus and purpose of your lesson. The first criterion listed here is importance and addresses the significance of the words surrounding the target word. This is a key criterion if students are choosing words within a content area to relate to the center word. In certain circumstances, the students might choose words through free association, and this criterion would not apply. For example, if students are writing a story and they are making up characters, they might put a character's name in the center and choose random words to associate with the character. These words are not tied to content and are not important until the students put them in a context. In some cases, the teacher assigns the descriptor words or asks students to use vocabulary words from a chapter in a textbook. In this case, importance is not a key criterion that is particularly helpful.

Similarly, with the second criteria, accuracy is important when students are relating information to content. The student must apply the descriptors accurately in terms of grammatical usage and meaning in the sentence. The third criterion refers to relevancy. This again reflects the prompt. If students are asked to elaborate on a weather disaster and they make a statement about a sunny day, they have not made a statement relevant to disasters unless it's during a heat wave! The fourth criterion addresses sentence variety. This is based on the students' prior knowledge about sentence structure and how to vary it. In the English or language arts class, sentence variety might be an important criterion, whereas in the science class this may not be a useful criterion. The fifth criterion is interesting. This is a totally subjective criterion and one the teacher may want to avoid. I like to use it, because I ask the students to reread their sentences and if they sound boring, to adjust them so that they are more exciting. Students know they can do this by changing the verb, adding adjectives and adverbs, or perhaps changing the sentence structure. The last criterion is organization. This may refer to the sentence itself or how the sentences are organized (which is denoted in the little boxes).

Figure 11.4   Sample: Bruce's Linear Graphic Organizer (Elaborate)

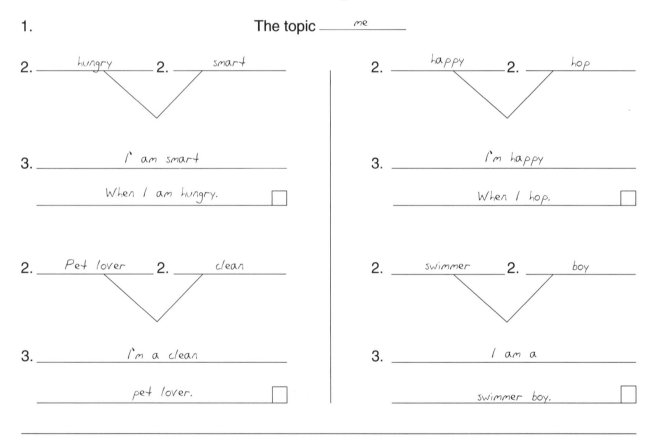

Name: _Bruce_ _____ **Date:** _____

Elaborate

1. State the idea or topic.

2. List eight related ideas, vocabulary words, adjectives, problems, and so on next to each number 2.

3. On the lines below the V, combine the two words into an interesting sentence without using "and."

4. Put a code in each box according to order, main idea/detail, or supporting evidence.

1.   The topic ____ _me_ ____

2. ____ _hungry_ ____   2. ____ _smart_ ____   2. ____ _happy_ ____   2. ____ _hop_ ____

3. ____ _I am smart_ ____   3. ____ _I'm happy_ ____
   ____ _When I am hungry._ ☐   ____ _When I hop._ ☐

2. ____ _Pet lover_ ____   2. ____ _clean_ ____   2. ____ _swimmer_ ____   2. ____ _boy_ ____

3. ____ _I'm a clean_ ____   3. ____ _I am a_ ____
   ____ _pet lover._ ☐   ____ _swimmer boy._ ☐

Not every lesson will require all six elements. Different lessons require different criteria. Remember, like the graphic organizers themselves, the rating scales and rubrics are flexible tools and should reflect the objectives of the lesson.

Let's take a look at the scores Joyce receives in the *Jack and the Beanstalk* example (Figure 11.5). Because Joyce chooses important words or ideas from the story, she receives a 5 in this area. She combines the words to make sentences that are all true except for the sentence, "Jack's mother was so shy she sent Jack to sell the cow." Joyce assumes this is the reason the mother sent Jack to sell the cow. This may or may not be true. Because she formulates the sentence based on an assumption that she cannot justify, Joyce receives a 3 in the area of accuracy. All the statements that Joyce makes are relevant. Even though Jack's mother may not have been shy, it is relevant that Jack went to sell the cow. Joyce scores a 5 in relevancy. The next criterion addresses how varied the sentences are. Joyce's sentence structures are fairly similar, because at her grade level students are just starting to understand sentence variety. She demonstrates an average amount of variety, and receives a 3. Joyce's sentences are fairly interesting and detailed, and rate a 4 in this category. Last of all, Joyce orders her sentences and can justify her reason for ordering them this way. She receives a 5 in organization.

The rating scale is turned into a rubric in Figure 11.6, and Joyce's scores are marked with asterisks.

This chapter addresses the skill of elaboration, using the forced association strategy in a graphic organizer format. The format allows students to use the creative thinking skill process to produce vivid language. By using this simple structure with students, their creative thinking skills will improve along with their knowledge about content. The Wheel of Words graphic organizer can be used in many ways to help students think about content in interesting ways.

In a time of standards and testing, it is easy to forget to use creative thinking. Most teachers will emphasize critical thinking skills because they think students will do better on tests. Research indicates that creative thinkers prefer to learn through the creative process (Sternberg, 1997). When differentiating for all students, it is important to remember that

Figure 11.5   Sample: Joyce's *Jack and the Beanstalk* Creative Thinking Rating Scale (Elaborate)

Criteria	Probing Question	Rating
Importance	To what degree are the elements important?	5
Accuracy	To what degree are the statements accurate?	3
Relevancy	To what degree are the statements relevant?	5
Variety	To what degree are the sentences varied?	3
Interesting	To what degree are the sentences detailed and interesting?	4
Organization	To what degree are the sentences organized?	5

creative thinkers do learn better, faster, and remember more when using the skills described in Chapters 8–11. Differentiated instruction must allow for a variety of instruction so that all students can learn.

In the next chapter, we will fine-tune our use of graphic organizers by looking at how to organize and manage different structures so that we get the most out of using them. Activity grids provide an overall structure that will demonstrate how to integrate graphic organizers into a unit of study. Before we move on, let's review a few key points about elaboration.

Figure 11.6   Sample: Joyce's *Jack and the Beanstalk* Creative Thinking Rubric (Elaborate)

1	2	3
Few elements stated, only some are important.	Some elements stated, most are important.	All elements stated are important. *
Some sentences are inaccurate.	Most sentences are accurate but assumptions and inferences may not be accurate. *	All statements are accurate.
Some statements are relevant.	Most statements are relevant.	All statements are relevant. *
Basic sentence structure may include "and."	Sentences well written but most have similar sentence structure.*	Great sentences with varied sentence structure. *
Sentences are not interesting due to lack of detail in the sentences.	Some sentences are interesting with some details in the sentences.	Interesting sentences with many details. *
Sentences are ordered incorrectly.	One sentence is ordered incorrectly.	Sentences are in order and the order can be justified. *

 KEY POINTS TO REMEMBER ABOUT ELABORATING

1. To elaborate means to describe something in detail.

2. Details are specific pieces of information that include facts, time sequences, cause and effect sequences, or episodes.

3. Elaboration often includes descriptive or vivid language, and can help build vocabulary.

4. Elaboration builds upon known information or ideas.

5. Elaboration involves taking an idea and improving it so that it is better in some way.

6. Elaborative thinking promotes depth of understanding and improves communication skills.

7. Elaboration may be communicated through visual forms.

? PAUSE FOR REFLECTION AND DISCUSSION

1. Why might student achievement increase when students become better at elaboration?

2. How might you apply this skill in your classroom?

3. How does the skill of elaboration promote vocabulary building and why is this important?

4. Why does elaboration promote depth of knowledge about the content?

5. How might you differentiate the lesson using the "elaborate" graphic organizer?

PART IV

Teachers as Practitioners: Thinking About What Works

Putting It All Together

Final Remarks

12

Putting It All Together

Curriculum Designs and Units of Study

Graphic organizers work well with any curricular or instructional approach. The organizers in this book will work particularly well for schools that use *The New Taxonomy of Educational Objectives* (Marzano & Kendall, 2007) to guide their curriculum writing, because the organizers are specifically designed to address symbolic representations of knowledge. For schools or districts that use the revised Bloom's Taxonomy (Anderson & Krathwohl, 2001) to guide their objectives, these cognitive graphic organizers will also serve well, as activities to target the learning objectives.

In *Understanding by Design* (McTighe & Wiggins, 2004), a backward design approach is recommended. Teachers follow a three-step model in which they (1) identify the desired results, (2) determine evidence, and (3) plan learning experiences and instruction. The cognitive graphic organizers fit well into the learning activities described in the third step of the backward design process. In looking at the design standards for the learning plan stage, McTighe and Wiggins recommend teachers use evaluation criteria (p. 24). The rating scales provide evaluation criteria so that teachers can give specific feedback on the thinking aspects of the lesson.

If schools are differentiating their curriculum using Tomlinson's model of differentiation (Tomlinson, 1999, 2003; Tomlinson & McTighe, 2006), teachers can use the six ways to differentiate to meet the learner's needs (see Chapter 2). These different ways to differentiate can be aligned with Tomlinson's planning model and equalizer. The graphic organizer activities are responsive to the student's readiness, interest, and style. Some districts do not use models but instead use particular textbooks. Other districts expect teachers to create their own lesson plan activities based on reference materials the teacher has gathered. Whether following a curriculum model, a textbook series, or designing your own lessons, teachers most often sprinkle graphic organizers throughout a unit of study. This sprinkling effect is generally a successful way to integrate them into the curriculum. There may be times, however, when teachers want to use a more articulated approach. This is when you might want to consider developing an activity grid.

CREATING AN ACTIVITY GRID

Using cognitive graphic organizers in an articulated way requires just a little more planning, but is easy to do when using an activity grid format. The activity grid can be used along with any curriculum model, in a textbook unit or teacher-designed unit of study. It can be used as a planning tool for the teacher or as an activity choice board for the students. You can use the activity grid as a planning tool to complement a unit of study using the following steps.

> ### How to Create an Activity Grid
>
> 1. Identify a unit of study.
> 2. Identify standards or objectives that are required in the unit of study.
> 3. Identify places in the unit to use differentiated instruction.
> 4. Identify which verbs you want to emphasize in the unit of study.
> 5. Create an activity grid using the target verbs in a prompt.
> 6. Articulate the complete differentiated learning experience.

When creating an activity grid, the first thing to do is to identify a unit of study that seems a little flat and could use more emphasis on critical and creative thinking through the use of graphic organizers. Next, be sure to connect your state standards and/or learning objectives to your graphic organizer activities. It will be up to you to differentiate—where in the unit these types of activities can occur, and which verbs you want to focus on. If you want to use a balance of critical and creative thinking graphic organizers, you can create a three-by-three grid and fill in at least one activity for each type of organizer from this book. If you want to add only creativity to the unit, you can design an activity grid that focuses just on creative thinking. You can accentuate the type of thinking you want your students to do by controlling the verb choices on the activity grid. Next, you can fill out the grid by taking each verb and turning it into a prompt for a lesson. The prompt can then be used with the corresponding graphic organizers in Chapters 3–11. The final step is to articulate the complete learning experience by differentiating the lesson based on the needs of your students and writing the lesson plan.

SAMPLE ACTIVITY GRID TEMPLATES

Activity grid templates are created in different sizes and different shapes according to your needs. The first template (Figure 12.1 on page 170) is a simple three-by-three grid with one critical or creative thinking skill word in each box. Each verb refers to a graphic organizer lesson. The Figure 12.1 template appeals to teachers who favor a more linear style of thinking, whereas the web format (Figure 12.2 on page 170) often appeals to teachers who are random thinkers. Like our students, we all have different thinking styles! The templates in Figures 12.1 and 12.2 show the verbs in the order they are presented in this book. Teachers can place the verbs in any order they choose to fit the lesson or unit that is being taught.

SAMPLE LESSONS

In a fourth-grade social studies unit, the teacher focuses on amendments to the Constitution and in particular the Bill of Rights (adapted from Donna Curtis, fourth-grade teacher). She decides she will use the graphic organizers to help her students understand this particular unit, and creates the activity grid in Figure 12.3.

In a middle school literacy unit, the teacher focuses on the story *The Field of the Dogs* by Katherine Paterson. She creates the activity grid in Figure 12.4 to use with her students (adapted from Susan Weber).

In Figure 12.5, an eleventh grade AP biology teacher focuses her activity grid on genetics (adapted from Carolyn Shorey Dupee).

The activity grid based on a seventh-grade math unit introducing algebra is an example of a smaller activity grid. The teacher incorporates graphic organizers into the math class because "The NCTM's [National Council of Teachers of Mathematics] *Principles and Standards for School Mathematics* (2000) speaks to the need for students to make conjectures, experiment with problem solving strategies, argue about mathematics, and justify their thinking" (Kenney, Hancewicz, Heuer, Metsisto, & Tuttle, 2005, p. 72).

Figure 12.1 Graphic Organizer Activity Grid Template

Assume	Infer	Analyze
Prioritize	Judge	Brainstorm
Connect	Create	Elaborate

Figure 12.2 Graphic Organizer Activity Web Template

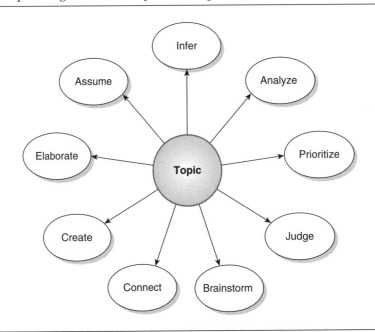

Figure 12.3 Sample: Donna Curtis's Bill of Rights Linear Activity Grid

What might you **assume** about having cameras in the courtroom?	What can you **infer** about the tension that exists between privacy and security rights?	**Analyze** what would happen if the U.S. Congress could and did appeal the Bill of Rights.
Prioritize the first amendment freedoms from least to most important to you.	**Judge** whether we should say the Pledge of Allegiance in class each day.	**Brainstorm** problems faced by those who framed the Constitution.
Connect the idea of freedom of speech to a person, place, and thing.	**Create** a classroom bill of rights.	**Elaborate** on the issues involved in protecting the Sixth Amendment rights of poor people.

Source: Adapted from the work of Donna Curtis, Forest Hills Consolidated School, Jackman, Maine.

Figure 12.4 Sample: Susan Weber's *The Field of the Dogs* Linear Activity Grid

What might you **assume** about bullying in this story?	What can you **infer** about the problem of bias in the media?	**Analyze** what are the effects of snow in the story?
Prioritize in which setting Josh is most vulnerable to his bully.	**Judge** what would have happened if the dogs had accepted Josh as one of their own?	**Brainstorm** ways Josh could have made friends.
Connect the idea of moving to a new community to a person, place, and thing.	**Create** a map of Josh's community including the field of dogs.	**Elaborate** on the sensory language that describes the setting.

Source: Adapted from the work of Susan Weber, Lewiston Middle School, Lewiston, Maine.

Figure 12.5 Sample: Carolyn Shorey-Dupee's Biology Linear Activity Grid

What might you **assume** about genetic engineering?	What can you **infer** about inheriting traits from your parents?	**Analyze** what are the problems of screening for genetic conditions.
Prioritize a list of the most effective strategies in determining possible genetic defects before birth.	**Judge** whether we should conduct stem cell research.	**Brainstorm** problems associated with chromosomal mutations.
Connect the idea of cloning to a person, place, and thing.	**Create** a pedigree for a homozygous recessive condition so the least number of individuals inherit the condition.	**Elaborate** on heredity.

Source: Adapted from the work of Carolyn Shorey-Dupee, Edward Little High School, Auburn, Maine.

Figure 12.6   Sample: Jessica West's Algebra Linear Activity Grid

Analyze the problem of only using tables to analyze data.	What can you **infer** about the use of algorithms?
Prioritize the advantages of using coordinate graphs.	**Judge** whether you think symbolic rules are important.
Connect the meaning of the x axis to a person, place, and thing.	**Create** a new mathematical symbol for a variable.

Source: Adapted from the work of Jessica West, Hodgkins Middle School, Augusta, Maine.

The graphic organizers give students a way to argue about math and justify their thinking. The grid in Figure 12.6 is adapted from one created by Jessica West on variables and patterns. In this example, a two-by-three grid works just fine. It's important to remember the purpose of the cognitive graphic organizer: to increase student achievement, help students make sense of information, allow students to chunk information, promote depth of learning, help students create mental models, and motivate students. If the graphic organizer does not accomplish these goals for the particular lesson you have in mind, you should think about choosing a different instructional strategy.

CREATING A UNIT CALENDAR

Once the teacher creates the activity grid, she can create a calendar that specifies which day she uses which organizer. An activity grid calendar (Figure 12.7) shows when the teacher uses a graphic organizer as well as other types of activities. This sample calendar for the middle school example, *The Field of the Dogs*, shows that the teacher plans to spend two weeks on the book. The calendar of activities addresses the story content, as well as the objectives and standards she must cover. In a reading unit, the activities can be organized according to pre-reading, during reading, and follow-up activities.

In this example, the teacher decides to use the idea of moving to a new place as a hook. This is considered a pre-reading activity. She is well aware that many of her students have never moved and may not understand the anxiety and the excitement that people experience when they relocate. The teacher uses this activity as a way for students who have moved to share firsthand experiences with those students who can only imagine what it must be like. The small group responses on the graphic organizer provide a focus for a whole class discussion about moving.

The teacher plans graphic organizer activities on Thursday, Friday, and Monday as ongoing reading activities. On the second Monday, she gives students a choice of two different graphic organizers. The students are all reading the same book, but they are doing different graphic organizers with different prompts, to allow for different learning strengths and styles. Notice on the following Wednesday, students have a choice again. Wednesday, Thursday, and Friday's graphic organizer lessons are summary lessons and are used as a follow-up to review the story content.

GRAPHIC ORGANIZERS IN COORDINATION WITH OTHER INSTRUCTIONAL STRATEGIES

In blocking out the activities in Figure 12.7, the teacher is mindful that she needs to vary the types of activities. Because she plans to use a lot of graphic organizers in a short amount of time, she decides to use hands-on activities on both Tuesdays and a summation activity on the first Wednesday. In the Bloom's Taxonomy cube activity on Tuesday, the students make a cube (Drapeau, 1998; Wormelli, 2005) and write a verb from each level of the taxonomy on the face of the cube. Students play with a partner, toss the cube, and create a question using the verb on the top of the cube. The other student answers the question, and the first student either accepts the answer or not. They discuss the answers and continue playing until it is time to stop. For students who struggle, the teacher provides the questions. These questions are written directly on the cube. This is easier to play because students do not have to create their own questions. The teacher can create basic questions so that struggling students are successful. The game is played in the same way except the student who tosses the cube answers the question on the top of the cube and the other student accepts the answer or not.

The "So Far" strategy noted on Wednesday is used to review the story during reading. The "So Far" activity uses the 3, 2, 1 prompt that can be used with a variety of descriptors. In this case, the teacher focuses the prompt on remembering, connecting to interest, and pointing out the main idea.

The *Jeopardy* game is always a hit with students. It is a great way to review information as well as allow students to see the categories that exist in a context. One way to play this is to make four teams (or as many as you like). Students sit in rows. The first person in the row answers the question. After they answer, they move to the end of the row. Another way to organize students is to make groups of four (or more) and let students work together to answer questions.

It is effective practice to alternate the graphic organizer activities with other instructional strategies, but sometimes the graphic organizer can be part of an activity. In this

Figure 12.7 Sample: *The Field of the Dogs* Unit Calendar

Monday	Tuesday	Wednesday	Thursday	Friday
Connect the idea of moving to a new community to a person, place, and thing.	Bloom's Taxonomy cube activity.	So far: Three things I want to remember, two things that are interesting, and one main idea.	What can you **infer** about the problem of bias in the media?	**Elaborate** on the sensory language that describes the setting.
Monday	**Tuesday**	**Wednesday**	**Thursday**	**Friday**
Brainstorm ways Josh could have made friends. Or What might you **assume** about bullying in this story?	*Jeopardy* categories to include: plot, setting, character, theme, point of view.	**Analyze** the effects of snow in the story. Or **Prioritize** in which setting Josh is most vulnerable to his bully.	**Judge** what would have happened if the dogs had accepted Josh as one of their own?	**Create** a map of Josh's community including the field of dogs.

174   TEACHERS AS PRACTITIONERS: THINKING ABOUT WHAT WORKS

way, the graphic organizer supports the use of the larger instructional strategy. For example, two students decide to create question and answer cards for a math concentration game. The questions are based on a fraction unit. For example, one card says, find an example of a mixed number. The matching card is 3½. Another card asks what is the first thing you need to do to solve 4½ + 6¼? The matching card says to convert the mixed number to an improper fraction. Although the activity is being used to review math content information, it is important for the students to create a game in which all students can be successful. The teacher knows the students have not considered who will be playing the game and what the needs of all students might be. The teacher feels the students ought to think carefully about their audience before they create their questions.

Instead of asking students directly if they think the game will work for all students, the teacher gives the two students the "assumption" graphic organizer to fill out so that they can make their own discoveries about their audience. The teacher asks the students to respond to the assumption, "We believe all students will have fun playing our concentration game." Because the graphic organizer asks them to verify their assumption, the students move around the room and ask other students if they think their concentration game will be fun. The students receive answers like "Maybe, if the questions aren't too hard" or "Maybe, if I can use my book to look up the answers."

What the creators of the concentration game soon realize is that the questions they have created may be too hard for some students and, if they are too hard, students will not have fun. The two students decide to make an easy and hard set of questions. They also decide to let students choose which level they want to play.

In this instance, the "assume" graphic organizer gave the students a structure so that they could collect information, make meaning of the information, and draw an appropriate conclusion. Instead of using the graphic organizer, the teacher could have told the students that their game would be too hard for some students, or the teacher could have questioned the students until they discovered that for themselves. Either way, the information would have been teacher directed rather than student initiated. By using the graphic organizer format, we can encourage students to become self-directed learners.

In some cases, multiple graphic organizers might constitute an instructional unit. Teachers can piggyback their graphic organizer lessons by using two or more graphic organizers in the same lesson. For example, groups of students might be asked to use the Rainbow of Ideas graphic organizer to brainstorm ways to solve the problem in the story. After they finish brainstorming, the students work individually to prioritize to determine their favorite idea and elaborate on it. This works well because the students have the advantage of generating many ideas by working together, but they do not have to negotiate with the group when it comes to deciding on their favorite idea. This decision is affected by personal choice and is best conducted individually.

In a unit on the Vietnam War, students might be asked to use the Rainbow of Ideas organizer to brainstorm events of the era in their small group. Then they use the Prioritizer graphic organizer, individually, to prioritize key significant events of the era from their brainstormed list. Finally, the teacher groups students according to who identified the same top key event. These new groups of students use the Wheel of Words to elaborate on the event. Then, they use the sentences that they come up with on the wheel to individually write a descriptive essay about the event.

The activity grid can be a type of multiple graphic organizer activity when it is used as a student choice board. Teachers create prompts that match up with graphic organizers in a three-by-three grid. Students choose three prompts in a row, column, or in a diagonal like in a tick-tack-toe game. Teachers can use this strategy at the end of a unit, story, or textbook chapter when students have enough information to answer all of the questions.

MANAGING DIFFERENTIATION AS YOU USE GRAPHIC ORGANIZERS

When we differentiate using graphic organizers, we must be adept at (1) managing time and (2) grouping students. If all students are using the open-ended prompt approach to differentiation (see Chapter 2), then there are minimal management problems. Theoretically, all students are doing the same activity at the same time. Some students will, however, finish at varying times due to the open-ended nature of the prompt and students' varying abilities. If some students or homogeneous groups of students are stuck, they will finish early (if they start at all) and if some students or homogeneous group of students find the prompt is too easy, they may also finish well before the others. To plan for this, you need to be available to help the struggling learners finish the activity while the more able students know what to do if they finish early. The teacher assigns them meaningful work to do. As described in Chapter 2, giving them another graphic organizer will not work! This is called "more of the same," and some of your brighter students will just slow down so that they don't have to do anything extra. Meaningful work might mean an extension activity that allows the student to research deeper into the content information. A few guiding questions can set these students on a quest for answers, while you work with the others finishing up the lesson. If the high-ability students do not finish their research by the time students are finished with the original activity, ask them to put their work aside and allow them to finish at another time.

The situation is different if the teacher groups students heterogeneously. All students should be able to contribute some ideas in their group. The teacher watches for students within the group who finish early. By this I mean, the group continues to work but some students have no more ideas. We hope these students are learning from the other students but in some instances the students no longer pay attention. The students' behavior turns disruptive or they sit there and space out. The teacher can manage this situation by having all students take on a role in the group such as timekeeper, note taker, illustrator, and so on.

This scenario changes with the directed prompt. Here, all of the students are doing the same graphic organizer, but some have a different prompt. Theoretically, finishing at different times should not be a problem because students are presented with levels of challenge commensurate with their ability level. There is a better chance of having all students finish at the same time. The students may work individually or in small groups with peers of similar ability. Teachers should be very cautious about making heterogeneous groups when using this type of differentiation.

The third way to differentiate using graphic organizers is to provide different resources. In this scenario, students can work in groups at similar reading levels. The students in the group can share sources and work together on the graphic organizer. Again, most groups of students should finish at about the same time because they are reading from sources that are at their level. If highly able students use sources below their ability level, they often finish quickly. When highly able students use higher-level reading material, they might take longer than other students. The information is usually denser. Often the struggling and unmotivated learners finish first when the teacher differentiates the resources. In this situation, these learners need to know what to do next because they won't push themselves to answer in more detail just because they have more time. Try grouping unmotivated students with motivated students with caution. Try giving unmotivated students resources that are interesting. Spend time with your unmotivated students. Personal attention sometimes is all they need.

The fourth way of differentiating with graphic organizers is to target different prompts and different graphic organizers but use the same resources. This works in classrooms where teachers have to use the same text for all students. Students can work in pairs or in small groups with others who have the same organizer and prompt. In this type of classroom, however, there may be many grouping arrangements. Although heterogeneous grouping works well with this type of differentiation, there may be individuals, pairs, and small groups all working in one class. The teacher is available to float and help those students who need help. Because there are diverse grouping arrangements, there is more possibility for noise and confusion. With this situation, it is important that teachers make sure the rules of the classroom are clear and that all students are engaged.

The fifth way of differentiating using graphic organizers is variety plus, in which students are able to choose their own graphic organizer, and the sixth way has students creating or modifying their own graphic organizer. These may be the easiest to manage because students tend to work individually or in pairs. As long as you have described how to use each graphic organizer and its accompanying rating scale, you can present the graphic organizers in folders and have the students choose the one they want to use or modify. They are working fairly independently at this point and you can be free to help those who need it. Again, some common problems—noise, different completion times, and the need to help some students—must be addressed. As with brainstorming, if the rules are set up, then the expectations are clear and students should feel comfortable being less dependent on the teacher to provide information.

 ## KEY POINTS TO REMEMBER

1. Graphic organizers can be sprinkled throughout a unit of study.

2. Teachers can plan their use of graphic organizers by creating an activity grid.

3. Activity grids can focus on critical thinking or creative thinking, or both types of thinking.

4. A calendar can help teachers see the balance between their use of graphic organizers and other instructional strategies.

5. Teachers need to think ahead about ways to manage differentiation and graphic organizer activities.

? PAUSE FOR REFLECTION AND DISCUSSION

1. How might the use of an activity grid help you to organize your graphic organizer lessons?

2. What other instructional strategies do you use that will complement the use of graphic organizer activities?

3. What do you assume about using the multiple graphic organizer activity with your class?

4. Brainstorm different places in a unit where a graphic organizer choice board might work.

5. How might you manage time and grouping with your differentiated instruction using graphic organizers?

13

Final Remarks

Essential FAQs

Here are some closing questions and answers to guide your use of graphic organizers as tools for critical and creative thinking and differentiation.

1. *How often should I use graphic organizers?*

   Keep track of the ones you use so that you have a true assessment of the frequency and type of graphic organizer that work best with students. In general, I recommend using cognitive graphic organizers at least twice a week. In this way, I know I'm doing critical and creative thinking skill lessons regularly and I'm promoting the use of cognitive graphic organizers as a habit. Students, with regular practice, will begin to process the steps on the organizers automatically. The more students use graphic organizers, the more students begin to think in formats and structures, which will also increase their ability to visualize, remember, arrange, and make meaning of information. Different units lend themselves to different uses of graphic organizers, but twice a week seems to work most of the time. Students may choose to use graphic organizers more than that if they wish.

2. *What happens if a student doesn't like to use graphic organizers?*

   Remember: the goal is to promote learning, not to make all students process information in the same way. Therefore, what I believe to be most important about cognitive graphic organizers is not the physical structures, but the delineation of the process. If students know and understand how to make a good judgment and do not want to use the graphic organizer, I think this is fine. Students can still use the rating scale or rubric as a self-assessment tool, regardless of the fact that their answers are not on a graphic organizer. If the student successfully learns the content, it is certainly unimportant to insist they use the graphic organizer. However, if the student makes a weak judgment and does not demonstrate that she has utilized a process to formulate or validate her judgment, then requiring the student to use the graphic organizer is recommended. If the student doesn't like to use graphic organizers but the state standard requires their use, then the objective of the lesson includes not only the content but also the graphic organizer itself. For example, the content standard in language arts in New Jersey states, "Students will use graphic organizers to build on experiences and extend learning." In this case, the students need to practice using graphic organizers if for no other reason than it is required of them.

3. *How do I know which graphic organizer to use when?*

If you are lucky enough to be able to create your own questions, you will need to consider how much prior knowledge and/or acquired knowledge your students have. You can then decide if you want to provide practice through a straight recall activity or if you want to promote critical and creative thinking through a graphic organizer activity. If you think students are ready to use critical and creative thinking, then choosing which graphic organizer to use is certainly the next consideration. If the objective of the lesson targets critical or creative thinking, you can readily substitute different verbs in different practice assignments. You may have already noticed and thought about how the graphic organizers presented in this book are interchangeable. For example, with the "assume" graphic organizer (Chapter 3), a teacher might ask students to respond to the prompt, "I assume the digestive system is important to our physical health." But the same teacher could ask the same students to use the "analyze" graphic organizer (Chapter 5) to respond to the prompt, "Analyze the digestive system," or ask students to prioritize the important parts of the digestive system by using the "prioritize" graphic organizer (Chapter 6). The teacher might want students to judge (Chapter 7) the digestive system in terms of its importance to physical health. To promote creative thinking, she can set this as a prompt and ask students to brainstorm reasons (Chapter 8) why the digestive system is important to our health. The teacher can ask students to connect (Chapter 9) the digestive system to a car or a home or a great meal. Students might be asked to create a model of the digestive system using the Idea Burst organizer (Chapter 10), or use elaborative language (Chapter 11) to describe the importance of the digestive system.

Therefore, it's important to consider what type of thinking you want your students to do and whether the type of cognitive processing involved will affect the learning outcome. If one particular type does not seem to make a significant difference, then perhaps any of the examples will serve the same purpose and work equally well. In looking at these examples, it is also clear that most students would not be successful with any of these prompts at the beginning of a unit. Because they need content information, these types of graphic organizers are best done later in a unit.

In some schools, teachers are not at liberty to create their own questions. They must use the language specifically stated in objectives or standards. If this is the case, the learning objective verb may not match any of the critical and creative thinking verbs articulated in the cognitive graphic organizers. For example, students are studying the civil rights movement in a twelfth-grade social studies class. The objective of the lesson states that the student should be able to "Describe the circumstances under which civil disobedience might be justified." Here we have the low-level verb "describe," but if we want students to use critical and/or creative thinking then we must bump up the level of questioning.

In this case, the teacher might decide to ask students to analyze the circumstances, prioritize the circumstances, or judge the circumstances leading to civil disobedience. In any of the responses using the critical thinking verbs listed, students would need to incorporate the description of the circumstances under which civil disobedience might be justified in their high-level thinking responses. If the teacher wants to foster creative thinking, then the teacher could ask students to brainstorm circumstances, relate the circumstances to a shoe, or elaborate on the circumstances. In both of these examples, students incorporate or at least cognitively process the description. This is because the high-level verb encompasses both high- and low-level thinking.

In another instance, the objective of the lesson might already target a high-level verb, such as in the prompt, "Evaluate the role of the media and public opinion in United States politics, including the ways government and media influence public opinion." In this example, the verb is "evaluate." In this case, it is best to use a graphic organizer that targets this same level of Bloom's Taxonomy. If students are asked to evaluate, they could use the "judge" graphic organizer or a graphic organizer specific to evaluation such as "prioritize."

Teachers often ask if the "analyze" graphic organizer can be substituted for "evaluate" because both are critical thinking skills. This is not recommended because evaluation is at a higher level than analysis. We do analyze when we evaluate, so it is part of the evaluation process. When students are asked to analyze, however, they are not necessarily expected to evaluate. Therefore, generally speaking, if the stated verb already targets a high level of Bloom's Taxonomy, only another verb at the same level ought to be substituted.

4. *How do I use graphic organizers with my textbook or teacher's manual?*

    Some teachers are fairly dependent upon students answering questions in their text or teacher's manual. If there is a list of chapter questions in a text, students can use graphic organizers to help them answer the questions. They can process their thoughts individually on the graphic organizer and share them with the group. The graphic organizer responses help to structure the group discussion. You can also have students work in pairs to fill out the graphic organizer and share their responses within a small group or with the class. Some of the questions in the text can be modified to match the target verbs in this book. With a quick change of the verb, you can replace a text question that focuses on low-level thinking with a critical and/or creative thinking verb to create more challenging or interesting questions.

5. *Can graphic organizers be used to review for a test?*

    It's important to use the graphic organizer to target the level of thinking that will be on the test. This will usually eliminate the creative thinking graphic organizers because most tests do not ask these types of questions. But we don't want to forget that some creative or unmotivated students may do the practice or homework if the review is presented in a more "playful" way. It's important to vary the type of graphic organizer to match students' styles and hook their interest. If a student is interested in car mechanics, then ask him to relate the digestive system to a car. Graphic organizers are flexible tools and should be used accordingly.

6. *Can multiple graphic organizers be used to promote content depth?*

    This question was answered in the last chapter, but here is a specific example that can be used in a writing class when students are asked to write a fictional piece. The graphic organizer prompts such as the following can be used to help students develop their fictional character.
    o What do you assume about the character?
    o What might you infer about this character?

    o Analyze your character.
    o Prioritize the personality characteristics you have created for your character.
    o Judge your character.

These tools are great ways for students to create well-developed characters. No teacher, however, would expect students to use every one of these graphic organizers when developing a character. In fact, some students are already fantastic writers and may not need to use any graphic organizer. Remember: When we differentiate, we do not require all students to do the same thing. You need to know which organizer to use in the pre-writing process with which student. You need to decide which tool will help increase the student's achievement and motivation (and produce a better product). You need to know if the tool will help the student make sense of the character, chunk the information, and promote depth in the writing piece. It is essential that you know why you are using the graphic organizer and how it is being used.

7. *Can graphic organizers be used in the research process?*

Regardless of whether you use a research model or not, graphic organizers can be used throughout the research process. Each step of the research process lends itself to particular types of graphic organizers. In the first step of a research model called the Independent Investigation Method (Nottage & Morse, 2003), students are asked what they know and what questions they have about a given topic. Students who are researching the same topic can work together to complete the "brainstorm" graphic organizer (Chapter 8).

In the second step of the research process, students are asked to set goals. Students might again use the "brainstorming" graphic organizer to help them develop questions to guide their research. They could also prioritize their questions (Chapter 6) to determine the degree of importance they place on answering particular questions. This may help them plan their time accordingly to reach their goals. Some students need to learn that they should spend more time investigating answers to questions that are of high priority.

In step three, students conduct their research from a variety of sources. It is not until we get to step four where students organize, analyze, and interpret their data that the graphic organizers can be useful again. Here, the critical thinking graphic organizers can be extremely helpful. As students gather their information and synthesize it, even the "judge" graphic organizer (Chapter 7) can be used to determine if they have enough evidence to make a meaningful conclusion.

In step five, students are asked to review their research to see if they have answered all of their research questions. Graphic organizers targeting assumptions and inferences can help students review their answers to their research questions. In step six, students can use the "create" graphic organizer (Chapter 10) to create a product. In the final or seventh step of the Independent Investigation Method, students are required to present their information to an audience. Again, the "create" graphic organizer (Chapter 10) can be used to create the presentation.

8. *How can I find the perfect graphic organizer?*

No graphic organizer is going to fit everyone's needs all of the time. Therefore, if you really want to find a perfect match to your content area, your grade level, and to your curriculum objectives, it may mean that some of the time, you might want to modify one that exists or create your own. I hope Chapter 2 of this book has given you the tools to do this. There are graphic tools on the computer and Internet sites to help you as well. When creating graphic organizers, there is just one rule to remember: simple steps and simple formats. Format complexity does not always help build meaning. It sometimes adds confusion. Keep it simple so that all students can be successful.

Always keep your students in mind. You have students who speak limited English. You have students with limited verbal ability. You have students who have difficulty remembering information. You have students who come to school hungry. You have students who only feel supported in school because there is no emotional support at home.

It's not about how fancy your graphic organizer is. It is what the students put into the structure that counts, and the way of doing so can advance their thinking and learning. Teachers send powerful messages, and perhaps the most powerful message of all is that we hold high expectations of our students. My hope is that the graphic organizers in this book help you to accomplish this goal. We should all strive to push students to produce their best work, as does Mr. Pitts, the English teacher, in this reflective poem Hilda Grant Jones wrote for the *Maine Educator* in January 2007.

From Your Student

High school English: Mr. Lonton Pitts.
Bald pate; coke-bottle glasses.
Brown gabardine pants
And short-sleeved shirt,
Each day some variation on the theme,
And always set off by a wild
Hawaiian tie, as if his soul
Were seeping out
In mango, frangipani, leis and palms.
"Class your first assignment will be
Tess of the d'Urbervilles,
by Thomas Hardy."
Okay, this one was mine,
A lead-pipe cinch.
This solitary kid, her lonely childhood
Peopled by Dickens, the Brontes,
Thackeray, Robert Louis Stevenson
and Sir Walter Scott,
Could take on Thomas Hardy in a
Cakewalk.

I tore through the book,
Slapped down the notes,
Dashed off my paper
With a fine panache—
Sat back, and waited for
    kudos to come.
The paper came back—
Without a grade, but a note:
"These things have all been said before.
I think you can do better:
Try again."
Stung, I slunk away
To read it all once more,
And in the process
Discovered Egdon Heath,
Located the center,
Felt the beating heart
And heard the voice.
So—Thank you, Thomas Hardy.
Thank you, Mr. Pitts.

Source: Hilda Grant Jones.

References

Alexander, P. A., Parsons, J. L., & Nash, W. R. (1996). *Toward a theory of creativity*. Washington, DC: National Association for Gifted Children.

Anderson, L. W., & Krathwohl, D. R. (Eds.). (2001). *A taxonomy for learning, teaching, and assessing: A revision of Bloom's Taxonomy of educational objectives*. New York: Longman.

Armstrong, T. (1994). *Multiple intelligence in the classroom*. Alexandria, VA: Association for Supervision and Curriculum Development.

Beers, S. Z. (2003). *Reading strategies for the content areas: Vol. 1. An ASCD action tool*. Alexandria, VA: Association for Supervision and Curriculum Development.

Bloom, B., Englehart, M., Furst, E., Hill, W., & Krathwohl, D. (1956). *Taxonomy of educational objectives: Handbook 1. Cognitive domain*. New York: Longmans, Green.

Burke, K. (1994). *How to assess authentic learning*. Palatine, IL: IRI/Skylight.

Chance, P. (1986). *Thinking in the classroom: A survey of programs*. New York: Teachers College Press.

Costa, A. L. (1991). *The school as a home for the mind*. Palatine, IL: IRI/Skylight.

Costa, A. L., & Garmston, R. J. (2001). Five human passions: The origins of effective thinking. In A. L. Costa (Ed.), *Developing minds: A resource book for teaching thinking* (3rd ed., pp. 18–22). Alexandria, VA: Association for Supervision and Curriculum Development.

Csikszentmihalyi, M. (1998). Letters from the field from Mihaly Csikszentmihalyi. *Roeper Review, 21*(1) 80–81.

Davis, G. (1992). *Creativity is forever*. Dubuque, IA: Kendall/Hunt.

Drapeau, P. (1998). *Great teaching with graphic organizers*. New York: Scholastic.

Drapeau, P. (2004). *Differentiated instruction: Making it work*. New York: Scholastic.

Erickson, H. L. (2007). *Concept-based curriculum and instruction for the thinking classroom*. Thousand Oaks, CA: Corwin Press.

Fogarty, R. (1994). *Teach for metacognitive cognition*. Palatine, IL: IRI/Skylight.

Forsten, C., Grant, J., & Hollas, B. (2003). *Differentiating textbooks strategies to improve student comprehension and motivation*. Peterborough, NH: Crystal Springs Books.

Friedman, T. L. (2005). *The world is flat*. New York: Farrar, Straus, and Giroux.

Futrell, M. H. (1987). A message long overdue. *Education Week, 7*(14), 9.

Gangwer, T. (2005). *Visual impact, visual teaching: Using images to strengthen learning*. San Diego, CA: The Brain Store.

Gardner, H. (1993). *Frames of mind: The theory of multiple intelligences*. New York: Basic Books.

Gardner, H. (1999). *Intelligence reframed*. New York: Basic Books.

Glasser, W. (1999). *Choice theory*. New York: Perennial.

Goleman, D., Kaufman, P., & Ray, M. (1992). *The creative spirit*. New York: Penguin.

Gregory, G., & Chapman, C. (2002). *Differentiated instructional strategies: One size doesn't fit all*. Thousand Oaks, CA: Corwin Press.

Gregory, G., & Kuzmich, L. (2004). *Data driven differentiation in the standards-based classroom*. Thousand Oaks, CA: Corwin Press.

Guilford, J. P. (1967). *The nature of human intelligence*. Columbus, OH: McGraw-Hill.

Guilford, J. P. (1977). *Way beyond the IQ*. Buffalo, NY: Creative Education Foundation.

Harris, R. (1998). *Introduction to creative thinking*. Retrieved June 25, 2007, from Virtual Salt at http://virtualsalt.com/crebook1.htm.

Harvey, S., & Goudvis, A. (2000). *Strategies that work*. Portland, ME: Stenhouse.

Heacox, D. (2002). *Differentiating instruction in the regular classroom*. Minneapolis, MN: Free Spirit Publishing.

Howard, D. L., & Fogarty, R. (2003). *The middle years: The essential teaching repertoire*. Chicago, IL: Fogarty and Associates.

Huitt, W. (1998). *Critical thinking: An overview*. Retrieved May 29, 2007, from Educational Psychology Interactive, Valdosta State University, GA, at http://chiron.valdosta.edu/whuitt/col/cogsys/critthnk.html.

Hyerle, D. (2004). *Student successes with thinking maps*. Thousand Oaks, CA: Corwin Press.

Institute of Advancement of Research in Education. (2003). *Graphic organizers: A review of scientifically based research* (Executive summary). Retrieved April 25, 2007, from Inspiration Software at http://www.inspiration.com/vlearning/research/index.cfm.

Intrator, S. (2004). The engaged classroom. *Educational Leadership, 62*(1), 23.

Jacobs, H. H. (2006). *Active literacy across the curriculum*. Larchmont, NY: Eye on Education.

Jensen, E. (2006). *Enriching the brain*. San Francisco, CA: Jossey-Bass.

Jones, H. G. (2007, January). From your student. *Maine Educator*, p. 4.

Kaplan, S. N. (2005). Layering differentiated curriculum for the gifted and talented. In F. A. Karnes & S. M. Bean (Eds.), *Methods and materials for teaching the gifted* (pp. 107–132). Waco, TX: Prufrock Press.

Kendall, J. S., & Marzano, R. J. (2000). *Content knowledge: A compendium of standards and benchmarks for K–12 education* (3rd ed.). Alexandria, VA: Association for Supervision and Curriculum Development; Aurora, CO: Mid-continent Research for Education and Learning.

Kenney, J. M., Hancewicz, E., Heuer, L., Metsisto, D., & Tuttle, C. L. (2005). *Literacy strategies for improving mathematics instruction*. Alexandria, VA: Association for Supervision and Curriculum Development.

Levine, M. (2002). *A mind at a time*. New York: Simon & Schuster.

Marzano, R. J. (2004). *Building background knowledge for academic achievement*. Alexandria, VA: Association for Supervision and Curriculum Development.

Marzano, R. J., & Kendall, J. S. (2007). *The new taxonomy of educational objectives*. Thousand Oaks, CA: Corwin Press.

Marzano, R. J., Norford, J. S., Paynter, D. E., Pickering, D. J., & Gaddy, B. B. (2001). *A handbook for classroom instruction that works*. Alexandria, VA: Association for Supervision and Curriculum Development.

Marzano, R. J., Pickering, D. J., & McTighe, J. (1993). *Assessing student outcomes: Performance assessment using the dimensions of learning model*. Alexandria, VA: Association for Supervision and Curriculum Development.

Marzano, R. J., Pickering, D. J., & Pollock, J. E. (2001). *Classroom instruction that works: Research-based strategies for increasing student achievement*. Alexandria, VA: Association for Supervision and Curriculum Development.

Marzano, R. J., & Pollock, J. E. (2001). Standards-based thinking and reasoning skills. In A. L. Costa (Ed.), *Developing minds: A resource book for teaching thinking* (3rd ed., pp. 29–34). Alexandria, VA: Association for Supervision and Curriculum Development.

Maxwell, J. C. (2003). *Thinking for a change*. New York: Center Street.

McTighe, J., & Wiggins, G. (2004). *Understanding by design*. Alexandria, VA: Association for Supervision and Curriculum Development.

Merkley, D. M., & Jefferies, D. (2001). Guidelines for implementing a graphic organizer. *Reading Teacher, 54*(4) 350–357.

Messina, J., & Messina, C. (1999). *Tools for improving your critical thinking: Stories off email postings to test your critical thinking*. Retrieved May 29, 2007, from Coping.org at http://www.coping.org/write/percept/logic.htm.

Michalko, M. (1998). *Cracking creativity: The secrets of creative genius*. Berkeley, CA: Ten Speed Press.

National Council of Teachers of Mathematics. (2000). *Principles and standards for school mathematics*. Reston, VA: Author.

National Education Goals Panel. (1991). *The national education goals report: Building a nation of learners*. Washington, DC: Author.

National Reading Panel. (2000). *Teaching children to read: An evidence-based assessment of the scientific research literature on reading and its implications for reading instruction*. Washington, DC: National Institute of Child Health and Human Development.

National Science Board Commission on Precollege Education in Mathematics, Science and Technology. (1983). *Educating Americans for the 21st century*. Washington, DC: National Science Board Commission.

Norris, S. P. (1985). Synthesis of research on critical thinking. *Educational Leadership, 42*(8), 40–45.

Nottage, C., & Morse, V. (2003). *IIM [Independent Investigation Method]: Seven easy steps to successful research*. Epping, NH: Active Learning Systems.

Nunley, K. F. (2006). *Differentiating in the high school classroom*. Thousand Oaks, CA: Corwin Press.

Osborn, A. F. (1963). *Applied imagination* (3rd ed.). New York: Scribner.

Parnes, S. (1988). *Visionizing: State-of-the-art processes for encouraging innovative excellence*. East Aurora, NY: D.O.K. Publishers.

Paul, R. (1999). *Critical thinking: Basic theory and instructional structures*. Sonoma, CA: Foundation for Critical Thinking.

Paul, R., & Elder, L. (2001). *Tools for taking charge of your learning and your life* (2nd ed.). Upper Saddle River, NJ: Prentice Hall.

Pink, D. H. (2006). *A whole new mind*. New York: Riverhead Books.

Polette, N. (1987). *The ABCs of books and thinking skills: A literature-based thinking skills program K–8*. O'Fallon, MO: Book Lures.

Reid, L. (1990). *Thinking skills resource book*. Mansfield, CT: Creative Learning Press.

Reiss, J. (2005). *Teaching content to English Language Learners*. White Plains, NY: Longman.

Silver, H. F., Strong, R. W., & Perini, M. J. (2000). *So each may learn integrating learning styles and multiple intelligences*. Alexandria, VA: Association for Supervision and Curriculum Development.

Sousa, D. A. (2001). *How the brain learns*. Thousand Oaks, CA: Corwin Press.

Sprenger, M. (2005). *How to teach so students remember.* Alexandria, VA: Association for Supervision and Curriculum Development.

Sternberg, R. J. (1996). *Successful intelligence: How practical and creative intelligence determine success in life.* New York: Simon & Schuster.

Sternberg, R. J. (1997). *Educational leadership.* Alexandria, VA: Association for Supervision and Curriculum Development.

Sternberg, R. J., & Grigorenko, E. L. (1993). Thinking styles and the gifted. *Roeper Review, 16*(2), 122–130.

Sternberg, R. J., & Williams, W. M. (1996). *How to develop student creativity.* Alexandria, VA: Association for Supervision and Curriculum Development.

Strangman, N., Hall, T., & Meyer, A. (2003). *Graphic organizers with UDL.* Wakefield, MA: National Center on Accessing the General Curriculum. Retrieved June 1, 2007, from http://www.cast .org/publications/ncac/ncac_goudl.html.

Sylwester, R. (2003). *A biological brain in a cultural classroom* (2nd ed.). Thousand Oaks, CA: Corwin Press.

Talents Unlimited. (1995). *A critical and creative thinking skills model: Awareness packet.* (ERIC Document Reproduction Service No. ED411382)

Tomlinson, C. A. (1999). *The differentiated classroom: Responding to the needs of all learners.* Alexandria, VA: Association for Supervision and Curriculum Development.

Tomlinson, C. A. (2003). *Fulfilling the promise of the differentiated classroom strategies and tools for responsive teaching.* Alexandria, VA: Association for Supervision and Curriculum Development.

Tomlinson, C. A., & Edison, C. (2003). *Differentiation in practice: A resource guide for differentiating curriculum grades K–5.* Alexandria, VA: Association for Supervision and Curriculum Development.

Tomlinson, C. A., & McTighe, J. (2006). *Integrating differentiated instruction and understanding by design.* Alexandria, VA: Association for Supervision and Curriculum Development.

Torrance, E. P. (1974). *Torrance tests of creative thinking.* Bensenville, IL: Scholastic Testing Service.

Torrance, E. P. (1987). Teaching for creativity. In S. G. Isaksen (Ed.), *Frontiers of creative research: Beyond the basic* (pp. 189–215). Buffalo, NY: Bearly Limited.

Torrance, E. P., & Safteer, H. T. (1990). *The incubation model of teaching: Getting beyond the Aha!* Buffalo, NY: Bearly Limited.

Tovani, C. (2000). *I read it, but I don't get it: Comprehension strategies for adolescent readers.* Portland, ME: Stenhouse.

Treffinger, D. J. (1995). *Creative problem solver's guidebook.* Sarasota, FL: Center for Creative Learning.

Treffinger, D. J., Isaksen, S. G., & Firestien, R. L. (1983). *Handbook of creative learning.* New York: Center for Creative Learning.

VanInwagen, P. (1997). *Inference is a guess you make.* East Windsor Hill, CT: Synergetics.

Willis, J. (2006). *Research-based strategies to ignite student learning.* Alexandria, VA: Association for Supervision and Curriculum Development.

Wolfe, P. (2001). *Brain matters: Translating research into classroom practice.* Alexandria, VA: Association for Supervision and Curriculum Development.

Wormelli, R. (2005). *Summarization in any subject.* Alexandria, VA: Association for Supervision and Curriculum Development.

Wormelli, R. (2006). *Fair isn't always equal: Assessing and grading in the differentiated classroom.* Portland, ME: Stenhouse.

Additional Reading

Adderholdt, M., & Goldberg, J. (1999). *Perfectionism: What's bad about being too good?* Minneapolis, MN: Free Spirit Publishing.

Alvermann, D. E., & Boothby, P. R. (1986). Children's transfer of graphic organizer instruction. *Reading Psychology, 7*(2), 87–100.

Beghetto, R. A. (2005, Spring). Does assessment kill student creativity? *The Educational Forum, 69,* 254–263.

Bender, W. N. (2005). *Differentiating math instruction strategies that work for K–8 classrooms!* Thousand Oaks, CA: Corwin Press.

Beyer, B. K. (1987*). Practical strategies for the teaching of thinking.* Boston, MA: Allyn & Bacon.

Beyer, B. K. (1991). *Teaching thinking skills: A handbook for elementary school teachers.* Boston, MA: Allyn & Bacon.

Beyer, B. K. (1991). *Teaching thinking skills: A handbook for secondary school teachers.* Boston, MA: Allyn & Bacon.

Brainstorming. (1996). Retrieved May 29, 2007, at http://members.optusnet.com.au/~charles57/ Creative/Techniques/brainstorm.htm.

Brandt, R. (1989). *Teaching thinking.* Alexandria, VA: Association for Supervision and Curriculum Development.

Bransford, J., Brown, A. L., & Cocking, R. R. (2000). *How people learn: Brain, mind, experience, and school* (Expanded ed.). Washington, DC: National Research Council.

Bromley, K., Irwin-De Vitis, L., & Modlo, M. (1995). *Graphic organizers: Visual strategies for active learners.* New York: Scholastic.

Brooks, J. G. (2004). To see beyond the lesson. *Educational Leadership, 62*(1), 9–12.

Burmark, L. (2002). *Visual literacy.* Alexandria, VA: Association for Supervision and Curriculum Development.

Caine, R. N., & Caine, G. (1997). *Making connections: Teaching and the human brain.* Alexandria, VA: Association for Supervision and Curriculum Development.

Carr, K. S. (1988, Winter). How can we teach critical thinking? *Childhood Education, 65,* 69–73. (ERIC Document Reproduction Service No. EJ326304)

Costa, A. L. (Ed.). (2001). *Developing minds: A resource book for teaching thinking* (3rd ed.). Alexandria, VA: Association for Supervision and Curriculum Development.

Cotton, K. (1991). Close-up #11: Teaching thinking skills. Retrieved May 4, 2007, from Northwest Regional Educational Laboratory's School Improvement Research Series at http://www .nwrel.org/scpd/sirs/6/cu11.html.

Csikszentmihalyi, M. (1990). *Flow: The psychology of optimal experience.* New York: HarperCollins.

Davis, G. A., & Rimm, S. B. (1998). *Education of the gifted and talented.* Boston, MA: Allyn & Bacon.

De Bono, E. (1971). *New think.* New York: Avon.

Elder, L. (1997). Critical thinking: The key to emotional intelligence. *Journal of Developmental Education, 21*(1), 40–41.

Elder, L., & Paul, R. (1994). Critical thinking: Why we must transform our teaching. *Journal of Developmental Education, 18*(1), 34–35.

Elder, L., & Paul, R. (1998). Critical thinking: Developing intellectual traits. *Journal of Developmental Education, 21*(3), 30–41.

Erickson, H. L. (1998). *Concept-based curriculum and instruction: Teaching beyond the facts.* Thousand Oaks, CA: Corwin Press.

Erickson, H. L. (2001). *Stirring the head, heart, and soul* (2nd ed.). Thousand Oaks, CA: Corwin Press.

Facione, P. A. (1990). *Critical thinking: A statement of expert consensus for purposes of educational assessment and instruction* (Executive summary of "The Delphi Report"). (ERIC Document Reproduction Service No. ED315423)

Gardill, M. C., & Jitendra, A. K. (1999). Advanced story map instruction: Effects on the reading comprehension of students with learning disabilities. *Journal of Special Education, 33*(1), 2–17.

Gerlic, I., & Jausovec, N. (1999). Multimedia: Differences in cognitive processes observed with EEG. *Educational Technology Research and Development, 47*(3), 5–14.

Gordon, W. J. J. (1961). *Synectics.* New York: Harper & Row.

Gordon, W. J. J., & Poze, T. (1980). *The new art of the possible.* Cambridge, MA: Porpoise Books.

Hall, T., Strangman, N., & Meyer, A. (2003). *Differentiated instruction and implications for UDL implementation.* Wakefield, MA: National Center on Accessing the General Curriculum. Retrieved August 20, 2006, at http://www.cast .org/publications/ncac/ncac_diffinstructudl .html.

Hyerle, D. (1996). *Visual tools for constructing knowledge.* Alexandria, VA: Association for Supervision and Curriculum Development.

Idol, L., & Croll, V. J. (1987). Story-mapping training as a means of improving reading comprehension. *Learning Disability Quarterly,* 10(3), 214–229.

Irvine, H. (1993). *A thinking approach to interdisciplinary experience.* Unionville, NY: Trillium Press.

Isaken, S., Dorval, B., & Treffinger, D. (1994). *Creative approaches to problem solving.* Dubuque, IA: Kendall/Hunt.

Jensen, E. (1998). *Teaching with the brain in mind.* Alexandria, VA: Association for Supervision and Curriculum Development.

Johnson, N. (1995). *Active questioning.* Marion, IL: Pieces of Learning.

Kagen, S. (1990). *Cooperative learning: Resources for teachers.* San Juan Capistrano, CA: Kagan Cooperative Learning.

Karnes, F. A., & Bean, S. M. (2005). *Methods and materials for teaching the gifted.* Waco, TX: Prufrock Press.

Kendall, J. S. (2000). Topics: A roadmap to standards. *NASSP Bulletin, 84*(620), 37–48.

Kingore, B. (1999). *Integrating thinking: Practical strategies and activities to encourage high-level responses.* Austin, TX: Professional Associates Publishing.

Kingore, B. (2004). *Differentiation: Simplified, realistic, and effective.* Austin, TX: Professional Associates Publishing.

Lynch, M., & Harris, C. R. (2001). *Fostering creativity in children K–8: Theory and practice.* Boston, MA: Allyn & Bacon.

Mamchur, C. (1996). *A teacher's guide to cognitive type theory and learning style.* Alexandria, VA: Association for Supervision and Curriculum Development.

Moore, D. W., & Readence, J. E. (1984). A quantitative and qualitative review of graphic organizer research. *Journal of Educational Research, 78*(1), 11–17.

Muirhead, B. D. (2002). Integrating critical thinking into online classes. *United States Distance Learning Association Journal, 16,* 1–8. (ERIC Document Reproduction Service No. EJ663103)

Novak, J. D. (1991). Clarify with concept maps. *Science Teacher, 58*(7), 45–49.

Parker, J. (1989). *Instructional strategies for teaching the gifted.* Boston, MA: Allyn & Bacon.

Paul, R. (1996). *How to teach through Socratic questioning.* Sonoma, CA: Foundation for Critical Thinking.

Paul, R., Binker, A. J. A., Jensen, K., & Kreklau, H. (1990). *Critical thinking handbook: 4th–6th grades.* Rohnert Park, CA: Foundation for Critical Thinking.

Perkins, D. (1995). *Outsmarting IQ: The emerging science of learnable intelligence.* New York: Free Press.

Potts, B. (1994). *Strategies for teaching critical thinking.* Retrieved May 5, 2007, from ERIC/AE Digest at http://ericae.net/edo/ed385606.htm.

Quinn, Q. (2005, November). *The key for two years' reading growth for one year of instruction: Assessment.* Paper presented at the Connecticut Reading Association Conference, Hartford, CT.

Raudsepp, E. (1981). *How creative are you?* New York: Pedigree Books.

Robb, L. (2000). *Teaching reading in the middle school.* New York: Scholastic.

Rowland, E., & Molotsky, L. (1994). *National Inventive Thinking Association: Resource of creative and inventive activities.* Richardson, TX: National Inventive Thinking Association.

Scanlon, D., Deshler, D. D., & Schumaker, J. B. (1996). Can a strategy be taught and learned in secondary inclusive classrooms? *Learning Disabilities Research & Practice, 11*(1), 41–57.

Schiever, S. (1991). *A comprehensive approach to teaching thinking.* Boston, MA: Allyn & Bacon.

Schwartz, R. J., & Parks, S. (1994). *Infusing the teaching of critical thinking into content instruction.* Pacific Grove, CA: Critical Thinking Books and Software.

Silverman, L. K. (2002). *Upside-down brilliance: The visual spatial learner.* Denver, CO: DeLeon Publishing.

Southern Maine Partnership. (2002). *Content area frameworks: Creating a bridge between the learning results and the classroom.* Gorham, ME: Author.

Sylwester, R. (1995). *A celebration of neurons: An educator's guide to the human brain.* Alexandria, VA: Association for Supervision and Curriculum Development.

Tomlinson, C. A., & Demirsky, S. (2000). *Leadership for differentiated schools and classrooms.* Alexandria, VA: Association for Supervision and Curriculum Development.

Udall, A. J., & Daniels, J. E. (1991). *Creating the thoughtful classroom: Strategies to promote student thinking.* Tucson, AZ: Zephyr Press.

Von Oech, R. (1983). *A whack on the side of the head.* New York: Warner Books.

Vygotsky, L. S. (1962). *Thought and language.* Cambridge, MA: MIT Press.

Vygotsky, L. S. (1978). *Mind in society.* Cambridge, MA: Harvard University Press.

Wiederhold, C. (1991). *The question matrix.* San Juan Capistrano, CA: Kagan Cooperative Learning.

Wiggins, A. (2007). *What is critical thinking?* Retrieved on May 29, 2007, at http://dusk.org/adam/criticalthinking/definitions.php.

Wiggins, G., & McTighe, J. (1998). *Understanding by design.* Alexandria, VA: Association for Supervision and Curriculum Development.

Wilhelm, J. D. (2001). *Improving comprehension with think-aloud strategies.* New York: Scholastic.

Index

Maine Educator, 181
Management strategies for
  differentiation, 15, 175–176
Math
  analysis in, 67, 68, 69
  assumptions in, 42, 43, 44
  brainstorming in, 112, 114
  creativity in, 138, 139, 140
  elaboration in, 155, 156, 157
  flexibility in, 123–124, 125, 126
  graphic organizers and, 9
  inferences in, 55, 56, 57
  judgment in, 94, 95, 96
  prioritizing in, 80, 83
Metacognition, 8
Metaphors, 3, 168
Middle grades
  analysis in, 68–69
  assumptions in, 42–43
  brainstorming in, 112–113
  creativity in, 139–140
  elaboration in, 156–157
  flexibility in, 124–125
  inferences in, 56
  judgment in, 94–95
  prioritizing in, 81–82
Motivation, fostering, 8
Multiple graphic organizers and
  content depth, 179–180

*New Taxonomy of Education Objectives,
  The,* 168
Nonlinguistic representations, 3
Nonverbal, 58
Note taking, 3

Objectives, setting, 4
Odyssey of the Mind, 110
Open-ended prompt, 16–17,
  19 (figure)
Organizing, 65
Oligarchic thinkers, 79
Outsiders, The, 112

Pace of instruction, 13
Paint Jar graphic organizer,
  58, 59 (figure), 61 (figure)
Planning tools, 144, 145 (figure)
Point of view, 53, 61
Preassessment, 23
Prediction, 28–29
Principles and generalizations, 19, 54
Principles and Standards for School
  Mathematics, 170
Prioritizer graphic organizer,
  83, 84 (figure)
Prioritizing
  applications, 79–83
  assessment, 88–89
  benefits of, 79
  defined, 76–77, 78 (figure)
  in elementary grades, 80–81

getting started using,
  83, 84–85 (figure)
in high school grades, 82–83
in middle grades, 81–82
purpose of, 78–79
sample lessons, 86–87
Problem solving, 5
Prompts
  directed, 17–20, 22, 175
  open-ended, 16–17, 19 (figure)
Purposes of graphic organizers, 6–8

Questions and cues, 4

Rainbow of Ideas graphic organizer,
  108, 111, 114, 115, 116 (figure)
Rating scales, 34–36, 132–133,
  149–150, 165
Reading and graphic organizers, 8–9
Recognition, providing, 3
*Regarding the Fountain: A Tale in
  Letters of Liars and Leaks,* 81
Relationships, 64
Research process and graphic
  organizers, 180
Resources make the difference
  differentiation, 23–25, 175–176
Resource variety, 14
Rollo Bones Canine Hypnotist,
  99, 100 (figure)
Rose-Colored Glasses graphic
  organizer, 121, 122, 125, 126,
  127 (figure), 130 (figure), 158
Rubrics, 34–36, 132–133, 149–150,
  165, 166 (figure)

Science
  analysis in, 68, 69
  assumptions in, 42, 43, 44
  brainstorming in, 112
  creativity in, 138, 139, 141
  elaboration in, 155, 156, 158
  flexibility in, 124, 125, 126
  graphic organizers and, 9
  inferences in, 55, 56, 57
  judgment in, 94, 95, 96
  prioritizing in, 81, 83
Selection of graphic organizers,
  33–34, 178–179, 180–181
Series of Unfortunate Events, A,
  58, 62–63 (figure)
Similes, 158
Social learning, 22
Social studies
  analysis in, 68, 69
  assumptions in, 42, 43, 44
  brainstorming in, 112
  creativity in, 138, 140, 141
  elaboration in, 155, 157, 158
  flexibility in, 124, 125, 126
  graphic organizers and, 9
  inferences in, 55, 56, 57

judgment in, 94, 95, 96
prioritizing in, 81, 83
Strategies That Work, 54
Summarizing, 3

Talents Unlimited model, 109
Target verbs, viii–ix
Teachers as critical and creative
  thinkers, x
Teacher's manuals, 179
*Teaching Thinking Skills: A Handbook
  for Elementary School
  Teachers,* 28
*Teaching Thinking Skills: A Handbook
  for Secondary School
  Teachers,* 28
Test preparation, 179
Textbooks, 179
Text modifications, 14
Thinking Maps, 3, 9
Thinking Skills Resource Book, 28
Thought Bubble graphic organizer,
  44, 45–46 (figure)
Three Little Pigs, The, 92
*Tools for Taking Charge of Your
  Learning and Your Life,* 38
Torrance Tests of Creative
  Thinking, 109
Transference, 32, 114
Trends in achievement, vi–vii

Understanding by Design, 168
Unit calendars, 172–173 (figure)

Variety plus differentiation,
  25–27, 176
Verbs
  create your own organizer, 28
  target, viii–ix
  thinking and reasoning
    skill, 5–6
  use of, 4–5
Visual brainstorming, 141
Visual learners, ,2, 12, 153
Vocabulary, 18, 152, 153, 166

Wheel of Words graphic organizer,
  158, 160 (figure), 162 (figure), 163
Whole New Mind, A, 135
Witches, The, 70, 73 (figure),
  74–75, 74 (figure)
Writing
  analysis in, 67, 68, 69
  assumptions in, 41, 42–43
  brainstorming in, 111–113
  creativity in, 138, 139, 140
  elaboration in, 155, 156, 157
  flexibility in, 123, 124, 125
  graphic organizers and, 9
  inferences in, 55, 56, 57
  judgment in, 94, 95, 96
  prioritizing in, 80, 81, 82

CORWIN PRESS

The Corwin Press logo—a raven striding across an open book—represents the union of courage and learning. Corwin Press is committed to improving education for all learners by publishing books and other professional development resources for those serving the field of PreK–12 education. By providing practical, hands-on materials, Corwin Press continues to carry out the promise of its motto: **"Helping Educators Do Their Work Better."**